Anonymous

Alciphron

Literally and completely translated from the Greek

Anonymous

Alciphron

Literally and completely translated from the Greek

ISBN/EAN: 9783337188122

Printed in Europe, USA, Canada, Australia, Japan

Cover: Foto ©ninafisch / pixelio.de

More available books at **www.hansebooks.com**

THE ATHENIAN SOCIETY'S
PUBLICATIONS

III

250 Copies of this work have been privately printed on ordinary paper solely for distribution amongst the Members of the Athenian Society. None of these copies are for sale.

5 Special Copies have also been privately printed on Japanese Vellum. None of these copies are for sale.

The Council of the Society pledge themselves never to reprint nor to re-issue in any form.

This Copy is No.

*LITERALLY AND COMPLETELY TRANSLATED
FROM THE GREEK, WITH INTRODUCTION
AND NOTES*

*ATHENS: PRIVATELY PRINTED FOR THE
ATHENIAN SOCIETY: MDCCCXCVI*

INTRODUCTION

ALCIPHRON was a Greek sophist, and one of the most eminent of the Greek epistolographers. We have no direct information of any kind respecting his life or the age in which he lived. Some assign him to the fifth century A.D.; others, to the period between Lucian and Aristaenetus (170-350 A.D.); while others again are of opinion that he lived before Lucian. The only circumstance that suggests anything in regard to the period at which he lived is the fact that, amongst the letters of Aristaenetus, there are two which passed between Lucian and Alciphron; and, as Aristaenetus is generally trustworthy,

we may infer that Alciphron was a contemporary of Lucian, which is not incompatible with the opinion, true or false, that he imitated him.

It cannot be proved that Alciphron, any more than Aristaenetus, was a real name. It is probable that there was a well-known sophist of that name in the second century A.D., but it does not follow that he wrote the letters.

The letters, as we have them, are divided into three books. Their object is to delineate the characters of certain classes of persons by introducing them as expressing their peculiar sentiments and opinions upon subjects with which they are familiar. For this purpose Alciphron chose country people, fishermen, parasites, and courtesans. All are made to express themselves in most elegant and graceful language, even where the

subjects are low and obscene. The characters are thus to some extent raised above the ordinary standard, without any great violence being done to the truth of the reality. The form of these letters is very beautiful, and the language in which they are written is the purest Attic. The scene is, with few exceptions, Athens and its neighbourhood; the time, some period after the reign of Alexander the Great, as is clear from the letters of the second book. The New Attic comedy was the chief source from which Alciphron derived his material, and the letters contain much valuable information in regard to the characters and manners he describes, and the private life of the Athenians. We come across some remarkably modern touches, as the thimble-rigger at the fair and the *claqueurs* at the theatre. Alciphron perhaps imitated

Lucian in style; but the spirit in which he treats his subjects is very different, and far more refined.

In the great majority of cases the names in the headings of the letters, which seem very clumsy in an English dress, are fictitious, and are purposely coined to express some characteristic of the persons between whom they are supposed to pass.

In the volume of "Lucian" in this series some account has been given of the courtesans of Athens. It will here be interesting to describe briefly another curious class of personages, the *parasites*—a word which has had a remarkable history.

Originally, amongst the Greeks, the parasites were persons who held special functions. They had a right, like the priests, to a certain portion of the sacrificial victims, and their particular duty was to look after the storage and keep of the sacred

corn, hence their name. They enjoyed an honourable position, and the Athenians resigned to them even the management of the temples, which gave them rank next to the priests.

Soon, after the example of Apollo, the richest citizens looked out for witty table - companions, to amuse them with jests, and flatter them in proportion to their importance and liberality. By degrees, however, these parasites, lending themselves to ridicule, fell into discredit and contempt. The name, diverted from its etymological signification, was applied to every haunter of the tables of the rich, to every sponger for a free meal, to every shameless flatterer who, in order to satisfy the needs of his stomach, consented to divert the company and patiently endure the insults which it pleased the master of the house to heap upon him.

At first this was by no means

the case with all parasites. Gaiety, audacity, liveliness, good humour, a knowledge of the culinary art, and sometimes even a certain amount of independence lent an additional charm to the members of the profession. One of the most famous of parasites was Philoxenus of Leucas, of whom we read in Athenaeus. It was his practice, whether at home or abroad, after he had been to the bath, to go round the houses of the principal citizens, followed by boys carrying in a basket oil, vinegar, fish-sauce, and other condiments. After he had made his choice, Philoxenus, who was a great gourmand, entered without ceremony, took his seat at table, and did honour to the repast before him. One day, at Ephesus, finding that there was nothing left in the market, he asked the reason. Being told that everything had been bought up

for a wedding festival, he washed
and dressed himself, and deliberately
walked to the house of the bride-
groom, by whom he was well received. He took his seat at table,
ate, drank, sang an epithalamium or
marriage - song, and delighted the
guests. "I hope you will dine here
to-morrow," said the host. "Yes,"
answered Philoxenus, "if you lay
violent hands upon the market as you
have done to-day." "I wish I had
a crane's neck," he sometimes ex-
claimed; "then I should be able to
relish the flavour of the food for a
longer time." Dionysius, the tyrant
of Syracuse, who knew that he was
very fond of fish, invited him to
dinner, and, while an enormous mullet
was set before himself, sent his guest
a very small one. Without being in
the least disconcerted, Philoxenus took
up the small fry, pretended to speak

to it, and put it close to his ear, as if to hear its reply. "Well," said Dionysius, somewhat annoyed, "what is the matter?" "I was asking him certain information about the sea which interests me; but he has been caught too young: this is his excuse for having nothing to tell me. The fish in front of you, on the contrary, is old enough to satisfy my curiosity." Dionysius, pleased with the rejoinder, sent on to him his own fish. To perpetuate his memory, Philoxenus composed a "Manual of Gastronomy," which was held in great repute.

Philoxenus, it must be admitted, was a very favourable specimen of his class. As a rule the parasites were among the most abject and worthless of men. "Selected for their profligacy, their impudence, or their wit, they were admitted to the tables of the wealthy, to promote licentious

mirth. This being the case, it does not seem at all unnatural that we should at the same time find them the friends and companions of the courtesans. Such characters could not but be mutually necessary to each other. The courtesan solicited the acquaintance of the parasite, that she might the more easily obtain and carry on intrigues with the rich and dissipated. The parasite was assiduous in his attention to the courtesan, as procuring through her means more easy access to his patrons, and was probably rewarded by them both, for the gratification which he obtained of the vices of the one and the avarice of the other."

The name parasite first assumed a dishonourable signification in the works of the writers of the Middle and New Comedy. The first who so used it is said to have been Alexis.

In the later comedians they are stock characters, whose chief object was to get a dinner without paying for it. They are divided into different classes. There were the γελωτοποιοὶ, or jesters, who, in order to secure an invitation, not only endeavoured to amuse, but endured the grossest insults and personal ill-treatment (cf. Book III., Letters 6, 7, 49). They had notebooks, in which they kept a collection of jokes ready for use. The κόλακες, or flatterers, endeavoured to get invitations by playing upon the vanity of their prospective patrons. The θεραπευτικοὶ, or "officious" parasites, tried to curry favour by services of the lowest and most degrading character, which are detailed in the sixth book of Athenaeus. They haunted the markets, wrestling-schools, baths, and other public places in search of patrons.

The Romans also had their parasites. As the stern rigour of the Republic relaxed and degenerated into the splendour and dissipation of a despotic government, the Roman parasites became less respectable and more profligate. But it does not appear that in the most licentious ages of the Empire they ever equalled in meanness or in vice those worthless characters described in such lively colours by Athenaeus, Alciphron, and the comic poets of Greece. Frequent allusions to them are found in Horace, Juvenal, Plautus, and particularly in Terence.

The latinized forms of the names of Greek gods and goddesses (such as Jupiter for Zeus) have been preserved in the translation as being more familiar, although, strictly speaking, they cannot be regarded as correct.

THE LETTERS
OF
ALCIPHRON

ΑΛΚΙΦΡΟΝΟΣ
ΡΗΤΟΡΟΣ
ΕΠΙΣΤΟΛΑΙ.

LIBER PRIMUS.

I.

Εὔδιος Φιλοσκάφῳ.

Χρηστὴν ἡμῖν ἡ θάλασσα τοτήμερον εἶναι τὴν γαλήνην ἐστόρεσεν. Ὡς γὰρ τρίτην ταύτην εἶχεν ὁ χειμὼν ἡμέραν, καὶ λάβρως κατὰ τοῦ πελάγους ἐπέπνεον ἐκ τῶν ἀκρωτηρίων οἱ βορεῖς, καὶ ἐπεφρίκει μὲν πόντος μελαινόμενος, τοῦ ὕδατος δὲ ἀφρὸς ἐξηνθήκει, πανταχοῦ τῆς θαλάσσης ἐπαλλήλων ἐπικλωμένων τῶν κυμάτων, τὰ μὲν γὰρ ταῖς πέτραις προσηράσσετο, τὰ δὲ εἴσω ἀνοιδοῦντα ἐρρήγνυτο, ἀεργία παντελὴς ἦν· καὶ τὰ ἐπὶ ταῖς ἠϊόσι καταλαβόντες καλύβια, ὀλίγα ξυλισάμενοι κομμάτια, ὅσα οἱ ναυπηγοὶ πρώην ἐκ τῶν

THE LETTERS OF ALCIPHRON

BOOK I.

LETTER I.

EUDIUS TO PHILOSCAPHUS.

HAPPILY for us, the sea to-day is smooth and calm again. The storm lasted for three days: the north winds blew violently from the headlands towards the open; the blackening sea grew rough, the waters were white with foam; the billows everywhere broke over each other, some dashing against the rocks, while others swelled and burst. It was utterly impossible to work: we betook ourselves to the huts on the bank, collected a few fragments of wood, the remains of the oaks which had been

δρυῶν, ἃς ἐξέτεμον, ἀπέλιπον, ἐκ τούτων πῦρ ἀνάψαντες τὸ πικρὸν τοῦ κρυμοῦ παρεμυθούμεθα. Τετάρτη δὲ αὕτη ἐπιλαβοῦσα ἡμᾶς ἀλκυονὶς ὡς οἶμαι ἡμέρα, ἔστι γὰρ τοῦτο τῷ καθαρῷ τῆς αἰθρίας τεκμαίρεσθαι, πλοῦτον ἀθρόον ἀγαθῶν ἔδειξεν. Ὡς γὰρ ὤφθη μὲν ὁ ἥλιος, πρώτη δὲ ἀκτὶς εἰς τὸ πέλαγος ἀπέστιλβε, τὸ πρώην νεωλκηθὲν σκαφίδιον σπουδῇ κατεσύραμεν· εἶτ᾽ ἐνθέμενοι τὰ δίκτυα ἔργων εἰχόμεθα. Μικρὸν δὲ ἄπωθεν τῆς ἀκτῆς χαλάσαντες, φεῦ τῆς εὐοψίας, ὅσον ἰχθύων ἐξειλκύσαμεν· μικροῦ καὶ τοὺς φελλοὺς ἐδέησε κατασῦραι ὕφαλον τὸ δίκτυον ἐξωγκωμένον. Εὐθὺς οὖν ὀψῶναι πλησίον, καὶ ὑπὲρ αὐτῶν καταβαλόντες ἀργύριον, τὰς ἀσίλλας ἐπωμίους ἀνελόμενοι, καὶ τὰς ἑκατέρωθεν σπυρίδας ἐξαρτήσαντες, ἄστυδ᾽ ἐκ Φαλήρων ἠπείγοντο. Πᾶσι δὲ τούτοις ἠρκέσαμεν ἡμεῖς· καὶ πρὸς τούτοις ἀπηνεγκάμεθα γαμεταῖς καὶ παιδίοις ὄγκον οὐκ ὀλίγον ἔχειν τῶν λεπτομερῶν ἰχθύων, οὐκ εἰς μίαν, ἀλλ᾽ εἰ χειμὼν ἐπιλάβοιτο, καὶ εἰς πλείους ἡμέρας ἐμφορῆσαι.

felled by the ships' carpenters, and lighted a fire to relieve the piercing cold. At last the fourth day came, a truly halcyon day, as we may conclude from the clearness of the air, and brought us wealth and fortune in abundance. For, as soon as the sun rose, and its first beams glittered on the sea, we quickly launched our little bark, which had lately been drawn up on land, and, putting our nets aboard, set to work. We cast them not far from land. Ha ! what an enormous haul we made ! The heavily-laden net, carried under water, almost dragged down the corks with it. Immediately the fish salesmen gathered round, with their yokes over their shoulders, from which hung baskets on either side ; and, having purchased our fish for money down, hastened from Phalerum to the city. We had enough to satisfy them all, and besides, took back to our wives and children a quantity of small fry, enough to keep them not only for one, but for several days, if bad weather should come on.

II.

Γαληνὸς Κύρτωνι.

Μάτην ἡμῖν πάντα πονεῖται, ὦ Κύρτων, δι' ἡμέρας μὲν ὑπὸ τῆς εἴλης φλεγομένοις, νύκτωρ δὲ ὑπὸ λαμπάσι τὸν βυθὸν ἀποξύουσι. Καὶ τὸ λεγόμενον δὴ τοῦτο εἰς τὸν τῶν Δαναΐδων τοὺς ἀμφορέας ἐκχέομεν πίθον· οὕτως ἄπρακτα καὶ ἀνήνυτα μοχθοῦμεν. Ἡμῖν μὲν γὰρ οὐδὲ ἀκαλήφης ἐστὶν ἢ πελωρίδος ἐμπλῆσαι τὴν γαστέρα· ὁ δεσπότης δὲ συλλέγει καὶ τοὺς ἰχθύας καὶ τὰ κέρματα. Οὐκ ἀπόχρη δὲ αὐτῷ τοσαῦτα ἔχειν παρ' ἡμῶν, ὁ δὲ διερευνᾶται καὶ τὸ σκαφίδιον συνεχῶς. Καὶ πρώην, ὅτ' ἐκ Μουνυχίας ἐπέμψαμεν αὐτῷ κομιοῦντα τὸ ὀψώνιον Ἕρμωνα τουτονὶ τὸν μειρακίσκον, σπόγγους ἡμῖν ἐπέτατte καὶ τὰ ἐκ τῆς θαλάσσης ἔρια ἃ φύεται ἐπιεικῶς ἐν Εὐρυνόμης λίμνῃ.[1] Ὡς δ' ὁ μὲν οὔπω ταῦτα προσαπῄτει, καὶ ὁ Ἕρμων

[1] Locus corruptus.

II.

GALENUS TO CYRTON.

ALL our labour is in vain, Cyrton! By day we are scorched by the heat of the sun, by night we explore the deep by the light of torches, and yet, in the words of the proverb, we are pouring the contents of our pitchers into the cask of the Danaides—so idle and useless are our efforts! We have not even sea nettles or Pelorian mussels to fill our belly; but the master collects both the fish and the money. But all that he gets from us is not enough for him : he is continually searching our little bark. Only lately, when we sent the lad Hermon to him from Munychia with the fish, he ordered us to bring him some sponges and sea-wool, which grows in fairly large quantities in the pool of Eurynome. Before he had finished giving these orders,

ἀφεὶς τὸ φορτίον αὐτοῖς ἰχθύσιν, ἀφεὶς δὲ καὶ ἡμᾶς αὐτῷ τῷ σκάφει, ᾤχετο ἐπὶ λέμβου κωπήρους, Ῥοδίοις τισὶ βαλαυστιουργοῖς ἀναμιχθείς. Καὶ ὁ μὲν δεσπότης οἰκέτην, ἡμεῖς δὲ συνεργὸν ἀγαθὸν ἐπενθήσαμεν.

Hermon left his load of fishes, the boat, and ourselves, and went off on a rowing-boat, with some Rhodian dyers whose acquaintance he had made. Thus the master has to mourn the loss of a slave; we, that of a true companion.

ΑΛΚΙΦΡΟΝΟΣ ΡΗΤΟΡΟΣ

III.

Γλαῦκος Γαλατείᾳ.

Χρηστὸν ἡ γῆ καὶ ἡ βῶλος ἀκίνδυνον. Οὐ μάτην γοῦν ἀνεισιδώραν ταύτην ὀνομάζουσιν Ἀθηναῖοι ἀνιεῖσαν δῶρα, δι' ὧν ἐστι ζῆν καὶ σώζεσθαι. Χαλεπὸν ἡ θάλαττα καὶ ἡ ναυτιλία ῥιψοκίνδυνον. Ὀρθῶς ἐγὼ τοῦτο κρίνω πείρᾳ καὶ διδασκαλίᾳ μαθών. Ποτὲ γὰρ ὄψον ἀποδόσθαι βουληθεὶς ἤκουσα ἑνὸς τῶν ἐν τῇ Ποικίλῃ διατριβόντων ἀνυποδήτου καὶ ἐνερόχρωτος στιχίδιον ἀποφθεγγομένου, τὴν ἀπόνοιαν τῶν πλεόντων ἐπιστύφοντος, ἔλεγε δὲ Ἀράτου τινὸς εἶναι σοφοῦ τὰ μετέωρα· καὶ ἦν ὅσον ἀπομνημονεύσαντα οὐχ' ὅλον εἰπεῖν ὧδε εἰρημένον ΟΛΙ'ΓΟΝ ΔΕ' ΔΙΑ' ΞΥ'ΛΟΝ Ἄἴ"Δ' ΕΡΥ'ΚΕΙ. Τί οὖν,

III.

Glaucus to Galatea.

Happy is he who lives on land! Husbandry involves no danger. With good reason, then, do the Athenians name it Aneisidora, because it bestows gifts, whereby we live and enjoy health. The sea is cruel, and a sailor's life is full of perils. My judgment is right: I have learnt this by experience and instruction. I remember that, once, when I wanted to sell some fish, I heard one of those fellows who hang about the Painted Porch, a bare-footed wretch with livid features, reciting verses and declaiming against the folly of sailors. He said that the verses were written by a certain Aratus, an astronomer. I cannot repeat all that he said; but, as far as I remember, one of the verses ran as follows:

A thin partition keeps off destruction.

γύναι, οὐ σωφρονοῦμεν, καὶ ὀψὲ τοῦ καιροῦ φεύγομεν τὴν πρὸς τὸν θάνατον γειτνίασιν, καὶ ταῦτα ἐπὶ παιδίοις ζῶντες· οἷς εἰ καὶ μηδὲν μέγα παρέχειν δι' ἀχρηματίαν ἔχομεν, τάδε παρέξομεν καὶ χαριούμεθα, τὸ τὰς τρικυμίας καὶ τοὺς ἐκ βυθοῦ κινδύνους ἀγνοῆσαι, γεωργίᾳ δὲ συντραφῆναι, καὶ τὸν ἀσφαλῆ καὶ ἀδεᾶ βίον ἀσπάσασθαι.

Why, then, wife, should we not be wise, and, even though it be late, avoid a life that is so near to death? We have children; and, although our poverty prevents us from leaving them anything considerable, we shall at least be able to leave them in blessed ignorance of the stormy waves and the dangers of the deep. They will be brought up to an agricultural life, and will enjoy a life of security, untroubled by alarm.

IV.

Κύμωθος Τριτωνίδι.

Ὅσον ἡ θάλαττα τῆς γῆς διαλλάττει, τοσοῦτον καὶ ἡμεῖς οἱ ταύτης ἐργάται τῶν κατὰ πόλεις ἢ κώμας οἰκούντων διαφέρομεν. Οἱ μὲν γὰρ ἢ μένοντες εἴσω πυλῶν τὰ δημοτικὰ διαπράττουσιν ἢ γεωργίᾳ προσανέχοντες τὴν ἐκ τῆς βώλου πρὸς διατροφὴν ἀναμένουσιν ἐπικαρπίαν· ἡμῖν δέ, οἷς ὁ βίος ἐν ὕδασι, θάνατος ἡ γῆ, καθάπερ τοῖς ἰχθύσιν ἥκιστα δυναμένοις ἀναπνεῖν τὸν ἀέρα. Τί δὴ οὖν παθοῦσα, ὦ γύναι, τὴν ἀκτὴν ἀπολιποῦσα καὶ τὰ νήματα τοῦ λίνου, ἄστυδε θαμίζεις, Ὠσχοφόρια καὶ Λήναια ταῖς πλουσίαις Ἀθηναίων συνεορτάζουσα; Οὐκ ἔστι τοῦτο σωφρονεῖν, οὐδὲ ἀγαθὰ διανοεῖσθαι· οὐχ οὕτω δέ σε ὁ πατὴρ ἐκ τῆς Αἰγίνης, οὗ τεχθῆναί

IV.

CYMOTHUS TO TRITONIS.

THERE is as much difference between us, toilers on the sea, and those who live in cities and villages, as there is between sea and land. They either remain within the gates and occupy themselves with public affairs, or, devoting themselves to agriculture, wait quietly for the crops that are their support; but we, whose life is spent upon the water, find land death to us, even as the fishes, who are unable to breathe the air. Whatever, then, is the matter with you, my dear Tritonis, that you leave the shore and your yarn, and are constantly running into the city, visiting the Oschophoria and Lenaea in the company of wealthy Athenian ladies? This shows a want of prudence and modesty. It was not for this purpose that your father brought you up in

σε καὶ τραφῆναι συνέβη, μυεῖσθαι ὑπ' ἐμοὶ γάμῳ παρέδωκεν. Εἰ τὴν πόλιν ἀσπάξῃ, χαῖρε καὶ ἄπιθι· εἰ δὲ τὰ ἐκ θαλάττης ἀγαπᾷς, ἐπάνιθι, εἰς τὸν ἄνδρα, τὸ λῷον ἑλομένη. Λήθη δέ σοι ἔστω μακρὰ τῶν κατ' ἄστυ τούτων ἀπατηλῶν θεαμάτων.

Aegina and gave you to me in marriage. If you are so fond of the city, farewell; go; but, if you love the sea, return to your husband; that is the best thing you can do; but forget for ever these delusive city spectacles.

V.

Ναυβάτης Ῥοδίῳ.

Οἴει μόνος πλουτεῖν, ὅτι τοὺς παρ' ἐμοὶ θητεύοντας δελεάζων ἄγεις ὡς σεαυτὸν περιουσίᾳ μισθωμάτων, καὶ εἰκότως. Σοί μὲν γὰρ ὁ βόλος ἤνεγκε πρώην χρυσοῦ κόμματα Δαρεικοῦ τῆς ἐπὶ Σαλαμῖνι ναυμαχίας ἴσως λείψανα, καταδύσης οἶμαι νηὸς Περσικῆς αὐτοῖς ἀνδράσι καὶ αὐτοῖς χρήμασιν, ὅτε ἐπὶ τῶν προγόνων τῶν ἡμετέρων ὁ Θεμιστοκλῆς ὁ τοῦ Νεοκλέους ἤρατο τὸ μέγα κατὰ τῶν Μήδων τρόπαιον· ἐγὼ δὲ ἀγαπῶ τὴν τῶν ἀναγκαίων εὐπορίαν ἐκ τῆς καθημερινῆς ἐργασίας τῶν χειρῶν ποριζόμενος. Ἀλλ' εἰ πλουτεῖς, σὺν δικαίῳ πλούτει· γινέσθω δέ σοι ὁ πλοῦτος μὴ κακίας ἀλλὰ καλοκἀγαθίας ὑπηρέτης.

V.

NAUBATES TO RHODIUS.

You flatter yourself that you alone are wealthy, because you are able to entice my sailors with the offer of a higher salary.. And no wonder; for only recently a lucky cast brought you in a quantity of golden darics, probably a relic of the battle of Salamis. Perhaps a Persian ship went to the bottom there with the crew and all the treasures on board, at the time when Themistocles, son of Neocles, in the days of our forefathers, set up his great trophy in honour of his victory over the Medes. I, for my part, am content if I can procure the necessaries of life, by the daily work of my hands. If you are wealthy, do not forget what is just: let your wealth be to you an assistance in performing, not unjust, but good and generous actions.

VI.

Πανόπη Εὐθυβόλῳ.

Ἡγάγου με, ὦ Εὐθύβολε, οὐκ ἀπερριμμένην γυναῖκα, οὐδὲ μίαν τῶν ἀσήμων, ἀλλ' ἐξ ἀγαθοῦ μὲν πατρὸς, ἀγαθῆς δὲ μητρὸς γεγονυῖαν. Σωσθένης ὁ Στειριεὺς ἦν μοι πατὴρ, καὶ Δαμοφίλη μήτηρ, οἵ με ἐγγυητὴν ἐπίκληρον ἐπὶ παίδων ἀρότῳ γνησίων συνῆψάν σοι γάμῳ. Σὺ δὲ ῥᾴδιος ὢν τὼ ὀφθαλμὼ, καὶ πρὸς πᾶσαν ἡδονὴν ἀφροδισίων κεχυμένος, ἀτιμάσας ἐμὲ καὶ τὰ κοινὰ παιδία, Γαλήνην καὶ Θαλασσίωνα, ἐρᾷς τῆς Ἑρμιονίτιδος μετοίκου, ἣν ἐπὶ κακῷ τῶν ἐρώντων ὁ Πειραιεὺς ἐδέξατο. Κωμάζουσι γὰρ εἰς αὐτὴν ἡ πρὸς θάλασσαν νεολαία, καὶ ἄλλος ἄλλο δῶρον ἀποφέρει· ἡ δὲ εἰσδέχεται καὶ ἀναλοῖ Χαρύβδεως δίκην.

VI.

PANOPE TO EUTHYBOLUS.

WHEN you married me, Euthybolus, you did not marry an outcast or one of the common herd, but the daughter of respectable parents. Sosthenes of Stiria was my father: Damophile, my mother. I was their sole heiress; and they consented to our union, in the hope of our having lawful children. But, notwithstanding, you are ever casting amorous glances upon the women, and are addicted to every kind of wanton pleasure: you neglect me and our children, Galene and Thalassion : you are enamoured of the strange woman from Hermione, who has arrived in Piraeus, to the misfortune of husbands and wives. The young fishermen of the coast hold orgies at her house: each gives her different presents ; and she accepts and swallows all, like

Σὺ δὲ ὑπερβαίνων τὰς ἁλιευτικὰς δωροφορίας, μαινίδας μὲν ἢ τρίγλας οὔτε φέρεις, οὔτε θέλεις διδόναι· ἀλλ' ὡς ἀφηλικέστερος καὶ γυναικὶ πάλαι συνὼν καὶ παιδίων οὐ μάλα νηπίων πατὴρ, παραγκωνίσασθαι τοὺς ἀντεραστὰς βουλόμενος, κεκρυφάλους Μιλησίους, καὶ Σικελικὸν ἱμάτιον, καὶ ἐπ' αὐτῷ χρυσίον εἰσπέμπεις. Ἢ οὖν πέπαυσο τῆς ἀγερωχίας καὶ τοῦ λάγνος εἶναι καὶ θηλυμανὴς ἀπόσχου, ἢ ἴσθι με παρὰ τὸν πατέρα οἰχησομένην, ὃς οὐδ' ἐμὲ περιόψεται, καὶ σὲ γράψεται παρὰ τοῖς δικασταῖς κακώσεως.

Charybdis. But you, more lavish than a fisherman can afford to be, are not satisfied with giving her sprats or mullets : although you are getting old, have been married a long time, and are the father of grown-up children, in your desire to oust your rivals, you send her Milesian hair-nets, Sicilian dresses, and even gold. Either give up this insulting conduct, your debauchery, and your madness for women, or I tell you plainly that I will go back to my father, who will know how to protect me and will summon you before the court for your cruel behaviour towards me.

VII.

Θάλασσιος Ποντίῳ.

Ἔπεμψά σοι ψήτταν καὶ σανδάλιον καὶ κεστρέα καὶ κήρυκας πέντε καὶ τριάκοντα· σὺ δέ μοι τῶν ἐρετμῶν δύο πέμψον, ἐπειδὴ τἀμὰ κατεάγετο. Ἀντίδοσις γὰρ ἡ παρὰ φίλων εἰς φίλους· ὁ γὰρ προχείρως καὶ θαρσαλέως αἰτῶν, εὔδηλός ἐστιν ὡς ἅπαντα κοινὰ τὰ πρὸς τοὺς φίλους καὶ τὰ τῶν φίλων ἔχειν ἡγούμενος.

VII.

THALASSIUS TO PONTIUS.

I SEND you a plaice, a sole, a mullet, and three dozen purple-fish: send me two oars for them, for mine are broken. The presents one friend makes to another are simple exchanges. He who asks for a thing boldly and without ceremony thereby declares that he considers the possessions of friends are common, and that he has a right to share what belongs to his friends.

VIII.

Εὐκόλυμβος Γλαύκῃ.

Οἱ τὴν γνώμην ἀμφίβολοι τὴν παρὰ τῶν εὐνοούντων κρίσιν ἐκδέχονται. Κἀγὼ τὰ πολλὰ ταῖς αὔραις διαλαλήσας (οὐδὲ γὰρ οὐδὲν πρὸς σὲ ἐθάρρουν, ὦ γύναι), νῦν ἐξαγορεύω, καὶ δέομαι τὸ λῷον εὑρημένην συμβουλεῦσαι. Ἄκουε δὲ ὡς ἔχει, καὶ πρὸς ὅτι σε δεῖ τὴν γνώμην ἐξενεγκεῖν. Τὰ ἡμέτερα, ὡς οἶσθα, παντελῶς ἐστιν ἄπορα, καὶ βίος κομιδῇ στενός· τρέφει γὰρ οὐδὲν ἡ θάλασσα. Ὁ λέμβος οὖν οὗτος, ὃν ὁρᾷς, ὁ κωπήρης, τοῖς πολλοῖς ἐρέταις κατηρτυμένος, Κωρύκιόν τι σκάφος, λῃσταὶ δὲ θαλάσσης τὸ ἐν αὐτῷ σύστημα. Οὗτοί με κοινωνὸν ἐθέλουσι λαβεῖν τοῦ τολμήματος, πόρους ἐκ πόρων εὐμεγέθεις ὑπισχνούμενοι. Πρὸς μὲν οὖν τὸν χρυσόν, ὃν ἐπαγγέλλονται,

VIII.

Eucolymbus to Glauce.

Those who are undecided in their minds wait for some kind friend to advise them. So I, who have often addressed myself to the winds—since I never had the courage to consult you, my dear wife—have now decided to speak out, and beg you to assist me with your advice, if you have anything better to suggest. Listen now to the state of things as to which I want your opinion. My affairs are, as you know, in a very embarrassed condition, and I find it very hard to get a living, for there are hardly any fish in the sea. This rowing-boat which you see, with its numerous crew, is a Corycian bark manned by pirates. They want me to become a partner in their venture, and promise me vast wealth. I confess that my mouth waters for the

καὶ τὴν ἐσθῆτα κέχηνα· ἀνδροφόνος δὲ οὐχ ὑπομένω γενέσθαι, οὐδὲ μιᾶναι λύθρῳ τὰς χεῖρας, ἃς ἡ θάλαττα ἐκ παιδὸς εἰς δεῦρο καθαρὰς ἀδικημάτων ἐφύλαξε· μένειν δὲ πενίᾳ συζῶντα χαλεπὸν καὶ οὐ φορητόν. Τούτων σὺ τὴν αἵρεσιν ταλάντευε· ὅπου γὰρ ἂν ῥέψῃς, ὦ γύναι, ἅπαξ, ἐκεῖ σε ἀκολουθήσω· ἀποκόπτειν γὰρ εἴωθε γνώμης ἡ τῶν φίλων συμβουλὴ τὸ ἀμφίβολον.

gold and garments which they hold out
to me as an inducement; but I have not
the heart to become a murderer and stain
with gore these hands of mine, which the
sea has kept pure from evil-doing, from
my childhood to the present day; and
yet, on the other hand, it is hard and
unendurable to live in continual poverty.
The decision of my choice lies in your
hands: to whatever course you are favour-
ably inclined, I will follow you, dear wife;
for the advice which friends give us often
cuts the knot of indecision.

IX.

Αἰγιαλεὺς Στρουθίωνι.

Βάλλ ἐς μακαρίαν· ὡς ἐναντίως ἡμῖν, καὶ κατὰ τὴν παροιμίαν ἐπὶ τὰ Μανδραβούλου χωρεῖ τὰ πράγματα. Τὸ μὲν γὰρ ἐπὶ λεπτῶν κερμάτων ἀποδίδοσθαι καὶ ὠνεῖσθαι τὰ ἐπιτήδεια, λιμηρὰν φέρει τὴν παραμυθίαν. Ὥρα οὖν σε συμπράττοντα ἡμῖν, ὦ Στρουθίων, τὴν παρ' ἡμῶν ἐξ ὧν ἂν ἡ θάλαττα πορίξῃ παραμυθίαν ἐκδέχεσθαι. Βούλομαι δὲ πρὸς ἕνα τῶν λακκοπλούτων διὰ σοῦ προξένου ἢ πρὸς Ἐρασικλέα τὸν Σφήττιον, ἢ πρὸς Φιλόστρατον τὸν Χολαργέα οἰκείως ἔχειν, ὡς αὐτὸς ἐπὶ φερνείων κομίζειν αὐτῷ τοὺς ἰχθύας· πάντως γὰρ πρὸς τῇ καταβολῇ τἀργυρίου ἔσται παρ' αὐτῷ τις διὰ σοῦ παραμυθία ἢ Διονυσίων ἢ Ἀπατουρίων τελουμένων. Καὶ ἄλλως ἐκ τῆς πικρᾶς τῶν

IX.

AEGIALEUS TO STRUTHION.

CONFOUND it, how unlucky I am! All my affairs go wrong, and, as the proverb says, after the fashion of Mandrabulus. It is a sorry comfort to be always buying and selling the necessaries of life for worthless bits of money! It is time for you to help me, Struthion; you shall share the fruits of my labours on the sea. I want, through your recommendation, to get on familiar terms with one or two of our city millionaires, such as Erasicles of Sphettus or Philostratus of Cholargus, that I may take my baskets of fish to them in person. By this means, in addition to the price of the fish, I hope through your interest to get some trifle at their house on the day of the festival of Dionysia or Apaturia. Besides this, they will save us from the

ἀγορανόμων ἐξελοῦνται ἡμᾶς χειρὸς, οἳ καθεκάστην ἐπὶ τῷ σφετέρῳ κέρδει εἰς τοὺς ἀπράγμονας ἐμφοροῦσιν ὕβρεις. Πολλοῦ δὲ δύνασθαι τοὺς παρασίτους ὑμᾶς παρὰ τοῖς νέοις καὶ πλουσίοις οὐ λόγος ἀλλ' ἔργον ἔδειξεν.

cruel hands of the market - inspectors, who, for their own profit, daily heap insults upon the inoffensive. Not only report, but also experience proves that you parasites have great influence with the young and wealthy.

X.

Κέφαλος Ποντίῳ.

Τὴν μὲν θάλατταν, ὡς ὁρᾷς, φρίκη κατέχει, καὶ τὸν οὐρανὸν ὑποβέβηκεν ἀχλὺς, καὶ πάντα πανταχόθεν συννέφελα, καὶ οἱ ἄνεμοι πρὸς ἀλλήλους ἀρασσόμενοι ὅσον οὔπω κυκήσειν τὸ πελαγος ἐπαγγελλονται. Ἀλλὰ καὶ οἱ δελφῖνες ἀνασκιρτῶντες καὶ τῆς θαλάττης ἀνοιδουμένης λείως ἐφαλλόμενοι, χειμῶνα καὶ τάραχον ἐπιόντα μηνύουσι. Ταύρου δέ φασιν ἐπιτολὴν κατ᾽ οὐρανὸν οἱ τὰ μετέωρα δεινοὶ τανῦν ἐστάναι. Πολλάκις οὖν σώζονται ὑπ᾽ ἀσφαλείας οἱ προμηθούμενοι φυλάξασθαι τὸν κίνδυνον· εἰσὶ δὲ οἳ παραδόντες ἑαυτοὺς ἅπαξ τῷ πελάγει ὑπ᾽ ἀμηχανίας τῇ τύχῃ τοὺς οἴακας ἐπιτρέπουσι φέρεσθαι. Ὅθεν ἀκούομεν τοὺς μὲν κατὰ τὸ Μαλέας ἀκρωτήριον, τοὺς δὲ κατὰ τὸν Σικελικὸν πορθμὸν, ἄλλους δὲ εἰς τὸ Λυκιακὸν πέλα-

X.

CEPHALUS TO PONTIUS.

THE surface of the ocean, as you see, is already rough ; a thick mist has overspread the heavens ; the sky is everywhere covered with clouds. The winds, driven together, threaten every moment to disturb the sea. The dolphins, leaping lightly over the swelling waves, herald the approach of stormy weather: those who are skilled in astronomy say that Taurus is rising in the heavens. Those who take due precautions against dangers for the most part come off uninjured ; but there are others who, from despair, abandon themselves to the waves of their own free will, and leave the guidance of the helm to chance. Hence we hear that some are carried along by the current to the promontory of Malea, and others to the Sicilian strait or the Lycian Sea, dashed

γος ρύμῃ φερομένους ἐποκέλλειν ἢ καταδύεσθαι. Ἔστι δὲ οὐδὲν τούτων πρὸς χειμῶνα καὶ κίνδυνον ὁ Καφηρεὺς ἐπιεικέστερος. Ἀναμείναντες οὖν ἀπολῆξαι τὸ κλυδώνιον κα ἰκαθαρὰ ναἰθρίαν γενέσθαι, περινοστήσομεν ἄχρι καὶ αὐτοῦ τοῦ Καφηρέως τῶν ἀκτῶν ἵν' εἴ πού τι τῶν ἐκ ναναγίας ἀποπτυσθὲν εὑρεθείη σῶμα, τοῦτο περιστείλαντες ταφῇ καλύψωμεν. Οὐ γὰρ ἄμισθον τὸ εὖ ποιεῖν, κἂν μὴ παραχρῆμα τῆς εὐεργεσίας ἡ ἀντίδοσις φαίνηται. Τρέφει δὲ οὐδὲν ἧττον τοὺς ἀνθρώπους πρὸς τοῖς ἐλπιζομένοις ἀγαθοῖς, καὶ διαχεῖ τὴν καρδίαν τὸ συνειδός, καὶ μάλισθ' ὅταν εἰς τοὺς ὁμοφύλους οὐκ ἔτ' ὄντας τὴν εὐποιίαν καταβάλλωνται.

upon the rocks, and swamped. The promontory of Caphareus is no better for ships in stormy weather. Therefore, let us wait until the sea is calm, and the air has cleared, before we explore the coast near this headland: perhaps we may find a body thrown up, the remnant of a shipwrecked crew, to which we may pay the honours of burial. A good action never misses its reward, even though it does not follow immediately upon the deed. The approval of the conscience, in addition to the hope of reward, supports and cheers the heart exceedingly, especially when we do a kindness to those of our fellows who are no more.

XI.

Θυνναῖος Σκοπέλῳ.

Ἀκήκοας ἀκουσμάτων βαρυτάτων, ὦ Σκόπελε; Στόλον Ἀθηναῖοι διανοοῦνται πέμπειν εἰς τὴν ὑπερορίαν, ναυμαχεῖν ἐθέλοντες. Καὶ ἤδη μὲν ἡ Πάραλος καὶ ἡ Σαλαμινία αἱ μάλιστα ταχυναυτοῦσαι πρόδρομοι λύουσι τῶν ἠϊόνων τὰ πρυμνήσια, τοὺς μαστῆρας, οἳ μέλλουσιν ἐπαγγέλλειν, παρ' οὗ καὶ ὅτε δεῖ ἀπιέναι πολεμήσοντας ἐνθέμεναι. Χρεία ταῖς λοιπαῖς ναυσὶ τὸ στρατιωτικὸν τάγμα δεχομέναις ἐρετῶν πλειόνων καὶ οὐχ ἥκιστα ἐμπείρων ἀνέμοις καὶ κύμασιν ἀπομάχεσθαι. Τί οὖν, ὦ βέλτιστε, δρῶμεν; φεύγομεν ἢ μένομεν; Ἀνδρολογοῦσι δ' ἐκ Πειραιῶς καὶ Φαληρόθεν καὶ Σουνίου καὶ μέχρι τῶν αὐτῷ Γεραιστῷ προσοίκων ὁρίων τοὺς τῆς θαλάττης ἐργάτας. Πῶς δὲ καὶ ἡμεῖς, οἱ μηδὲ τὴν ἀγορὰν εἰδύτες, ὑπομείναιμεν πυρα-

XI.

THYNNAEUS TO SCOPELUS.

HAVE you heard the important news, Scopelus? The Athenians are thinking of sending a fleet to foreign parts, to carry on a naval campaign. The Paralus and Salaminia, the swiftest vessels afloat, leading the way, are already unmoored, and have taken on board the commissioners who are to settle the time and starting-point of the expedition. The rest of the ships, which are to transport the troops, require the services of a number of oarsmen, who have had experience in contending with the winds and waves. What are we to do then, my good friend? Shall we run away or stay? Everywhere, from Piraeus, Phalerum, and Sunium, as far as the neighbourhood of Geraestus, they are enlisting sailors. How should we be able to remain quiet in the ranks and to

τάττεσθαι, καὶ ὁπλομάχοις ἀνδράσιν ὑπηρετεῖσθαι; Δυοῖν δὲ ὄντοιν χαλεποῖν, τοῦ τε φεύγειν ἐπὶ τέκνοις καὶ γυναιξὶ, τοῦ τε μέλλειν ξίφεσιν ὁμοῦ καὶ θαλάττῃ παραδιδόναι τὸ σῶμα, τοῦ μένειν ὄντος ἀλυσιτελοῦς, τὸ φεύγειν ἐφάνη λυσιτελέστερον.

obey the orders of men in arms, we who know nothing even about the contests of the law courts ? We have a choice of two evils : to leave our wives and children and take to flight, or to expose our lives to the perils of the sword and the sea. Since it is useless to remain, flight seems preferable.

XII.

Ναυσίβιος Πρυμναίῳ.

Ἡγνόουν ὅσον εἰσὶ τρυφερὰ καὶ ἁβρόβια τῶν Ἀθήνῃσι πλουσίων τὰ μειράκια. Ἔναγχος δὲ Παμφίλου μετὰ τῶν συνηλικιωτῶν μισθουμένου τὸ σκαφίδιον, ὡς ἂν ἔχῃ γαληνιῶντος τοῦ πελάγους περιπλεῖν ἅμα καὶ συμμετέχειν ἡμῖν τῆς ἄγρας τῶν ἰχθύων, ἔγνων, ἡλίκα αὐτοῖς ἐκ γῆς καὶ θαλάττης πορίζεται τρυφήματα. Οὐ γὰρ ἀνεχόμενος τῶν ξύλων τῆς ἁλιάδος, ἐπί τε ταπήτων τινῶν ξενικῶν καὶ ἐφεστρίδων κατακλιθεὶς (οὐ γὰρ οἷός τε ἔφασκεν εἶναι κεῖσθαι, ὡς οἱ λοιποί, ἐπὶ τῶν καταστρωμάτων, τὴν σανίδα οἶμαι νομίζων λίθου τραχυτέραν), ᾔτει παρ' ἡμῶν σκιὰν αὐτῷ μηχανήσασθαι, τὴν τοῦ ἱστίου σινδόνα ὑπερπετάσαντας, ὡς οὐδαμῶς οἷός τε ὢν φέρειν τὰς ἡλιακὰς ἀκτῖνας. Ἡμῖν δὲ οὐ μόνον τοῖς ταύτην ποιουμένοις τὴν ἐργασίαν, ἀλλὰ καὶ πᾶσιν ἁπαξαπλῶς, ὅσοις μὴ περιουσία πλούτου πρόσεστι, σπουδάζεται ἔστιν οὗ δυναμένοις

XII.

NAUSIBIUS TO PRYMNAEUS.

I DID not know how luxurious and effeminate the sons of our wealthy Athenians were. But, lately, when Pamphilus and some of his friends hired my skiff, that they might go for a sail as the sea was calm and take part in a fishing-expedition, I learned what luxuries they provided themselves with both on land and sea. Finding the wooden seats in the boat disagreeable, Pamphilus stretched himself out upon some foreign carpets and rugs, declaring that he could not lie down upon the bare boards, which he no doubt thought harder than stone. He next asked us to make an awning for him, by spreading out the linen sails overhead, because he could not endure the heat of the sun's rays: whereas not only we sailors, but all who are only moderately

τῇ εἴλῃ θέρεσθαι· ἐν ἴσῳ γὰρ κρυμὸς καὶ θάλαττα. Φερομένων δὲ ἅμα οὐ μόνος οὐδὲ μετὰ μόνων τῶν ἑταίρων ὁ Πάμφιλος, ἀλλὰ καὶ γυναίων αὐτῷ περιττῶν τὴν ὥραν πλῆθος συνείπετο, μουσουργοὶ πᾶσαι (ἡ μὲν γὰρ ἐκαλεῖτο Κρουμάτιον, καὶ ἦν αὐλητρίς· ἡ δὲ Ἐρατώ, καὶ ψαλτήριον μετεχειρίζετο· ἄλλη δὲ Εὐεπής, αὕτη δὲ κύμβαλα ἐπεκρότει). Ἐγένετο οὖν μοι μουσικῆς ἡ ἄκατος πλέα, καὶ ἦν ᾠδικὸν τὸ πέλαγος, καὶ πᾶν θυμηδίας ἀνάμεστον. Πλὴν ἐμέ γε ταῦτα οὐκ ἔτερπεν, οὐδὲ γὰρ οὐκ ὀλίγοι τῶν ὁμοβίων καὶ μάλιστα ὁ πικρὸς Γλαυκίας Τελχῖνος ἦν μοι βασκαίνων βαρύτερος. Ἐπεὶ δὲ τὸν μισθὸν πολὺν κατεβάλετο, τἀργύριόν με διέχει, καὶ νῦν ἐκείνου τοὺς ἐπιθαλαττίους ἀγαπῶ κώμους, καὶ τοιοῦτον δεύτερον ἐπιστῆναί μοι ποθῶ δαπανηρὸν καὶ πολυτελῆ νεανίσκον.

wealthy, as a rule seek every opportunity of warming ourselves in the sun; for the sea and cold go together. Certainly Pamphilus had not merely brought his male friends, but he was accompanied by a number of very pretty women, all musicians. The name of one was Crumatium, who played on the flute; another, Erato, was a harpist; and Euepes beat the cymbals. Thus my bark was full of music, the sea resounded with song, and mirth and gaiety prevailed. To me alone this afforded no enjoyment. For several of my fellows, especially the spiteful Glaucias, with his jealousy, caused me more uneasiness than a Telchinian. However, the ample payment he gave me cheered me; and now I am so fond of these pleasure-parties on the sea, that I wish I could find another of these generous and wealthy young men.

XIII.

Αὐχένιος Ἀρμενίῳ.

Εἰ μέν τι δύνασαι συμπράττειν, καὶ δῆτα λεγε πρός με, οὐ πρὸς ἑτέρους ἔκπυστα ποιῶν τἀμά· εἰ δὲ μηδὲν οἷός τε εἶ ὠφελεῖν, γενοῦ μοι τανῦν Ἀρεοπαγίτου στεγανώτερος. Ἐγὼ δὲ ὅπη ποτὲ τἀμά σοι διηγήσομαι· ἔρως με οὐκ ἐᾷ παρεμπεσὼν ὑπὸ τοῦ λογισμοῦ κυβερνᾶσθαι, ἀλλὰ τὸ νῆφον ἐν ἐμοὶ συνεχῶς ὑπὸ τοῦ πάθους βυθίζεται. Πόθεν γάρ ποτε εἰς ἁλιέα δύστηνον ἀγαπητῶς τὴν ἀναγκαίαν ἐκπορίζοντα διατροφὴν ἔρως ἐνέσκηψε, καὶ ἐντακεὶς οὐκ ἀνίησιν, ἀλλ' ἴσα τοῖς πλουσίοις καὶ ὡρικοῖς νεανίσκοις φλέγομαι; καὶ ὅ ποτε γελῶν τοὺς ἐκ τρυφῆς πάθει δουλεύοντας, ὅλος εἰμὶ τοῦ πάθους· γαμησείω νῦν, καὶ τὸν Ὑμέναιον ἐκφαντά-

XIII.

Auchenius to Armenius.

IF you can help me, tell me frankly, but do not talk of my affairs to anyone else ; but, if you cannot, at least be more secret than a member of the Areopagus. Meanwhile, this is the state of affairs. Love has attacked my heart, and will not allow me to be guided by reason. All sense is swamped within me by this passion. How ever has it come to pass that love has violently attacked me, a poor fisherman, who was till lately quite satisfied if he could make enough to live upon ? It has taken deep hold of me and will not let me go, and I am as much inflamed as any rich and handsome young man. I, who once laughed at those whose effeminacy made them the slaves of their passion, am now entirely in its power; I want a wife, and I can think of no-

ζομαι, τὸν παῖδα τῆς Τερψιχόρης. Ἔστι δὲ ἡ παῖς, ἧς ἐρῶ, τὸ τῶν μετοίκων θυγάτριον τῶν ἐξ Ἑρμιόνης οὐκ οἶδ' ὅπως εἰς Πειραιᾶ φθαρέντων. Ἄλλην μὲν οὖν δοῦναι προῖκα οὐκ ἔχω, ἐμαυτὸν δὲ δείξας, οἷός εἰμι θαλαττουργὸς, εἰ μὴ μαίνοιτο ὁ ταύτης πατὴρ, οἶμαι παρέξειν ἐπιτήδειον νυμφίον.

thing but Hymenaeus, son of Terpsichore. The girl I love is the daughter of one of those foreigners who, somehow or other, have migrated from Hermione to Piraeus, to our sorrow. I have certainly no dowry to offer; but I hope, if I introduce myself as what I am, a simple fisherman, that I shall be considered an eligible suitor, unless her father is mad.

XIV.

Ἐγκύμων Ἁλικτύπῳ.

Ἡρόμην ἰδὼν ἐπὶ τῆς ἠϊόνος τῆς ἐν Σουνίῳ παλαιὸν καὶ τετρυχωμένον δίκτυον ὅτου εἴη, καὶ τίνα τρόπον οὐκ ἐξογκούμενον ἀποσχισθὲν, ἤδη δὲ καὶ ὑπὸ χρόνου παλαιότητος διερρωγὸς ἀπέκειτο. Οἱ δὲ ἔφασαν σὸν κτῆμα γεγονέναι πρὸ τούτων τεττάρων ἐτῶν, εἶθ' ὑφάλῳ προσομιλῆσαν πέτρᾳ, κατὰ μέσον ἀποσχισθῆναι τῶν πλεγμάτων· σοῦ δὲ ἐξ ἐκείνου μήτε ἀκέσασθαι, μήτε ἀνελέσθαι βουληθέντος, μεῖναι, μηδενὸς τῶν περιοικούντων ὡς ἀλλοτρίου θιγγάνειν ἐπιχειρήσαντος. Ἐγένετο οὖν οὐκ 'κείνων μόνον, ἀλλὰ καὶ σοῦ τοῦ ποτε δεσπότου λοιπὸν ἀλλότριον. Αἰτῶ οὖν σε τὸ τῇ φθορᾷ καὶ τῷ χρόνῳ μὴ σόν. Σὺ δ' ὃ παντελῶς ἀπωλείᾳ προσένειμας, ἥκιστα ζημιούμενος, ἕτοιμος ἔσο πρὸς τὴν δόσιν.

XIV.

Encymon to Halictypus.

I LATELY saw, on the beach at Sunium, an old net torn and full of holes. I asked whose it was, and why it was lying there, as it had evidently not been broken by too heavy a load, but its rents were the result of age. I was told that it had belonged to you four years ago; that it had become entangled in a sunken reef, and its meshes torn in the middle. It appears that, since then, as you did not care either to mend or take it away, it has remained where it is, since none of the neighbours ventured to touch it, as they did not consider it belonged to them. Thus, not only these people, but you, the former owner, have abandoned your rights of possession. I therefore ask you to give me what is spoilt by age, and is really no longer your property. You can, without any loss to yourself, hand over to me that which you have already doomed to destruction.

XV.

Ἁλίκτυπος Ἐγκύμονι.

Δυσμενὴς καὶ βάσκανος ὁ τῶν γειτόνων ὀφθαλμός, φησὶν ἡ παροιμία. Τίς γάρ σοι τῶν ἐμῶν φροντίς; τί δὲ τὸ παρ' ἐμοῦ ῥαθυμίας ἠξιωμένον κτῆμα σὸν εἶναι νομίζεις; εἶργε τὰς χεῖρας, μᾶλλον δὲ τὰς ἀπλήστους ἐπιθυμίας· μὴ δέ σε ἡ τῶν ἀλλοτρίων ὄρεξις ἀδίκους αἰτεῖν χάριτας ἐκβιαζέσθω.

XVI.

Ἐγκύμων Ἁλικτύπῳ.

Οὐκ ᾔτησά σε ἃ ἔχεις, ἀλλ' ἃ μὴ ἔχεις. Ἐπεὶ δὲ οὐ βούλει, ἃ μὴ ἔχεις, ἕτερον ἔχειν, ἔχε ἃ μὴ ἔχεις.

XV.

HALICTYPUS TO ENCYMON.

THERE is a proverb: A neighbour's eye is spiteful and envious. How do my affairs concern you? By what right do you claim what it has pleased me to neglect? Hold your hands, or rather your insatiable desires; let not a greedy longing for what belongs to others force you to ask unreasonable favours.

XVI.

ENCYMON TO HALICTYPUS.

I DID not ask you for anything that is yours, but for something that is not. Since you will not let anyone else have it, very well; keep what you have not got.

XVII.

Εὐσάγηνος Λιμενάρχῳ.

Οὐκ ἐς κόρακας φθαρήσεται ὁ σκοπιωρὸς ὁ Λέσβιος; Φρίκῃ σκιερὰν κατὰ μέρος τὴν θάλατταν ἰδὼν ἀνεβόησεν, ὡς πλήθους ὅλου προσιόντος θύννων ἢ πηλαμίδων. Καὶ ἡμεῖς πεισθέντες, τῇ σαγήνῃ μονονουχὶ τὸν κόλπον ὅλον περιελάβομεν εἶτα ἀνιμώμεθα, καὶ τὸ βάρος μεῖζον ἦν ἢ κατὰ φορτίον ἰχθύων. Ἐλπίδι οὖν καὶ τῶν πλησίον τινὰς ἐκαλοῦμεν μερίτας ἀποφαίνειν ἐπαγγελλόμενοι, εἰ συλλάβοιντο ἡμῖν καὶ συμπονήσαιεν. Τέλος μόγῳ πολλῷ δείλης ὀψίας εὐμεγέθη κάμηλον ἐξειλκύσαμεν μυδῶσαν ἤδη καὶ σκώληξιν ἐπιβρύουσαν. Τοιαῦτα θηράσας, οὐχ ἵνα ἐπιγελάσῃς ἐδήλωσα, ἀλλ' ἵνα μάθῃς, αἷς καὶ πόσαις μηχαναῖς ἡ τύχη ἐμὲ τὸν ἀτυχῆ καταγωνίζεται.

XVII.

EUSAGENUS TO LIMENARCHUS.

CONFOUND that Lesbian watcher! When he saw the sea in some parts growing black and rough, he shouted out, as if a large shoal of young or old tunnies was approaching. Believing him, we almost completely surrounded the bay with our nets; then we hauled them up, and they felt heavier than is usual after a catch. In a state of expectation, we summoned the neighbours, promising them a share in the spoil if they would assist and aid us in our labours. At length, after great efforts, at nightfall we brought to land—an enormous camel, quite rotten and alive with worms. I have told you of this catch of ours, not to make you laugh, but that you may know how completely and by what means fortune overwhelms my unlucky self.

XVIII.

Εὔπλοος Θαλασσέρωτι.

Ὑπερμαξᾷς ἢ μέμηνας· ἀκούω γάρ σε λυρῳδοῦ γυναικὸς ἐρᾶν, καὶ ὡς ἐκείνην φθειρόμενον, πᾶσαν τὴν ἐφήμερον ἄγραν κατατίθεσθαι. Ἀπήγγειλε γάρ μοι τοῦτο γειτόνων ὁ βέλτιστος Σωσίας. Ἔστι δὲ τῶν ἐπιεικῶς τὴν ἀλήθειαν τιμώντων, καὶ οὐκ ἄν ποτε ἐκεῖνος εἰς ψευδηγορίαν ὠλίσθησεν. Οὗτος ἐκεῖνος Σωσίας ὁ τὸν χρηστὸν καὶ ἡδὺν γάρον ἑψῶν ἐκ τῶν λεπτοτέρων ἰχθύων, οὓς ἐγκολπίζεται τῇ σαγήνῃ. Πόθεν οὖν, εἰπέ μοι, μουσικῆς σοι διάτονον καὶ χρωματικὸν καὶ ἐναρμόνιον μέλος ἐστίν, ὡς αὐτὸς ἔφασκεν ἐπαγγέλλων; Ὁμοῦ γὰρ τῇ ὥρᾳ τῆς παιδίσκης ἠράσθης καὶ τοῖς κρούμασι. Πέπαυσο ἐς ταῦτα δαπανώμενος, μή σε ἀντὶ τῆς θαλάτ-

XVIII.

EUPLOUS TO THALASSEROS.

You must be suffering from the effects of high feeding, or else you are mad. I hear that you are madly enamoured of a singing-woman, and that, in paying ruinous visits to her, you squander all your daily profits. I have heard this from our excellent neighbour Sosias, who has a great respect for the truth, and would never be betrayed into falsehood: I mean the Sosias who is so skilful at making that excellent savoury broth from the little fish which he snares in his nets. Tell me, then, what has given you the idea of music, of the diatonic, harmonic, and chromatic styles, as he said, when he informed me about it? You are in love both with the girl's beauty and her music, as it seems. Leave off spending your money on such things, else you will

της ή γη ναυηγὸν ἀποφήνη ψιλώσασα τῶν χρημάτων, καὶ γένηταί σοι τὸ της ψαλτρίας καταγώγιον ὁ Καλυδώνιος κόλπος ἢ τὸ Τυρρηνικὸν πέλαγος, καὶ Σκύλλα ἡ μουσουργὸς, οὐκ ἔχοντί σοι Κράταιϊν ἐπικαλεῖσθαι, εἰ δεύτερον ἐφορμᾳ.

suffer shipwreck on land instead of on sea; you will be stripped of your substance, and the abode of this singing-woman will prove as dangerous to you as the gulf of Calydon, the Tyrrhenian sea, or Scylla the songstress, since you will not be able to call upon Crataiis, if she attacks you a second time.

XIX.

Θαλασσέρως Εὐπλόῳ.

Τηνάλλως ποιεῖς τὴν πρός με νουθεσίαν, ὦ Εὔπλοε. Ἐγὼ γὰρ οὐκ ἂν ἀποσταίην τῆς ἀνθρώπου, θεῷ μυσταγωγοῦντι πυρφόρῳ καὶ τοξοφόρῳ πειθόμενος. Καὶ ἄλλως ἡμῖν τὸ ἐρᾶν συγγενές, τῆς θαλαττίας θεοῦ τεκούσης τοῦτο τὸ παιδίον. Ἡμέτερος οὖν πρὸς μητρὸς ὁ Ἔρως, καὶ ὑπὸ τούτου βληθεὶς τὴν καρδίαν, ἔχω πρὸς θαλάττῃ τὴν κόρην, Πανόπῃ νομίζων ἢ Γαλατείᾳ ταῖς καλλιστευούσαις τῶν Νηρηίδων συνεῖναι.

XIX.

THALASSEROS TO EUPLOUS.

YOUR exhortations are useless, Euplous. It is quite impossible for me to give up this girl, now that I follow the god who has initiated me into the mysteries, the god who is armed with torch and bow. Besides, love is quite natural to us toilers on the sea: was not a goddess of the sea the mother of the winged boy? thus Love is related to us on the mother's side. Smitten by him to the heart, I enjoy the company of my girl on the shore, and think that in her I possess a Panope, or Galatea, the most beautiful of the Nereids.

XX.

Θερμολέπυρος Ὠκίμωνι.

Σχέτλια πεπόνθαμεν· τοῖς γὰρ ἄλλοις οὖθαρ καὶ μῆτραι καὶ ἧπαρ δρόσῳ προσεοικὸς διὰ τὴν ἐκ τῆς πιότητος λεπτότητα παρέκειτο, ἡμῖν δὲ ἔτνος ἦν τὸ βρῶμα· καὶ οἱ μὲν Χαλυβώνιον ἔπινον, ἐκτροπίαν δὲ ἡμεῖς καὶ ὀξίνην. Ἀλλ' ὦ μοιραῖοι θεοὶ καὶ μοιραγέται δαίμονες, δοίητε παρατροπὴν τῆς ἀδίκου ταύτης τύχης, καὶ μὴ τοὺς μὲν διηνεκεῖ φυλάττετε εὐτυχίᾳ, τοὺς δὲ τῷ λιμῷ συνοικίζετε. Ἡ γὰρ φορὰ τῆς εἱμαρμένης τὰ τοιαῦτα κατηνάγκασεν. Ἄδικα πάσχομεν πρὸς αὐτῆς οἱ λεπτῇ καὶ στενῇ κεχρημένοι τῇ τύχῃ.

XX.

Thermolepyrus to Ocimon.

I HAVE been disgracefully treated! The other guests were served with sow's udder and womb, and liver, which from the delicacy of its fat might have been compared to dew, while we had nothing but pea-soup. They drank wine from Chalybon: we had wine that had gone off, as sour as vinegar. O gods and spirits, who preside over and regulate our destinies, avert from us such injustice of fortune: do not keep some in a state of perpetual happiness, and give others hunger for a constant companion. The course of destiny has reduced humanity to melancholy necessities. But we, whose lot is poor and miserable, are treated by her with the most cruel injustice.

XXI.

Κωνωποσφράντης Ἰσχολίμῳ.

Ἀνεμιαίους ἐλπίδας ἔσχον ἐπὶ τῷ μειρακίῳ Πολυκρίτῳ. Ὤιμην γὰρ αὐτὸν, εἰ τεθναίη αὐτῷ ὁ πατὴρ, χύσιν ἂν ἐργάσασθαι τῆς οὐσίας πολλὴν, καὶ ἀδηφαγοῦντα καὶ καθηδυπαθοῦντα μετά τε ἡμῶν μετά τε τῶν ἑταιρῶν, ὅσαι κατὰ τὴν ὥραν πρωτεύουσιν, ἐξαντλοῦντα ἢ τὸ πᾶν ἢ τὸ πολὺ τῆς οὐσίας. Ὁ δὲ, ἐπειδὴ Κρίτων αὐτῷ ὁ γεννήσας ἀπεγένετο, σιτεῖται μὲν ὀψὲ τῆς ἡμέρας, καὶ τοῦτο ὀψὲ τῆς ὥρας ἡλίου λοιπὸν ἀμφὶ δύσιν ἔχοντος. Σιτεῖται δὲ οὐδὲν τῶν πολυτελῶν, ἀλλ' ἄρτον τὸν ἐξ ἀγορᾶς καὶ ὄψον, εἴποτε εὐημερίας ἡμέραν ἐπιτελοίη, δρυπετεῖς ἢ φαυλίας. Διαμαρτὼν οὖν τῆς θαυμαστῆς ταύτης ἐλπίδος οὐκ οἶδ' ὅ τι καὶ δράσαιμι· εἰ γὰρ ὁ τρέφων δεῖται τοῦ θρέψοντος, τί ἂν εἴη ὁ τρέφεσθαι ὀφείλων; λιμώττοντα δὲ λιμώττοντι συνεῖναι διπλοῦν τὸ βάρος.

XXI.

CONOPOSPHRANTES TO ISCHOLIMUS.

MY hopes of the young Polycritus have deceived me. I thought that, if his father should die, he would spend his money freely in feasting and all kinds of pleasure with us and in the company of beautiful women, and that he would have got rid of all his fortune, or the greater part of it, in this manner. Quite a mistake! ever since his father Criton died, he only takes one meal a day, and that quite late, just before sunset. He eats no expensive dishes, but common bread from the market, and, when he wants to have a regular feast, he adds some over-ripe figs and half-rotten olives. Having been thus deceived in my wonderful expectations, I do not know what I am to do. For, if the supporter himself needs some one to support him, what is to become of him who needs to be supported? It is a double misfortune for one hungry man to associate with another.

XXII.

Εὔβουλος Γεμέλλῳ.

Παρέκειτο μὲν ἡμῖν ὁ Γέλωνος τοῦ Σικελιώτου πλακοῦς ἐπώνυμος. Ἐγὼ δὲ καὶ τῇ θέᾳ μόνον πρὸς τὰς καταπόσεις εὐτρεπιζόμενος ηὐφραινόμην. Μέλλησις δὲ ἦν πολλὴ περιστεφόντων τραγημάτων τὰ πέμματα· ἦν δὲ ὁ καρπὸς τῆς πιστάκης καὶ βάλανοι φοινίκων καὶ κάρυα τῶν ἐλύτρων ἐξῃρημένα. Ἐγὼ δὲ πρὸς ταῦτα ἕκαστα ἐχθρὰ βλέπων ἀνέμενον ἐπαφήσειν ἐμαυτὸν ἐγχανὼν τῷ πλακοῦντι· οἱ δὲ καὶ τὸ ἐντραγεῖν ἐπὶ μήκιστον ἐξέτειναν, καὶ κύλικος συνεχὲς περισοβουμένης διατριβὰς καὶ μελλησμοὺς ἐνεποίουν. Τέλος, ὥσπερ ἐκ συνθήματος τὴν ἐμὴν ἀναρτῶντες ἐπιθυμίαν, ὁ μέν τις κάρφος λαβὼν ἐξεκάθαιρε τὰ ἐνιζάνοντα τῶν βρωμάτων τοῖς ὀδοῦσιν ἰνώδη· ὁ δὲ ὑπτιάσας ἑαυτὸν οἷος ἦν ὕπνῳ κατέχεσθαι μᾶλλον ἢ τῆς τραπέζης

XXII.

Eubulus to Gemellus.

One of these cheese-cakes called after Gelon of Sicily was set before us. The very sight of it delighted me, and I was all eagerness to devour it; but this moment was put off for some time, for the cakes were surrounded with all kinds of sweets, made of pistachios, dates, and nuts out of the shell. I regarded all this with an unfriendly eye; and waited, with my mouth wide open, until it should be time to attack the cake. But the guests were an unconscionably long time finishing the sweetmeats, and the continual circulation of the wine-cup caused further delay. At last, as if it had been agreed to torture me with suspense, one of them began to clean his teeth with a piece of stick, another stretched himself on his back, as if he were more inclined to sleep than

φροντίζειν· εἶτα ἄλλος ἄλλῳ διελέγετο, καὶ πάντα μᾶλλον ἐπράττετο, ἢ ὁ ἡδὺς ἐκεῖνος καὶ ποθητὸς ἡμῖν πλακοῦς εἰς ἀπόλαυσιν ἤρχετο. Τέλος, οἷα εἰκὸς, οἱ θεοὶ κατοικτείραντες τὸ κατάξηρον τῆς ἐμῆς ἐπιθυμίας, μόλις ποτὲ ἱμείροντά με τοῦ πλακοῦντος ἀπογεύσασθαι παρεσκεύασαν. Ταῦτά σοι γράφω οὐ τοσοῦτον ἐπὶ τοῖς ἡδέσιν ἡσθεὶς, ὅσον ἐπὶ τῇ παρολκῇ τῆς βραδυτῆτος ἐκτακείς.

to trouble himself about eating; then they began chattering, and nothing seemed farther from their thoughts than to give me a chance of enjoying the delicious and longed-for cake. At last, I believe, the gods had compassion upon my consuming desire, and, after long delay, procured me a taste of the cake I had so eagerly longed for. I write this, not so much with a feeling of pleasure, as of weariness and exhaustion after my prolonged waiting.

XXIII.

Πλατύλαιμος Ἐρεβινθολέοντι.

Οὐπώποτε ἐγὼ κατὰ τὴν Ἀττικὴν ὑπέμεινα τοιοῦτον χειμῶνα. Οὐ γὰρ μόνον ἐκ παραλλήλων φυσῶντες, μᾶλλον δὲ φύρδην φερόμενοι κατεκτύπουν ἡμῶν οἱ ἄνεμοι, ἀλλ' ἤδη καὶ χιὼν πυκνὴ καὶ ἐπάλληλος φερομένη, πρῶτον μὲν τοὔδαφος ἐκάλυπτεν· ἔπειτα οὐκ ἐπιπολῆς, ἀλλ' εἰς ὕψος ᾔρετο τῆς νιφάδος χῦμα πάμπολυ, ὡς ἀγαπητὸν εἶναι τὸ θυρίον ἀνοίξαντα τῆς οἰκίας τὸν στενωπὸν ἰδεῖν. Ἐμοὶ δὲ οὔτε ξύλον οὔτε ἄσβολος παρῆν. Πῶς γὰρ ἢ πόθεν; ὁ κρυμὸς δὲ εἰσεδύετο μέχρι μυελῶν αὐτῶν καὶ ὀστέων. Ἐβουλευσάμην οὖν Ὀδύσσειον βούλευμα, δραμεῖν εἰς τοὺς θόλους ἢ τὰς καμίνους τῶν βαλανείων· ἀλλ' οὐδὲ ἐκεῖσε συνεχώρουν οἱ τῶν ὁμοτέχνων περὶ ταῦτα κυλινδούμενοι· καὶ γὰρ αὐτοὺς ἡ παραπλησία θεὸς ἠνόχλει, Πενία. Ὡς οὖν

XXIII.

PLATYLAEMUS TO EREBINTHOLEON.

I HAVE never experienced so severe a winter in Attica. Not only did the winds, blowing side by side or rather rushing together in confusion, fall violently upon us, but a steady fall of deep snow covered the ground : it did not stop at the surface, but rose to such a height, that, when you opened the door, you could hardly see the street that led to our house. As you may imagine, I had neither wood nor fuel, and the cold pierced me to the very marrow. I then bethought myself of a plan worthy of Ulysses—to run to the vapour-rooms or furnaces of the public baths. But even there my fellow-labourers, who were already assembled, refused to allow me to enter, for we were all of us tormented by the same goddess—Poverty.

ἠσθόμην οὐκ εἶναί μοι εἰς ταῦτα εἰσιτητέον, δραμὼν ἐπὶ τὸ Θρασύλλου βαλανεῖον ἰδιωτικῆς οἰκίας, εὗρον τοῦτο κενόν· καὶ καταβαλὼν ὀβολοὺς δύο, καὶ τὸν βαλανέα τούτοις ἵλεων καταστήσας, ἐθερόμην, ἄχρις οὗ τὸν νιφετὸν μὲν πηγυλὶς διεδέξατο, καὶ ὑπὸ τοῦ κρύους τοῦ μεταξὺ διεροῦ παγέντος πρὸς ἀλλήλους ἐδέδεντο οἱ λίθοι. Μετὰ δὲ τὸ ἀποβράσαι τὸ δριμὺ, προσηνὴς ὁ ἥλιος ἐλευθέραν μοι τὴν πρόσοδον καὶ περιπάτους ἀνειμένως ἀπέφηνεν.

As soon as I saw that there was no getting in there, I ran to the private bath of Thrasyllus, and this time I found nobody. Having appeased the bath-keeper with a couple of obols, I succeeded in warming myself. After this, the snow was succeeded by frost, the cold dried up the moisture, and the stones on the roads became icebound. At last, the temperature became milder, and the gentle sunbeams permitted me to go out again freely, and to take my usual walks abroad.

XXIV.

Ἀμνίων Φιλομόσχῳ.

Ἀπέκειρεν ἡμῶν ἡ χάλαζα βαρέως ἐμπεσοῦσα τὰ λήϊα, καὶ λιμοῦ φάρμακον οὐδέν. Ὠνεῖσθαι δ᾽ ἡμῖν ἐπακτοὺς πυροὺς οὐχ οἷόν τε διὰ σπάνιν κερμάτων. Ἔστι δέ σοι, ὡς ἀκούω, τῆς πέρυσιν εὐετηρίας λείψανα. Δάνεισον οὖν μοι μεδίμνους εἴκοσιν, ὡς ἂν ἔχοιμι σώζεσθαι αὐτὸς καὶ ἡ γυνὴ καὶ τὰ παιδία. Καρπῶν δὲ εὐφορίας γενομένης, ἐκτίσομεν αὐτὸ τὸ μέτρον, καὶ λώϊον, ἐάν τις εὐθηνία γένηται. Μὴ δὴ περιΐδῃς ἀγαθοὺς γείτονας εἰς στενὸν τοῦ καιροῦ φθειρομένους.

XXIV.

AMNION TO PHILOMOSCHUS.

A VIOLENT hailstorm has ruined our crops, and I see no remedy against famine, for our poverty prevents us from buying imported corn. I have been told that you still have something left from your abundant harvest of last year. Lend me then twenty bushels, to save the lives of myself, my wife, and my children. If I have a good harvest, I will return it to you; yea, with interest, if I have an abundant crop. Do not desert, in time of need, such good neighbours, who are for the moment in difficulties.

XXV.

Εὔστολος Ἐλατίωνι.

Οὐδέν με τῆς γῆς ἀμειβομένης τῶν πόνων ἄξιον, ἔγνων ἐμαυτὸν ἐπιδοῦναι θαλάττῃ καὶ κύμασι. Ζῆν μὲν γὰρ καὶ τεθνάναι μεμοίραται ἡμῖν, καὶ οὐκ ἔστι τὸ χρέος φυγεῖν κἂν ἐν οἰκίσκῳ τὶς καθείρξας αὑτὸν τηρῇ· ἐναργὴς γὰρ ἡ ἡμέρα ἐκείνη, καὶ τὸ πεπρωμένον ἄφυκτον, ὥστε τὸ ζῆν οὐχ ὑπὸ τούτων ταλαντεύεται, ἀλλ ὑπὸ τῇ τύχῃ βραβεύεται. Ἤδη γάρ τινες μὲν ἐπὶ γῆς ὠκύμοροι, ἐπὶ θαλάττης δὲ μακρόβιοι κατεβίωσαν. Ὥστε εἰδὼς ταῦθ᾽ οὕτως ἔχειν, ἐπὶ ναυτιλίαν βαδιοῦμαι, καὶ ἀνέμοις ὁμιλήσω καὶ κύμασι. Κρεῖττον γὰρ ἐπανήκειν ἐκ Βοσπόρου καὶ Προποντίδος νεόπλουτον, ἢ καθήμενον ἐπὶ ταῖς τῆς Ἀττικῆς ἐσχατιαῖς λιμῶδες καὶ αὐχμηρὸν ἐρυγγάνειν.

XXV.

EUSTOLUS TO ELATION.

SINCE the land does not sufficiently repay me for my labours, I have resolved to intrust my fortunes to the sea and the waves. Life and death are allotted to us by destiny: it is impossible for a man to escape the payment of this debt, even if he shut himself up in a cell. The day of death is fixed inevitably, and fate is unavoidable. Life, therefore, does not depend upon the profession which we choose: it is subject to the arbitrament of fortune. Besides, many have perished in their youth on land, while others have lived to a great age at sea. Convinced of the truth of this, I will turn my attention to a seafaring life, and will live in the company of the winds and waves. It is better for me to return home from the Bosphorus and Propontis with newly-acquired wealth, than to live, in a remote corner of Attica, a life of misery and poverty.

XXVI.

Ἀγελαρχίδης Πυθολάῳ.

Μέγα, ὦ φίλε, κακὸν οἱ κατὰ τὴν πόλιν τοκογλύφοι. Ἐγὼ γὰρ, οὐκ οἶδα τί παθὼν, δέον παρὰ σὲ ἢ παρά τινα ἄλλον τῶν κατ' ἀγρὸν γειτόνων ἐλθεῖν, ἐπεὶ κατέστην ἐν χρείᾳ χρημάτων, βουλόμενος ἐπὶ Κολωνῷ πρίασθαι χωρίον, ξεναγήσαντός μέ τινος τῶν ἀστικῶν ἐπὶ τὰς Βυρτίας θύρας ἀφικόμην. Εἶτα καταλαμβάνω πρεσβύτην, ὀφθῆναι ῥικνὸν, συνεσπακότα τὰς ὀφρῦς, χαρτίδια ἀρχαῖά τινα, σαπρὰ δὲ διὰ τὸν χρόνον, ὑπὸ κορέων καὶ σητῶν ἡμίβρωτα, διὰ χειρὸς κατέχοντα. Εὐθὺς μὲν οὖν μόλις με προσεῖπε, ζημίαν ἡγούμενος τὴν προσηγορίαν· εἶτα τοῦ προξένου φήσαντος, ὡς δεοίμην χρημάτων, πόσων ἤρετο ταλάντων; Ἐμοῦ δὲ θαυμάσαντος τὴν

XXVI.

AGELARCHIDES TO PYTHOLAUS.

MY good friend, usurers are a great curse in the city. I do not know what was the matter with me. When I might have applied to you or one of my neighbours in the country, when I wanted some money to pay for a field which I had bought at Colonus, I allowed myself to be taken by one of the inhabitants of the city to Byrtius's door. There I found an old man, with shrivelled face and frowning brows, holding in his hand some dirty old pieces of paper, half eaten by bugs and moths. At first, he hardly spoke to me, apparently considering talking to be loss of time. When my introducer told him that I wanted money, he asked, "How many talents?" When I expressed my astonishment at the mention of such a sum, he immediately put on an

ὑπερβολὴν, διέπτυεν εὐθέως, καὶ δῆλος ἦν δυσχεραίνων· ὅμως ἐδίδου καὶ ἀπῄτει γραμματεῖον, καὶ ἐπὶ τῷ ἀρχαίῳ τόκον βαρὺν καὶ τὴν οὐσίαν ὑποθέσει μηνὸς εἰσέτι μοι· μέγα τὶ κακὸν εἰσὶν οἱ περὶ τὰς ψήφους καὶ τῶν δακτύλων τὰς κάμψεις εἰλινδούμενοι· μή μοι γένοιτο ἀγροίκων ἔφοροι δαίμονες, μὴ λύκον ἔτι, μὴ δανειστὴν ἰδεῖν.

air of contempt and made no secret of his impatience. However, he agreed to lend me the sum I wanted, and required my bond, in which I promised to pay him back the principal with enormous interest, and my property was to be security for a month. I repeat it—such people are a curse, who revel in the occupation of counting and reckoning on the fingers. O ye gods who protect the husbandman, preserve me from ever seeing a wolf or a money-lender again!

XXVII.

'Ανίκητος Φοιβιανῇ.

Φεύγεις με, ὦ Φοιβιανή, φεύγεις, καὶ ταῦτα ἀρτίως ὅλον τὸν ἀγρὸν ἀπενεγκαμένη. Τί γὰρ οὐ τῶν ἐμῶν λαβοῦσα ἔχεις; οὐ σῦκα; οὐ τυρὸν ἐκ ταλάρων; οὐκ ἀλεκτορίδων ζεῦγος; οὐ τὰ λοιπὰ τρυφήματα πάντα ἔστι σοι ἐξ ἐμοῦ; οὕτως ὅλον με αὐτὴ κατὰ τὴν παροιμίαν ἀνατρέψασα δουλεύειν ἀπηνάγκασας. Σὺ δὲ οὐδεμίαν ὥραν ἔχεις ἐμοῦ διακαῶς φλεγομένου. Ἀλλὰ χαῖρε καὶ ἄπιθι· ἐγὼ δὲ οἴσω βαρέως μὲν, οἴσω δὲ ὅμως τὴν ἀτιμίαν.

XXVII.

Anicetus to Phoebiane.

You avoid me now, Phoebiane; you avoid me, although you have just lately robbed me of all my property. What is there of mine that you have not had? Figs, fresh cheeses in baskets, a pair of fowls, not to mention all the other dainties? Thus, after having, in the words of the proverb, completely ruined me, you have forced me to become your slave. And yet you pay no heed to my burning love? Farewell: leave me. I will endure your treatment with sorrow, but yet with firmness.

XXVIII.

Φοιβιανὴ Ἀνικήτῳ.

Ὠδίνουσά με ἀρτίως ἥκειν ὡς ἑαυτὴν ἡ τοῦ γείτονος μετέπεμψατο γυνή· καὶ δῆτα ᾔειν ἀραμένη τὰ πρὸς τὴν τέχνην. Σὺ δὲ ἐξαπιναίως ἀναστὰς ἐπειρῶ τὴν δέρην ἀνακλάσας κῦσαι. Οὐ παύσῃ τρικόρωνον καὶ ταλάντατον γερόντιον πειρῶν τὰς ἐφ᾽ ἡλικίας ἀνθοῦσας ἡμᾶς ὥς τις ἄρτι νεάζειν ἀρχόμενος; οὐχὶ τῶν κατ᾽ ἀγρὸν πόνων ἀφεῖσαι, ἀεργὸς τῶν ἰδίων προϊστάμενος; οὐχὶ τοὐπτανείου καὶ τῆς ἐσχάρας ὡς ἀδύνατος ὢν ἐξέωσαι; πῶς οὖν τακερὸν βλέπεις βλέμμα καὶ ἀναπνεῖς; Πέπαυσο Κέκροψ ἄθλιε, καὶ τρέπου κατὰ σεαυτόν, ὦ πρέσβυ.

XXVIII.

PHOEBIANE TO ANICETUS.

A NEIGHBOUR, who was in labour, just now sent for me, and I was on the way to her with the necessary appliances, when you suddenly came upon me, violently held back my neck, and wanted to kiss me. You decrepit and wretched old man, will you never leave off persecuting with your overtures, as if you were a young man, us girls who are in the prime of life? Have you not been obliged to give up your work in the fields, since you are unable to look after your own affairs? Have you not been driven from the kitchen and the hearth as incompetent? What then is the use of these tender glances, these long-drawn sighs? Stop it, you miserable Cecrops, and mind your own business.

XXIX.

Γλυκέρα Βακχίδι.

Ὁ Μένανδρος ἡμῖν ἐπὶ τὴν τῶν Ἰσθμίων θέαν εἰς τὴν Κόρινθον ἐλθεῖν βεβούληται. Ἐμοὶ μὲν οὐ κατὰ νοῦν· οἶδας γὰρ οἶόν ἐστιν ἐραστοῦ τοιούτου καὶ βραχὺν ὑστερῆσαι χρόνον, ἀποτρέπειν δὲ οὐκ ἐνῆν μὴ πολλάκις ἀποδημεῖν εἰωθότα. Οὐδ' ὅπως αὐτὸν παρεγγυήσω μέλλοντα ἐπιδημήσειν ἔχω, οὐδ' ὅπως μή, βουλόμενον αὐτὸν σπουδασθῆναι ὑπὸ σοῦ, κἀμοί τινα φέρει φιλοτιμίαν, τοῦτο λογίζομαι, οἶδα γὰρ τὴν οὖσαν ἡμῖν ἑταιρίαν πρὸς ἀλλήλας. Δέδοικα δέ, ὦ φιλτάτη, οὐ σὲ τοσοῦτον (χρηστοτέρῳ γὰρ ἤθει κέχρησαι τοῦ βίου), ὅσον αὐτὸν ἐκεῖνον. Ἐρωτικὸς γάρ ἐστι δαιμονίως καὶ Βακχίδος οὐδ' ἂν

XXIX.

GLYCERA TO BACCHIS.

MENANDER has made up his mind to make a journey to Corinth, to see the Isthmian games. I do not at all approve of this idea. You know what it is to be deprived of the company of a lover such as he is, even for a little while; but I had no right to try and dissuade him, since he is hardly ever absent. He intends to stay in your town: I don't know whether I ought to intrust him to your care or not; for I know that he is anxious to win your friendship, and this certainly makes me somewhat jealous. I am aware of our mutual friendship, but I am afraid, my dear, not so much of you—for I know that your character is more honourable than your manner of life—as of Menander. He is terribly amorous, and, besides, even the gloomiest

τῶν σκυθρωποτάτων τὶς ἀπόσχοιτο. Τὸ μὲν γὰρ δοκεῖν αὐτὸν οὐκ ἔλαττον τοῦ σοὶ ἐντυχεῖν ἢ τῶν Ἰσθμίων ἕνεκεν τὴν ἀποδημίαν πεποιῆσθαι, οὐ πάνυ πείθομαι. Ἴσως αἰτιάσῃ με τῆς ὑποψίας. Συγγίνωσκε δὲ ταῖς ἑταιρικαῖς, ὦ φιλτάτη, ζηλοτυπίαις. Ἐγὼ δὲ οὐ παρὰ μικρὸν ἡγοῦμαι Μενάνδρου διαμαρτεῖν ἐραστοῦ. Ἄλλως τε κἄν μοι κνισμός τις πρὸς αὐτὸν ἢ διαφορὰ γένηται, δεήσει με ἐπὶ τῆς σκηνῆς ὑπὸ Χρεμητός τινος ἢ Διφίλου πικρῶς λοιδορεῖσθαι. Ἐὰν δὲ ἐπανέλθῃ μοι, οἷος ᾤχετο, πολλὴν εἴσομαί σοι χάριν. Ἔρρωσο.

of men would not be proof against the charms of Bacchis. I do not feel at all sure that he is not taking this journey rather for the sake of making your acquaintance than for the Olympian games. Perhaps you will think me suspicious. My dear friend, you must pardon the jealousy which is so natural to us girls. It is no trifle for me to lose a lover like Menander; especially as, if any irritation or quarrel should arise between us, I should be obliged to put up with the railleries and insults of a Chremes or Diphilus on the stage. I shall be extremely grateful to you, if he should return to me as he started. Farewell.

XXX.

Βακχὶς Ὑπερίδῃ.

Πᾶσαί σοι ἴσμεν αἱ ἑταῖραι χάριν, καὶ ἑκάστη γε ἡμῶν οὐχ ἧττον ἢ Φρύνη· ὁ μὲν γὰρ ἀγὼν μόνος Φρύνης, ὃν ὁ παμπόνηρος Εὐθίας ἐπανείλετο, ὁ δὲ κίνδυνος ἁπασῶν. Εἰ γὰρ αἰτοῦσαι παρὰ τῶν ἐραστῶν ἀργύριον οὐ τυγχάνομεν, ἢ τοῖς διδοῦσιν ἐντυγχάνουσαι ἀσεβείας κριθησόμεθα, πεπαῦσθαι κρεῖττον ἡμῖν τοῦ βίου τούτου, καὶ μηκέτι ἔχειν πράγματα, μήτε τοῖς ὁμιλοῦσι παρέχειν. Νῦν δ' οὐκ ἔτι τὸ ἑταιρεῖν αἰτιασόμεθα, ὅτι πονηρὸς Εὐθίας ἐραστὴς εὑρέθη, ἀλλ' ὅτι ἐπιεικὴς Ὑπερίδης, ζηλώσομεν. Πολλὰ τοίνυν ἀγαθὰ γένοιτό σοι τῆς φιλαν-

XXX.

BACCHIS TO HYPERIDES.

ALL we girls are grateful to you: there is not one of us who is not as much obliged as Phryne. Certainly she alone was concerned in the dangerous action, which that vile Euthias brought against her, but the danger threatened us all alike. For, if we are to ask our lovers for presents in vain, or are to be accused of impiety if we bestow our favours upon generous clients, it will be better to give up our present mode of life, and to avoid exposing ourselves and others who consort with us to annoyances on our account. But now we shall no longer be blamed on account of our profession, because Euthias has shown himself a disloyal lover; but, since Hyperides is just and good, we shall continue it in the future with increased zest. May your humanity

θρωπίας. Καὶ γὰρ ἑταίραν χρηστὴν σεαυτῷ περιεποιήσω, καὶ ἡμᾶς ἀμειψομένας σε ἀντ' ἐκείνης παρεσκεύασας. Εἰ δὲ δὴ καὶ τὸν λόγον γράψαις τὸν ὑπὲρ τῆς Φρύνης, τότε ἂν ὡς ἀληθῶς χρυσοῦν αἱ ἑταῖραί σε στήσαιμεν, ὅπη ποτὲ βούλει τῆς Ἑλλάδος.

meet with its due reward. You have gained a respectable mistress for your own benefit, and, in her person, you have saved us all; for which our gratitude is due to you. If you would only publish the speech which you delivered on her behalf, then we girls promise to erect in your honour a golden statue, in whatever part of Greece you please.

XXXI.

Βακχὶς Φρύνῃ.

Οὐ τοσοῦτόν σοι τοῦ κινδύνου συνηχθέσθην, ὦ φιλτάτη, ὅσον, ὅτι πονηροῦ μὲν ἀπηλλάγης ἐραστοῦ, χρηστὸν δὲ εὗρες Ὑπερίδην, συνήσθην. Τὴν γὰρ δίκην σοι καὶ πρὸς εὐτυχίαν γεγονέναι νομίζω· διαβόητον γάρ σε οὐκ ἐν ταῖς Ἀθήναις μόνον, ἀλλὰ καὶ ἐν τῇ Ἑλλάδι ἁπάσῃ ὁ ἀγὼν ἐκεῖνος πεποίηκεν. Εὐθίας μὲν γὰρ ἱκανὴν τιμωρίαν δώσει τῆς σῆς ὁμιλίας στερούμενος· ὑπὸ γὰρ ὀργῆς μοι δοκεῖ κινηθεὶς διὰ τὴν ἔμφυτον ἀμαθίαν ὑπεράραι τὸ μέτρον τῆς ἐρωτικῆς ζηλοτυπίας. Καὶ νῦν ἐκεῖνον ἐρῶντα μᾶλλον εὖ ἴσθι ἢ Ὑπερίδην. Ὁ μὲν γὰρ διὰ τὴν τῆς συνηγορίας χάριν δῆλός ἐστι σπουδά-

XXXI.

BACCHIS TO PHRYNE.

THE sympathy which I felt for you in your hour of danger, my dearest friend, was not so great as is my present joy, now that you have got rid of a worthless lover and found an honest friend in Hyperides. It is my opinion that this suit has been very fortunate for you; for the trial has made your name famous, not only in Athens, but throughout the whole of Greece. Euthias will be sufficiently punished by the loss of your favours. Owing to his natural stupidity, he appears to have gone beyond the limits of the jealousy of a lover in the excitement of his anger; be assured that he loves you at the present moment more than Hyperides himself. The latter certainly wishes to be regarded with favour by you in return for having undertaken your

ξεσθαι βουλόμενος καὶ ἐρώμενον ἑαυτὸν ποιῶν· ὁ δὲ τῷ ἀποτεύγματι τῆς δίκης παρώξυνται. Προσδέχου δὴ πάλιν δι' αὐτοῦ δεήσεις καὶ λιτανείας καὶ πολὺ χρυσίον. Μὴ δὴ καταδιαιτήσῃς ἡμῶν, ὦ φιλτάτη, τῶν ἑταιρῶν· μὴ δὲ Ὑπερίδην κακῶς δόξαι βεβουλεῦσθαι ποιήσῃς, τὰς Εὐθίου ἱκεσίας προσιεμένη· μὴ δὲ τοῖς λέγουσί σοι, ὅτι, εἰ μὴ τὸν χιτωνίσκον περιρρηξαμένη τὰ μαστάρια τοῖς δικασταῖς ἀπέδειξας, οὐδὲν ὁ ῥήτωρ ὠφέλει, πείθου. Καὶ γὰρ αὐτὸ τοῦτο, ἵνα ἐν καιρῷ γένηταί σοι, ἡ ἐκείνου παρέσχε συνηγορία.

defence, and to gain your affection; but the passion of the other has been only more violently whetted by the loss of his case. You may expect from him, then, fresh entreaties, supplications, and presents in abundance; but, my dear girl, do not prejudice our cause, or, by listening to the entreaties of Euthias, cause it to be thought that Hyperides has done wrong in taking our part. Neither believe those who tell you that the orator's efforts would have been unavailing, unless you had rent your clothes and shown your bare breasts to the judges. Why, this very argument, so opportunely employed, was the result of his exertions on your behalf.

XXXII.

Βακχὶς Μυρρίνῃ.

Μὴ δὴ κρείττονος εἴη σοι τυχεῖν ἐραστοῦ, δέσποινα Ἀφροδίτη, ἀλλ' Εὐθίας σοι, ὃν νῦν περιέπεις, συγκαταβιώη. Τάλαινα γυνὴ τῆς ἀνοίας, ἥτις τῷ τοιούτῳ θηρίῳ προσέφθαρσαι. Πλὴν ἴσως τῷ κάλλει πεπίστευκας. Φρύνην γὰρ ὑπεριδὼν δηλονότι στέρξει Μυρρίνην. Ἀλλ' ἔοικας κνίσαι τὸν Ὑπερίδην βεβουλῆσθαι ὡς ἔλαττόν σοι νῦν προσέχοντα. Κἀκεῖνος ἑταίραν ἔχει ἀξίαν ἑαυτοῦ, καὶ σὺ ἐραστήν σοι πρέποντα. Αἴτησόν τι παρ' αὐτοῦ, καὶ ὄψει σεαυτὴν ἢ τὰ νεώρια ἐμπεπρηκυῖαν, ἢ τοὺς νόμους καταλύουσαν. Ἴσθι γοῦν, ὅτι παρὰ πάσαις ἡμῖν ταῖς τὴν φιλανθρωποτέραν Ἀφροδίτην προτιμώσαις μεμίσησαι.

XXXII.

BACCHIS TO MYRRHINE.

No, so help me, Venus, may you never find a better lover! may you spend all your life with Euthias, with whom you are so infatuated! Unhappy woman! how foolish you are to attach yourself to a monster like that, merely because of your confidence in your beauty! Of course he will despise Phryne and love Myrrhine. No doubt your object was to irritate Hyperides, who at this moment treats you with neglect. He in truth possesses a mistress who is worthy of him; and you have a lover who is admirably suited to you. But only ask him for a present: you will soon see if he does not accuse you of having tried to set fire to the dockyards or of having broken the laws. To tell the truth, you have made yourself hateful to all of us, who have regard for a more honourable attachment.

XXXIII.

Θαῒς Θετταλῃ.

Οὐκ ἄν ποτ' ᾠήθην ἐκ τοσαύτης συνηθείας ἔσεσθαί μοι τινὰ πρὸς Εὐξίππην διαφοράν. Καὶ τὰ μὲν ἄλλα, ἐν οἷς αὐτῇ χρησίμη γέγονα ὑπὸ τὸν ἀπὸ τῆς Σάμου κατάπλουν, οὐκ ὀνειδίζω. Ἀλλὰ Παμφίλου, γινώσκεις τοῦτο καὶ σὺ ὅσον, ἡμῖν διδόντος ἀργύριον, ὅτι ταύτῃ ποτὲ ἐντυγχάνειν ἐδόκει τὸ μειράκιον, οὐ προσιέμην. Ἀλλὰ καλῶς ἡμᾶς ἀντὶ τούτων ἠμείψατο, τῇ κάκιστα ἀπολουμένῃ Μεγάρᾳ χαρίζεσθαι θέλουσα· πρὸς ἐκείνην δ' ἦν τις παλαιά μοι διὰ Στράτωνα ὑπόνοια. Ἀλλὰ ταύτην μὲν οὐδὲν ᾤμην ποιεῖν παράλογον κακῶς λέγουσάν με. Ἁλῶα δ' ἦν, κἀπὶ τὴν παννυχίδα πᾶσαι, ὥσπερ ἦν εἰκὸς, παρ' ἡμῖν. Ἐθαύμαζον δὲ τῆς Εὐξίππης·

XXXIII.

THAIS TO THESSALE.

I SHOULD never have believed that, after so long an intimacy with Euxippe, I should quarrel with her. I do not reproach her with the many services I have rendered her since she arrived here from Samos. You know what a handsome present Pamphilus offered me; but I refused to have anything to do with him, because I knew that he had already become acquainted with her. By way of rewarding my kindness handsomely, she is endeavouring to curry favour with that accursed woman Megara, of whom I have long had my suspicions, on account of Straton. So there is nothing astonishing in her speaking ill of me. It was the festival of Ceres, and we were all assembled according to custom at my house, to spend the night. I was sur-

τὸ μὲν γὰρ πρῶτον, κιχλίζουσα μετ' ἐκείνης καὶ μωκωμένη, τὴν δυσμένειαν ἐνεδείκυτο, εἶτα φανερῶς ποιήματα ᾖδεν εἰς τὸν οὐκ ἔθ' ἡμῖν προσέχοντα ἐραστήν. Κἀπὶ τούτοις μὲν ἧττον ἤλγουν· ἀπαναισχυντήσασα δὲ εἰς τὸ φῦκός με καὶ τὸν παιδέρωτα ἔσκωπτεν. Ἐδόκει δέ μοι πάνυ κακῶς πράττειν, ὡς μηδὲ κάτοπτρον κεκτῆσθαι. Εἰ γὰρ οἶδεν ἑαυτὴν χρῶμα σανδαράχης ἔχουσαν, οὐκ ἂν ἡμᾶς εἰς ἀμορφίαν ἐβλασφήμει. Ἐμοὶ μὲν οὖν βραχὺ μέλει περὶ τούτων, ἀρέσκειν γὰρ τοῖς ἐρασταῖς, οὐχὶ Μεγάρᾳ καὶ Εὐξίππῃ βούλομαι ταῖς πιθήκοις. Δεδήλωκα δέ σοι, ἵνα μή μ' ἔτι μέμψῃ. Ἀμυνοῦμαι γὰρ αὐτὰς οὐκ ἐν σκώμμασιν, οὐδ' ἐν βλασφημίαις, ἀλλ' ἐν οἷς μάλιστα ἀνιάσονται. Προσκυνῶ δὲ τὴν Νέμεσιν.

prised at Euxippe's behaviour. At first, she kept on giggling with Megara, and, by mocking and mimicking me, showed her spitefulness; then she began to sing aloud some verses, containing allusions to a lover who had forsaken me. I did not mind this so much. But, at last, she lost all decency, and ridiculed my dye and rouge. She seems badly off herself: I don't believe she even possesses a mirror. For, if she saw how like yellow ochre her complexion was, she would not abuse me for being ugly. However, I care very little about this. I want to please my lovers, not monkeys like Megara or Euxippe. I have told you this, that you may not blame me afterwards; for, one day, I will revenge myself upon them, not with raillery or insult, but in such a manner as to make them feel it. I worship the goddess Nemesis.

XXXIV.

Θαῒς Εὐθυδήμῳ.

Ἐξ οὗ φιλοσοφεῖν ἐπενόησας, σεμνός τις ἐγένου, καὶ τὰς ὀφρῦς ὑπὲρ τοὺς κροτάφους ἐπῆρας. Εἶτα σχῆμα ἔχων καὶ βιβλίδιον μετὰ χεῖρας εἰς τὴν Ἀκαδημίαν σοβεῖς, τὴν δὲ ἡμετέραν οἰκίαν ὡς οὐδὲ ἰδὼν πρότερον παρέρχῃ. Ἐμάνης, Εὐθύδημε; οὐκ οἶδας, οἷός ἐστιν ὁ σοφιστὴς οὗτος ὁ ἐσκυθρωπακὼς καὶ τοὺς θαυμαστοὺς τούτους διεξιὼν πρὸς ὑμᾶς λόγους; Ἀλλ' ἐμοὶ μὲν πράγματα, πόσος ἐστὶν οἴει χρόνος, ἐξ οὗ παρέχει βουλόμενος ἐντυχεῖν. Προσφθείρεται δὲ Ἑρπυλλίδι τῇ Μεγάρας ἅβρᾳ. Τότε μὲν οὖν αὐτὸν οὐ προσιέμην, σὲ γὰρ περιβάλλουσα κοιμᾶσθαι μᾶλλον ἐβουλόμην, ἢ τὸ παρὰ πάντων σοφιστῶν χρυσίον. Ἐπεὶ δέ σε ἀποτρέπειν

XXXIV.

Thais to Euthydemus.

Since you have taken it into your head to study philosophy, you have become serious, and raise your eyebrows above your forehead. Then, assuming the philosopher's air, with a book in your hand, you strut proudly towards the Academy, passing by my house, as if you had never seen it before. Are you mad, Euthydemus? Don't you know what sort of man that scowling sophist is, who has so excited your admiration by his discourses? You don't know how long he has been pestering me, in order to gain my favours. He is also mad after Herpyllis, Megara's pet maid. At that time, I refused to receive him, for I preferred your kisses and embraces to all the gold of philosophers. But, since he seems to be the cause of your keeping

ἔοικε τῆς μεθ' ἡμῶν συνηθείας, ὑποδέξομαι αὐτόν· καὶ εἰ βούλει, τὸν διδάσκαλον τουτονὶ τὸν μισογύναιον ἐπιδείξω σοι νυκτὸς οὐκ ἀρκούμενον ταῖς συνήθεσιν ἡδοναῖς. Λῆρος ταῦτα εἰσὶ καὶ τῦφος καὶ ἐργολάβεια μειρακίων, ὦ ἀνόητε. Οἴει δὲ διαφέρειν ἑταίρας σοφιστήν; τοσοῦτον ἴσως, ὅσον οὐ διὰ τῶν αὐτῶν ἑκάτεροι πείθουσιν· ἐπεὶ ἕν γε ἀμφοτέροις τέλος πρόκειται τὸ λαβεῖν. Πόσῳ δὲ ἀμείνους ἡμεῖς καὶ εὐσεβέστεραι; Οὐ λέγομεν θεοὺς οὐκ εἶναι, ἀλλὰ πιστεύομεν ὀμνύουσι τοῖς ἐρασταῖς, ὅτι φιλοῦσιν ἡμᾶς. Οὐδ' ἀξιοῦμεν ἀδελφαῖς καὶ μητράσι μίγνυσθαι τοὺς ἄνδρας, ἀλλ' οὐδὲ γυναιξὶν ἀλλοτρίαις. Εἰ μὴ, ὅτι τὰς νεφέλας ὁπόθεν εἶεν, καὶ τὰς ἀτόμους ὁποῖαι, ἀγνοοῦμεν, διὰ τοῦτο ἥττους δοκοῦμέν σοι τῶν σοφιστῶν. Καὶ αὐτὴ παρὰ τούτοις ἐσχόλακα καὶ πολλοῖς διείλεγμαι. Οὐδεὶς ἑταίραις ὁμιλῶν τυραννίδας ὀνειροπολεῖ καὶ στασιάζει τὰ κοινά·

away from me, I will receive him; and,
if you like, I will prove to you that this
wonderful teacher, this woman-hater, is
not satisfied with ordinary enjoyments
during the night. You foolish young
man, all this display is simple nonsense,
mere artifice, a trap to fleece young men.
Do you think there is much difference
between a sophist and a woman? The
only difference is in their ways of persuasion; the object of their efforts is the
same—to get money. Indeed, our prin-
ciples are far better and more religious
than theirs: we do not deny the existence of the gods, but we believe our
lovers, when they swear that they adore
us. We also prevent men from com-
mitting incest and adultery. Only, because we are ignorant of the origin of
the clouds and the theory of atoms, you
consider us to be inferior to the sophists.
I myself have attended their lectures,
and have conversed with several of them.
The truth is, that none of those who
frequent the company of women trouble
themselves with idle dreams of upsetting

ἀλλὰ σπάσας τὸν ἑωθινὸν καὶ μεθυσθεὶς, εἰς ὥραν τρίτην ἢ τετάρτην ἠρεμεῖ. Παιδεύομεν δὲ οὐ χεῖρον ἡμεῖς τοὺς νέους. Ἐπεὶ σύγκρινον, εἰ βούλει, Ἀσπασίαν τὴν ἑταίραν, καὶ Σωκράτην τὸν σοφιστὴν, καὶ πότερος ἄμεινον αὐτῶν ἐπαίδευσεν ἄνδρας, λόγισαι· τῆς μὲν γὰρ ὄψει μαθητὴν Περικλέα, τοῦ δὲ Κριτίαν. Κατάβαλε τὴν μωρίαν ταύτην καὶ ἀηδίαν, ὁ ἐμὸς ἔρως, Εὐθύδημε (οὐ πρέπει σκυθρωποῖς εἶναι τοιούτοις ὄμμασι), καὶ πρὸς τὴν ἐρωμένην ἧκε τὴν ἑαυτοῦ, οἷος ἐπανελθὼν ἀπὸ Λυκείου πολλάκις τὸν ἱδρῶτα ἀποψώμενος, ἵνα μικρὰ κραιπαλήσαντες ἐπιδειξώμεθα ἀλλήλοις τὸ καλὸν τελος τῆς ἡδονῆς. Καὶ σοὶ νῦν μάλιστά γε φανοῦμαι σοφή. Οὐ μακρὸν δίδωσιν ὁ δαίμων χρόνον τοῦ ζῆν μὴ λάθῃς τοῦτον εἰς αἰνίγματα καὶ λήρους ἀναλώσας. Ἔρρωσο.

the state and seizing the supreme authority: they drink all the morning, get frightfully drunk, and then sleep it off till nine or ten o'clock. Again, we educate young men quite as well as they do. Compare, if you like, Aspasia the courtesan and the famous sophist Socrates; and consider which of them produced the best citizens. You will find that Pericles was the pupil of the former, Critias of the latter. Abandon this folly, shake off your disagreeable looks, my darling Euthydemus: your beautiful eyes were never intended to be scowling; return to your lady-love the same as when you used to visit her on the way from the Lyceum, wiping off the perspiration. Let us drink moderately, and prove to each other that pleasure is the aim of life. Then you will confess how learned I am! Besides, the Deity only allows us a short time to live; do not waste it foolishly in trying to solve riddles. Farewell.

XXXV.

Σιμαλίων Πετάλῃ..

Εἰ μὲν ἡδονὴν σοί τινα φέρειν ἢ φιλοτιμίαν πρός τινας τῶν διαλεγομένων οἴει τὸ πολλάκις ἡμᾶς ἐπὶ τὰς θύρας φοιτᾶν, καὶ τοῖς πεμπομένοις πρὸς τοὺς εὐτυχεστέρους ἡμῶν θεραπαινιδίοις ἀποδύρεσθαι, οὐκ ἀλόγως ἡμῖν ἐντρυφᾷς. Ἴσθι μέν τοι (καί τοι ποιῶν οἶδα πρᾶγμα ἀσύμφορον ἐμαυτῷ), οὕτω με διακείμενον ὡς ὀλίγοι τῶν ἐντυγχανόντων σοι νῦν ἀμεληθέντες ἂν διατεθεῖεν. Καί τοι γε ᾤμην τὸν ἄκρατον ἔσεσθαί μοι παρηγόρημα, ὃν παρ' Εὐφρονίῳ τρίτην ἑσπέραν πολύν τινα ἐνεφορησάμην, ὡς δὴ τὰς παρὰ τὴν νύκτα φροντίδας διωσόμενος· τὸ δὲ ἄρα ἐναντίως ἔσχεν. Ἀνερρίπισε γάρ μου τὴν ἐπιθυμίαν, ὥστε κλαίοντά με καὶ βρυχώμενον ἐλεεῖσθαι

XXXV.

SIMALION TO PETALE.

IF you think it is any satisfaction to you or that it adds to the gratification of your clients, to make me come repeatedly to your door and complain to your servants who are sent to more fortunate suitors, I cannot say you are wrong in treating me thus contemptuously. I know that my efforts are unavailing; but be assured that few of your favoured lovers would be so deeply affected by the loss of your affection as I am. I flattered myself that the quantity of wine I drank yesterday at Euphemius's would afford me some consolation, and help me to drive away my nightly cares; but it had just the contrary effect. It only fanned more violently the flame of my passion: I wept, I sobbed loudly, so that the better disposed of those around me

μὲν παρὰ τοῖς ἐπιεικεστέροις, γέλωτα δὲ τοῖς ἄλλοις παρέχειν. Μικρὰ δὲ ἔπεστί μοι παραψυχὴ καὶ μαραινόμενον ἤδη παραμύθιον, ὅ μοι ὑπὸ τὴν λυπρὰν τῷ συμποσίῳ μέμψιν προσέρριψας ἀπ' αὐτῶν περισπάσασα τῶν πλοκάμων, ὡς μὴ πᾶσι τοῖς ὑφ' ἡμῶν πεμφθεῖσιν ἀχθομένη. Εἰ δή σοι ταῦτα ἡδονὴν φέρει, ἀπόλαυε τῆς ἡμετέρας μερίμνης· κἂν ᾖ σοι φίλον, διηγοῦ τοῖς νῦν μὲν μακαριωτέροις ἡμῶν, οὐκ εἰς μακρὰν δέ, ἂν ὥσπερ ἡμεῖς ἔχωσιν, ἀνιασομένοις. Εὔχου μέν τοι μηδέν σοι νεμεσῆσαι ταύτης τῆς ὑπεροψίας τὴν Ἀφροδίτην. Ἕτερος ἂν λοιδορούμενος ἔγραφε καὶ ἀπειλῶν· ἀλλ' ἐγὼ δεόμενος καὶ ἀντιβολῶν, ἐρῶ γὰρ, ὦ Πετάλη, κακῶς. Φοβοῦμαι δὲ μὴ κάκιον ἔχων μιμήσομαί τινα τῶν περὶ τὰς ἐρωτικὰς μέμψεις ἀτυχεστέρων.

were moved to pity, while the rest laughed at me. There still remains for me a slight alleviation of my sorrow, a poor consolation, which, however, is now withering away and fading. I mean the flower which you plucked from your head when we quarrelled at supper, and threw at me, to show that you were not offended with everything I had sent you. But, if it amuses you, enjoy my grief; if it please you, tell the story of it to those who are now more fortunate than myself; it will perhaps soon be their turn to grieve, when they meet with similar treatment. However, pray to Venus that she be not angry with you for your pride. Another would have written a letter to you full of insults and threats: I prefer to address you with prayers and supplications, for I am desperately in love with you. Alas! in the excess of my grief, I am afraid of imitating those unfortunate lovers whose complaints only serve to increase their misfortune.

XXXVI.

Πετάλη Σιμαλίωνι.

Ἠβουλόμην μὲν ὑπὸ δακρύων ἑταίρας τρέφεσθαι οἰκίαν. Λαμπρῶς γὰρ ἂν ἔπραττον ἀφθόνων τούτων ἀπολαύουσα παρὰ σοῦ· νῦν δὲ δεῖ χρυσίου ἡμῖν, ἱματίων, κόσμου, θεραπαινίδων. Ἡ τοῦ βίου διοίκησις ἅπασα ἐντεῦθεν. Οὐκ ἔστιν ἐν Μυρρινοῦντι πατρῷον ἐμοὶ κτημάτιον, οὐδ᾽ ἐν τοῖς ἀργυρίοις ἐμοὶ μέταλλον, ἀλλὰ μισθωμάτια καὶ αἱ δυστυχεῖς αὗται καὶ κατεστεναγμέναι τῶν ἀνοήτων ἐραστῶν χάριτες. Σοὶ δὲ ἐνιαυτὸν ἐντυγχάνουσα ἀδημονῶ, καὶ αὐχμηρὰν μὲν ἔχω τὴν κεφαλήν, μηδὲ ἰδὼν τὸν χρόνον τοῦτον μύρον· τὰ δὲ ἀρχαῖα καὶ τρύχινα περιβαλλομένη Ταραντινίδια αἰσχύνομαι τὰς φίλας. Οὕτως ἀγαθόν τι μοι γένοιτο. Εἶτα οἴει μέ σοι

XXXVI.

PETALE TO SIMALION.

How I wish that a woman's house could be supported on tears! I should live right royally, for I know you would keep me abundantly supplied with them; but, as it is, unfortunately we want money, clothes, ornaments, and servants. Our arrangements depend entirely upon this. I have no patrimony at Myrrhinus, no share in the silver mines; I depend upon the little presents I receive, and the favours of foolish lovers, wrung only from them with many sighs and tears. I have known you now for more than a year, and I am no better for it. My hair is in disorder; it has not seen any oil all this time. I have only got one Tarentine tunic, so old and torn that I am perfectly ashamed to be seen in it by my friends. I hope I may have better

παρακαθημένην ποθὲν ζήσειν; Ἀλλὰ δακρύεις; πεπαύσῃ μετὰ μικρόν. Ἐγὼ δὲ ἂν μή τις ὁ διδοὺς ᾖ, πεινήσω τὸ καλόν. Θαυμάζω δέ σου καὶ τὰ δάκρυα ὡς ἔστιν ἀπίθανα. Δέσποινα Ἀφροδίτη, φιλεῖς, ἄνθρωπε, φιλεῖς, καὶ βούλει σοι τὴν ἐρωμένην διαλέγεσθαι, ζῆν γὰρ χωρὶς ἐκείνης μὴ δύνασθαι. Τί οὖν; οὐ ποτήρια ἐστὶν ἐπὶ τῆς οἰκίας ὑμῖν, μὴ χρυσία τῆς μητρὸς, μὴ δάνεια τοῦ πατρὸς κομιουμένοις; Μακαρία Φιλότης, εὐμενεστέροις ὄμμασιν εἶδον ἐκείνην αἱ Χάριτες, οἷον ἐραστὴν ἔχει Μενεκλείδην, ὃς καθ' ἡμέραν δίδωσί τι· ἄμεινον γὰρ ἢ κλάειν. Ἐγὼ δὲ ἡ τάλαινα θρηνῳδὸν, οὐκ ἐραστὴν ἔχω, στεφάνιά μοι καὶ ῥόδα ὥσπερ ἀώρῳ τάφῳ πέμπει, καὶ κλάειν δι' ὅλης φησὶ τῆς νυκτός. Ἐὰν φέρῃς τι, ἧκε μὴ κλαίων, εἰ δὲ μὴ, σεαυτὸν οὐχ ἡμᾶς ἀνιάσεις.

luck! And do you think that, while I stick to you, I shall be able to find other resources? You weep; be sure that won't last long. But I shall be finely hungry, unless I can find a lover to give me something. I wonder at your tears: how absurd they are! O lady Venus! You say, Simalion, that you are madly in love with a woman, and that you cannot live without her. Well, my friend, have you no valuable drinking-cups at home? has not your mother some jewellery? cannot you get some securities belonging to your father? Happy Philotis! the Graces have looked upon her with kindly eyes. What a lover she has in Meneclides, who gives her something every day. That is better than tears. As for me, unhappy girl, I have no lover, but a hired mourner, who sends me nothing but roses and garlands, as if to decorate an early grave for me, and declares that he weeps all night. If you can give me anything, come and see me, but—no tears. Otherwise, keep your grief to yourself, and do not worry me.

XXXVII.

Μυρρίνη Νικίππῃ.

Οὐ προσέχει μοι τὸν νοῦν ὁ Δίφιλος, ἀλλὰ ἅπας ἐπὶ τὴν ἀκάθαρτον Θετταλὴν νένευκε. Καὶ μέχρι μὲν τῶν Ἀδωνίων καὶ ἐπίκωμός ποτε πρὸς ἡμᾶς καὶ κοιμησόμενος ἐφοίτα, ἤδη μέν τοι ὡς ἄν τις ἀκκιζόμενος καὶ ἐρώμενον ἑαυτὸν ποιῶν, καὶ τά γε πλεῖστα ὑπὸ τοῦ Ἕλικος, ὁπότε μεθυσθείη, ὁδηγούμενος (ἐκεῖνος γὰρ τῆς Ἑρπυλλίδος ἐρῶν τὴν παρ' ἡμῖν ἠγάπα σχολήν)· νῦν μέν τοι δῆλός ἐστι μηδ' ὅλως ἡμῖν ἐντευξόμενος· τέσσαρας γὰρ ἑξῆς ἡμέρας ἐν τῷ Λύσιδος κήπῳ μετὰ Θετταλῆς καὶ τοῦ κάκιστ' ἀπολουμένου Στρογγυλίωνος, ὃς ταύτην αὐτῷ προὐμνηστεύσατο τὴν ἐρωμένην ἐμοί τι προςκρούσας, κραιπαλᾷ. Γραμματίδια μὲν οὖν καὶ θεραπαινίδων διαδρομαὶ καὶ ὅσα τοιαῦτα μάτην

XXXVII.

Myrrhine to Nicippe.

DIPHILUS no longer cares for me; he is altogether devoted to that dirty wretch Thessale. Until the day of the festival of Adonis, he used to come and sup and sleep with me from time to time, but since then he has put on an insolent and haughty air, and wants to be made much of. Whenever he was drunk, he was escorted by Helix, who was very fond of coming to stay at my house, since he was in love with Herpyllis. But now he makes no secret of it, that he does not intend to have anything more to do with me. For four whole days he has been on the drink in Lysis's garden, in the company of Thessale and that accursed Strongylion, who, out of spite against me, has introduced this new flame to him. Letters, my servants' journeys to and fro—all my

διήνυσται, καὶ οὐδὲν ἐξ αὐτῶν ὄφελος· δοκεῖ δέ μοι μᾶλλον ὑπὸ τούτων τετυφῶσθαι καὶ ὑπερεντρυφᾶν ἡμῖν. Λοιπὸν οὖν ἀποκλείειν, κἂν ἔλθῃ ποτὲ πρὸς ἡμᾶς κοιμηθησόμενος, εἰ δὴ κνίσαι ποτὲ ἐκείνην βουληθείη, διώσασθαι· εἴωθε γὰρ ἡ βαρύτης τῷ ἀμελεῖσθαι καταβάλλεσθαι. Ἐὰν δὲ μηδ᾽ οὕτως ἀνύοιμεν, θερμοτέρου τινὸς ἡμῖν ὥσπερ τοῖς σφόδρα κάμνουσι φαρμάκου δεῖ· δεινὸν γὰρ οὐ τοῦτο μόνον, εἰ τῶν παρ᾽ αὐτοῦ μισθωμάτων στερησόμεθα, ἀλλ᾽ εἰ Θετταλῃ γέλωτα παρέξομεν. Ἔστι σοι πειραθὲν, ὡς φῆς, πολλάκις ἐφ᾽ ἡλικίας φίλτρον. Τοιούτου τινὸς βοηθήματος δεόμεθα, ὃ τὸν πολὺν αὐτοῦ τύφον, ἀλλ᾽ οὖν καὶ τὴν κραιπάλην ἐκκορήσειεν. Ἐπικηρυκευσόμεθα δὴ αὐτῷ καὶ δακρύσομεν πιθανῶς, καὶ τὴν Νέμεσιν δεῖν αὐτὸν ὁρᾶν, εἰ οὕτως ἐμὲ περιόψεται ἐρῶσαν αὐτοῦ, καὶ τοιαῦτα ἄλλα ἐροῦμεν καὶ πλασόμεθα. Ἥξει γὰρ ὡς ἐλεῶν δήπου με καιομένην ἐπ᾽ αὐτῷ· μεμνῆσθαι γὰρ τοῦ παρελ-

efforts were fruitless and without result. I even think they have increased his pride and arrogance towards me. The only thing that remains for me to do is to shut my door against him, if ever he wants to spend the night with me, in order to vex her; insolence is generally overcome by contempt. But, even if this proves useless, then I must have recourse to a more drastic remedy, as in cases of severe illness; for it would be intolerable not only to lose the money I get out of him, but also to be Thessale's laughing-stock. You say you have a love-potion, which you have often tried upon young men. I need some assistance of the kind to cure him of his pride and fondness for drink. I will send to make overtures of peace and will try to soften him with my tears. I will tell him he must beware of the wrath of Nemesis, if he slights a heart so affectionate as mine. I will tell him other things of the same kind, and draw freely on my imagination. He will certainly come, moved to pity by my great affection. He will even allow

θόντος χρόνου καὶ τῆς συνηθείας ἔχειν καλῶς ἐρεῖ, φυσῶν ἑαυτὸν ὁ λάσταυρος. Συλλήψεται δὲ ἡμῖν καὶ ὁ "Ελιξ· ἐπ' ἐκεῖνον γὰρ ἡ Ἑρπυλλὶς ἀποδύσεται. Ἀλλ' ἀμφιβάλλειν εἴωθε τὰ φίλτρα καὶ ἀποσκήπτειν εἰς ὄλεθρον βραχύ μοι μέλει· δεῖ γὰρ αὐτὸν ἢ ἐμοὶ ζῆν ἢ τεθνάναι Θετταλῃ.

that it is only right to keep past times
and our old acquaintance in remembrance,
puffing himself up with pride, like the
wretch that he is. Helix also will help
me ; Herpyllis will see to him. But the
effect of philtres is doubtful; they sometimes prove fatal. But what do I care?
He must either live to be mine, or die
for Thessale.

XXXVIII.

Μενεκλείδης Εὐθυκλεῖ.

Οἴχεται Βακχὶς ἡ καλὴ, Εὐθύκλεις φίλτατε, οἴχεται, πολλά τέ μοι καταλιποῦσα δάκρυα καὶ ἔρωτος ὅσον ἡδίστου τὸ τέλος οὐ πονηροῦ τὴν μνήμην. Οὐ γὰρ ἐκλήσομαί ποτε Βακχίδος, οὐχ οὗτος ἔσται χρόνος. Ὅσην συμπάθειαν ἐνεδείξατο. Ἀπολογίαν ἐκείνην καλῶν οὐκ ἄν τις ἁμαρτάνοι τοῦ τῶι ἑταιρῶν βίου· καὶ εἰ συνελθοῦσαι ἅπασαι πανταχόθεν εἰκόνα τινὰ αὐτῆς ἐν Ἀφροδίτης ἢ Χαρίτων θεῖεν, δεξιὸν ἄν τι μοι ποιῆσαι δοκοῦσιν. Τὸ γὰρ θρυλλούμενον ὑπὸ πάντων, ὡς πονηραὶ, ὡς ἄπιστοι, ὡς πρὸς τὸ λυσιτελὲς βλέπουσαι μόνον, ὡς ἀεὶ τοῦ διδόντος, ὡς τίνος γὰρ οὐκ αἴτιαι κακοῦ τοῖς ἐντυγχάνουσι, διαβολὴν ἐπέδειξεν ἀφ' ἑαυτῆς

XXXVIII.

Meneclides to Euthycles.

She is dead, dear Euthycles! beautiful Bacchis is dead! She has left me nothing but tears that will ever flow and the remembrance of the sweetest love, that continued delightful to the end. Never shall I forget Bacchis: that moment will never be. What sympathy she had for all! One would be right in calling her a living justification of the life of a courtesan. I should think it an excellent idea, if all the women assembled from all parts and set up her statue in the temple of Venus or the Graces. It is a common reproach against such women that they are wicked, faithless, greedy after money: that their doors are always open to anyone who will give them money presents, and that they bring all kinds of misfortunes upon their lovers. She has shown by her example the injustice of such accusations: her honour-

ἄδικον οὕτω πρὸς τὴν κοινὴν βλασφημίαν τῷ ἤθει παρετάξατο. Οἶσθα τὸν Μήδειον ἐκεῖνον τὸν ἀπὸ τῆς Συρίας δεῦρο κατάραντα μεθ' ὅσης θεραπείας καὶ παρασκευῆς ἐσόβει, εὐνούχους ὑπισχνούμενος καὶ θεραπαίνας καὶ κόσμον τινὰ βαρβαρικόν· καὶ ὅμως ἄκοντα αὐτὸν οὐ προσίετο, ἀλλ' ὑπὸ τοὐμὸν ἠγάπα κοιμωμένη χλανίσκιον τὸ λιτὸν τοῦτο καὶ δημοτικόν, καὶ τοῖς παρ' ἡμῶν γλίσχρως αὐτῇ πεμπομένοις ἐπανέχουσα, τὰς σατραπικὰς ἐκείνας καὶ πολυχρύσους δωρεὰς διωθεῖτο. Τί δὲ τὸν Αἰγύπτιον ἔμπορον ὡς ὑπεσκοράκισεν, ὅσον ἀργυρίου προτείνοντα; Οὐδὲν ἐκείνης ἄμεινον εὖ οἶδ' ὅτι γένοιτ' ἄν. Ὡς χρηστὸν ἦθος οὐκ εἰς εὐδαίμονα βίον προαίρεσιν δαίμων τὶς ὑπήνεγκεν. Εἶτ' οἴχεται ἡμᾶς ἀπολιποῦσα, καὶ κείσεται λοιπὸν μόνη ἡ Βακχίς. Ὡς ἄδικον, ὦ φίλαι μοῖραι· ἔδει γὰρ αὐτῇ συγκατακεῖσθαί με καὶ νῦν ὡς τότε. Ἀλλ' ἐγὼ μὲν περίειμι, καὶ τροφῆς ψαύω, καὶ διαλέξομαι τοῖς ἑταίροις· ἡ δὲ οὐκ ἔτι με φαιδροῖς τοῖς ὄμμασιν ὄψεται μειδιῶσα, οὐδὲ ἴλεως καὶ εὐμενὴς διανυκτερεύσει

able conduct protected her from the general slander. You remember that Mede who came from Syria with a numerous suite and great pomp? He promised her eunuchs, slaves, and Oriental ornaments: but she rejected his advances. She was content to share my humble cloak, and, satisfied with my trifling presents, refused the gold and lavish presents of the satrap. Do you remember, also, how she rejected the Egyptian merchant, who offered her untold gold? There was never a better creature born; I am convinced of it. Why, with all her good qualities, did not Fortune guide her to a better choice? And now she is gone, she has left me, and for the future will rest alone in the grave! How unjust, O kindly Fates! why am I not united with her in death, as formerly in life? But alas! I still live, I eat my food, and hold converse with my friends; but she will never look upon me again with her bright eyes, with a smile upon her lips; nor, kind and gentle, will she pass the night with

τοῖς ἡδίστοις ἐκείνοις κολάσμασιν. Ἀρτίως μὲν οἷον ἐφθέγγετο, οἷον ἔβλεπεν, ὅσαι ταῖς ὁμιλίαις αὐτῆς Σειρῆνες ἐνίδρυντο, ὡς δὲ ἡδύ τι καὶ ἀκήρατον ἀπὸ τῶν φιλημάτων νέκταρ ἔσταξεν ἐπ' ἄκροις μοι δοκεῖ τοῖς χείλεσιν αὐτῆς ἐκάθισεν ἡ Πειθώ· ἅπαντα ἐκείνη γε τὸν κεστὸν ὑπεζώσατο, ὅλαις ταῖς Χάρισι τὴν Ἀφροδίτην δεξιωσαμένη. Ἔρρει τὰ παρὰ τὰς πόσεις μινυρίσματα, καὶ ἡ τοῖς ἐλεφαντίνοις δακτύλοις κρουομένη λύρα ἔρρει. Κεῖται δὲ ἡ πάσαις μέλουσα Χάρισι κωφὴ λίθος καὶ σποδιά. Καὶ Μεγάρα μὲν ἡ ἱππόπορνος ζῇ, οὕτω Θεαγένη συλήσασα ἀνηλεῶς, ὡς ἐκ πάνυ λαμπρᾶς οὐσίας τὸν ἄθλιον χλαμύδιον ἁρπάσαντα καὶ πέλτην οἴχεσθαι στρατευσόμενον. Βακχὶς δὲ ἡ τὸν ἐραστὴν φιλοῦσα ἀπέθανε. Ῥάων γέγονα πρὸς σέ ἀποδυράμενος, Εὐθόκλεις φίλτατε· ἡδὺ γάρ μοι δοκεῖ περὶ ἐκείνης καὶ λαλεῖν καὶ γράφειν· οὐδὲν γὰρ ἢ τὸ μεμνῆσθαι καταλέλειπται. Ἔρρωσο.

me in delightful encounters. But just
now, how she spoke, how she looked!
what charms were in her words! how
sweet and pure was the nectar that dis-
tilled from her kisses! It seems to me,
Persuasion sat upon her lips; girt with
the cestus, she went hand in hand with
Venus and the Graces. Now all the
ditties she used to sing as the wine went
round are over; the lyre, which she
smote with her ivory fingers, is silent:
she, who was the darling of all the
Graces, lies mute as a stone, mere dust
and ashes. And Megara, that fearful
prostitute, is still alive, after having so
mercilessly plundered Theagenes that, reduced to poverty from affluence, he has
snatched up a miserable cloak and shield,
and gone off as a soldier; while Bacchis,
who adored her lover, is dead. I feel
easier, my dearest Euthycles, now that
I have poured my lament into your ears;
for it is delightful to me to speak and
write of her, now that nothing is left to
me but the remembrance of her. Farewell.

XXXIX.

Μεγάρα Βακχίδι.

Σοὶ μόνῃ ἐραστὴς γέγονεν, ὃν φιλεῖς οὕτως, ὥστε μηδ' ἀκαρῆ πως αὐτοῦ διαζευχθῆναι δύνασθαι. Τῆς ἀηδίας, δέσποινα Ἀφροδίτη. Κληθεῖσα ὑπὸ Γλυκέρας εἰς τοσοῦτον χρόνον (ἀπὸ τῶν Διονυσίων γὰρ ἡμῖν ἀπήγγειλεν), οὐχ ἥκεις, εἰ μὴ δι' ἐκείνην, οὐδὲ τὰς φίλας ἰδεῖν γυναῖκας ἀνασχομένη. Σώφρων γέγονας σὺ καὶ φιλεῖς τὸν ἐραστήν. Μακαρία τῆς εὐφημίας· ἡμεῖς δὲ καὶ πόρναι καὶ ἀκόλαστοι. Ὑπῆρξε καὶ Φίλωνι συκίνη βακτηρία· ὀργίζομαι γὰρ νὴ τὴν μεγάλην θεόν. Πᾶσαι γὰρ ἦμεν, Θετταλη, Μυρρίνη, Χρυσίον, Εὐξίππη· ὅπου καὶ Φιλουμένη, καί τοι γεγαμημένη προσφάτως καὶ ζηλοτυπουμένη, τὸν

XXXIX.

Megara to Bacchis.

You alone have a lover, of whom you are so enamoured that you cannot endure to be separated from him for a moment. How impolite! by our lady Venus! Although you had been invited long ago by Glycera—since the Dionysia, she told us —you did not come; if you could not do so for her sake, I wonder how you could bear to refuse to join your friends. You have become modest, and are in love with your admirer. Does such a reputation make you happy? Well, we are only prostitutes and cannot control our passions. But, patience; Philo also had a staff of fig-tree wood: by the great goddess, I am angry with you. We were all present, Thessale, Myrrhine, Chrysium, Euxippe; and Philumena, who has recently married a jealous husband, put the worthy

καλὸν ἀποκοιμίσασα τὸν ἄνδρα, ὀψὲ μὲν, ὅμως δὲ παρῆν. Σὺ δὲ ἡμῖν μόνη τὸν Ἄδωνιν περιέψυχες, μή που καταλειφθέντα αὐτὸν ὑπὸ σοῦ τῆς Ἀφροδίτης ἡ Περσεφόνη παραλάβῃ. Οἷον ἡμῶν ἐγένετο τὸ συμπόσιον (τί γὰρ οὐχ᾽ ἅψομαί σου τῆς καρδίας), ὅσων χαρίτων πλῆρες. Ὠιδαὶ, σκώμματα, πότος εἰς ἀλεκτρυόνων ᾠδὰς, μύρα, στέφανοι, τραγήματα. Ὑπόσκιος τισὶ δάφναις ἦν ἡ κατάκλισις· ἓν μόνον ἡμῖν ἔλειπε, σύ· τὰ δ᾽ ἄλλα οὔ. Πολλάκις ἐκραιπαλήσαμεν, οὕτω δὲ ἡδέως ὀλιγάκις. Τὸ γοῦν πλεῖστον ἡμῖν παρασκευάσαν τέρψιν, δεινή τις φιλονεικία κατέσχε Θρυαλλίδα καὶ Μυρρίνην ὑπὲρ τῆς πυγῆς, πότερα κρείττω καὶ ἁπαλωτέραν ἐπιδείξει. Καὶ πρώτη Μυρρίνη τὸ ζώνιον λύσασα, βόμβυξ δ᾽ ἦν τὸ χιτώνιον, δι᾽ αὐτοῦ τρέμουσαν, οἷον πιμελὴ ἢ πηκτὸν γάλα, τὴν ὀσφῦν ἀνεσάλευσεν, ὑποβλέπουσα εἰς τοὐπίσω πρὸς τὰ κινήματα τῆς πυγῆς· ἠρέμα δ᾽ οἷον ἐνεργοῦσά τι ἐρωτικὸν ὑπεστέναξεν, ὥστε ἐμὲ, νὴ τὴν Ἀφροδίτην, καταπλαγῆναι. Οὐ μὴν ἀπεῖπέ γε ἡ Θρυαλλὶς, ἀλλὰ τῇ ἀκολασίᾳ

man to bed, and joined us, although she came late. But you alone carefully guarded your Adonis, lest, if you, his Venus, left him, Proserpine might claim him for her own. What a bout we had! how full of enjoyment! for I see no reason to spare your feelings. Songs, jests, drinking till cock-crow, perfumes, garlands, sweetmeats. The place where we sat down was shaded with laurels: only one thing was wanting —your company; nothing else. We have often got drunk before, but rarely so delightfully. But what afforded us the greatest amusement was a serious dispute between Thryallis and Myrrhine, as to which of them could show the finest and most delicate buttocks. Myrrhine first unloosed her girdle, and began to shake her loins, which quivered through her silken shift like fat or curdled milk, looking back complacently all the time at the movements of her rump, then, moving gently as if she were in the act, she sighed, so that, by Venus, I was struck with astonishment. Nor did Thryallis shrink from the contest, but, eager to

παρενδοκίμησεν αὐτήν οὐ γὰρ διὰ παραπετασμάτων ἐγώ, φησὶν, ἀγωνίσομαι, οὐδὲ ἀκκιζομένη, ἀλλ' οἷον ἐν γυμνικῷ· καὶ γὰρ οὐ φιλεῖ προφάσεις ἀγών. Ἀπεδύσατο τὸ χιτώνιον, καὶ μικρὸν ὑποσιμώσασα τὴν ὀσφῦν, ἰδοὺ, σκόπει τὸ χρῶμα, φησὶν, ὡς ἀκριβὲς, Μυρρίνη, ὡς ἀκήρατον, ὡς καθαρόν· τὰ πορφυρᾶ τῶν ἰσχίων ταυτί· τὴν ἐπὶ τοὺς μηροὺς ἔγκρισιν, τὸ μήτε ὑπέρογκον αὐτῶν μήτε ἄσαρκον, τοὺς γελασίνους ἐπ' ἄκρων. Ἀλλ' οὐ τρέμει, νὴ Δία, ὥσπερ ἡ Μυρρίνης, ἀλλ' ὑπομειδιῶσα τοσοῦτον παλμὸν ἐξειργάσατο τῆς πυγῆς, καὶ ἅπασαν αὐτὴν ὑπὲρ τὴν ὀσφῦν τῇδε καὶ τῇδε ὥσπερ ῥέουσαν περιεδίνησεν, ὥστε ἀνακροτῆσαι πάσας, καὶ νίκην ἀποφῆνασθαι τῆς Θρυαλλίδος. Ἐγένοντο δὲ καὶ περὶ ἄλλων συγκρίσεις, καὶ περὶ μασταρίων ἀγῶνες· τῆς μὲν γὰρ Φιλουμένης γαστρὶ ἀντεξετασθῆναι οὐδ' ἡτισοῦν ἐθάρσησεν· ἄτοκος γὰρ ἦν καὶ σφριγῶσα. Καταπαννυχίσασαι γοῦν καὶ τοὺς ἐραστὰς κακῶς εἰποῦσαι καὶ ἄλλων ἐπιτυχεῖν εὐξάμεναι (ἀεὶ γὰρ ἡδίων ἡ πρόσφατος ἀφροδίτη), ᾠχόμεθα

surpass her in wantonness, said, " I will not enter the lists with anything to cover me, or with any affectation, but just like the athletes at the games : the contest admits of no shuffling." She stripped off her shift, and, bending her loins upwards a little, she said, " Look at the colour, Myrrhine, how perfect it is, how pure, how irreproachable! Look at my hips, how they join the thighs, neither too fleshy nor too lean, and the dimples at their extremities." Then she showed her loins, not trembling, like Myrrhine's, and, with a smile, shook them with a quivering motion, and whirled her buttocks round in every direction so that they seemed like running water. Then we all clapped our hands and awarded the victory to Thryallis. We also had other contests, and compared each other's breasts ; nobody, however, ventured to dispute the palm with Philumena, who has never had a child and is plump and swelling. Having spent the night in this way and abused our lovers and prayed that we might find others—for the latest fancy is always the

ἔξοινοι. Πολλὰ δὲ κατὰ τὴν ὁδὸν κραιπαλήσασαι, ἐπεκωμάσαμεν Δεξιμάχῳ κατὰ τὸν χρυσοῦν στενωπὸν, ὡς ἐπὶ τὴν ἄγνον κατιόντι πλησίον τῆς Μενέφρονος οἰκίας. Ἐρᾷ γὰρ αὐτοῦ Θαὶς κακῶς, καὶ νὴ Δία εἰκότως· ἔναγχος γὰρ πλούσιον κεκληρονόμηκε πατέρα τὸ μειράκιον. Νῦν μὲν οὖν συγγνώμην ἔχομέν σοι τῆς ὑπεροψίας· τοῖς Ἀδωνίοις δὲ ἐν Κολυττῷ ἐστιώμεθα παρὰ τῷ Θετταλῆς ἐραστῇ· τὸν γὰρ τῆς Ἀφροδίτης ἐρώμενον ἡ Θετταλῆ στέλλει. Ὅπως δ' ἥξεις φέρουσα κήτιον καὶ κοράλλιον, καὶ τὸν σὸν Ἄδωνιν, ὃν νῦν περιψύχεις· μετὰ γὰρ τῶν ἐραστῶν κραιπαλήσομεν. Ἔρρωσο.

sweetest—we went away pretty well tipsy. After many drunken freaks on the way, we went to finish up at Deximachus's, in the Golden Alley, near the house of Meniphron as you go down towards Agnus. For Thais is desperately in love with him, and with good reason, by Jove; for the lad has just come in for a large fortune from his father. We will pardon you for your contemptuous treatment of us. On the day of the festival of Adonis we are going to have a feast at Colyttus at the house of Thessale's lover: for it is her turn to bedeck the lover of Venus. We will pardon you, on condition that you come and bring a dice-box and coral image, and your pet Adonis; for we shall have a jollification with our lovers. Farewell.

XL.

Φιλουμένη Κρίτωνι.

Τί πολλὰ γράφων ἀνιᾷς σεαυτόν; πεντήκοντά σοι χρυσῶν δεῖ, καὶ γραμμάτων οὐ δεῖ. Εἰ μὲν οὖν φιλεῖς, δύς· εἰ δὲ φιλαργυρεῖς, μὴ ἐνόχλει. Ἔρρωσο.

XL.

PHILUMENE TO CRITO.

WHY do you trouble yourself to write so often? I want fifty gold pieces, not letters. If you love me, give them to me; but if you are too fond of your money, don't bother me. Good-bye.

LIBER SECUNDUS.

I.

Λάμια Δημητρίῳ.

Σὺ ταύτης τῆς παρρησίας αἴτιος, τοσοῦτος ὢν βασιλεὺς, εἶτα ἐπιτρέψας καὶ ἑταίρᾳ γράφειν σοι, καὶ οὐχ ἡγησάμενος δεινὸν ἐντυγχάνειν τοῖς ἐμοῖς γράμμασιν, ὅλῃ μοι ἐντυγχάνων. Ἐγὼ, δέσποτα Δημήτριε, ὅταν μὲν ἔξω σε θεάσωμαι καὶ ἀκούσω μετὰ τῶν δορυφόρων καὶ τῶν στρατοπέδων καὶ τῶν πρεσβέων καὶ τῶν διαδημάτων, νὴ τὴν Ἀφροδίτην, πέφρικα καὶ δέδοικα καὶ ταράττομαι καὶ ἀποστρέφομαι ὡς τὸν ἥλιον, μὴ ἐπικαῶ τὰ ὄμματα· καὶ τότε μοι ὄντως ὁ πολιορκητὴς εἶναι δοκεῖς Δημήτριος. Οἷον δὲ καὶ βλέπεις τότε, ὡς πικρὸν καὶ πολεμικὸν καὶ

BOOK II.

I.

LAMIA TO DEMETRIUS.

You are to blame for the liberty I am taking; for you, though so mighty a monarch, have allowed a courtesan to write to you, and do not disdain to accept my letters, after you have accepted me. O my Lord Demetrius, when I see you in public, and in the midst of your body-guards and soldiers, and with the ambassadors, wearing your diadem, by Venus, I shudder and am afraid: I am confounded and turn my eyes away from you, as from the blazing sun, lest your splendour consume them: then in truth you appear to me as Demetrius, the besieger of cities.[1] How fierce and warlike is your look! Then I can hardly believe my own eyes, and I say to myself:

[1] He was called Poliorcetes.

ἀπιστῶ ἐμαυτῇ καὶ λέγω· Λάμια, σὺ μετὰ τοῦδε καθεύδεις; σὺ διὰ νυκτὸς ὅλης αὐτὸν καταυλεῖς; σοὶ νῦν οὗτος ἐπέσταλκε; σοὶ Γνάθαιναν τὴν ἑταίραν συγκρίνει; καὶ ἠλογημένη σιωπῶ καὶ εὐχομένη θεάσασθαι παρ' ἑαυτῇ. Καὶ ὅταν ἔλθῃς, προσκυνῶ σε, καὶ ὅταν περιπλακεὶς μέγα φιλῇς, πάλιν πρὸς ἐμαυτὴν τἀναντία λέγω· οὗτός ἐστιν ὁ πολιορκητής; οὗτός ἐστιν ὁ ἐν τοῖς στρατοπέδοις; τοῦτον φοβεῖται Μακεδονία; τοῦτον ἡ Ἑλλάς; τοῦτον ἡ Θρᾴκη; νὴ τὴν Ἀφροδίτην σήμερον αὐτοῖς τοῖς αὐλοῖς ἐκπολιορκήσω, καὶ ὄψομαι, τί με διαθήσει. Μεῖνον εἰς τρίτην, παρ' ἐμοὶ γὰρ δειπνήσεις, δέομαι. Τὰ Ἀφροδίσια ποιῶ ταῦτα κατ' ἔτος, καὶ ἀγῶνα ἔχω, εἰ τὰ πρότερα τοῖς ὑστέροις νικᾷ. Ὑποδέξομαι δέ σε ἐπαφροδίτως καὶ ὡς ἔνι μάλιστα πιθανῶς, ἄν μοι περιουσιάσαι γένηται ὑπὸ σοῦ, μηδὲν ἀνάξιον τῶν σῶν ἀγαθῶν ἐξ ἐκείνης τῆς ἱερᾶς νυκτὸς ἔτι πεποιηκυίᾳ, καί τοι σοῦ γε ἐπιτρέποντος, ὅπως ἂν βούλωμαι, χρῆσθαι τῷ ἐμῷ σώματι·

O Lamia, is this the man with whom you sleep? is this the man to whom you sing and play all night? is this the man who has just written to you? does he think Gnathaena as beautiful as yourself? But this does not grieve me: I silently utter a prayer that I may see you at my house. When you come, I adore you, and when you take me to your arms and kiss me fondly, I say to myself on the other hand: Is this the besieger of cities? is this the man of war? is this the terror of Macedonia, Greece, and Thrace? By Venus, I will take him by storm this day with my pipes alone, and I will see how he will treat me. Wait until the day after to-morrow, and you shall sup with me. I celebrate the feast of Venus every year, and I do all I can to make each succeeding feast surpass the last. I will receive you lovingly and winningly, if you assist me generously; for I have committed no act that should make me undeserving of your kindness since that blessed night, although you gave me permission to make what use I pleased of

ἀλλὰ κέχρημαι καλῶς καὶ ἀμίκτως πρὸς ἑτέρους. Οὐ ποιήσω τὸ ἑταιρικὸν, οὐδὲ ψεύσομαι, δέσποτα, ὡς ἄλλαι ποιοῦσιν· ἐμοὶ γὰρ ἐξ ἐκείνου, μὰ τὴν Ἄρτεμιν, οὐδὲ προσέπεμψαν ἔτι πολλοὶ, οὐδὲ ἐπείρασαν, αἰδούμενοί σου τὰς πολιορκίας. Ὀξύς ἐστιν ὁ Ἔρως, ὦ βασιλεῦ, καὶ ἐλθεῖν καὶ ἀναπτῆναι· ἐλπίσας πτεροῦται, καὶ ἀπελπίσας ταχὺ πτερορρυεῖν εἴωθεν ἀπογνωσθείς. Διὸ καὶ μέγα τῶν ἑταιρουσῶν ἐστι σόφισμα, ἀεὶ τὸ παρὸν τῆς ἀπολαύσεως ὑπερτιθεμένας ταῖς ἐλπίσι διακρατεῖν τοὺς ἐραστάς· (πρὸς ὑμᾶς δὲ οὐδὲ ὑπερτίθεσθαι ἔξεστιν, ὥστε φόβον εἶναι κόρον)· λοιπὸν ἡμᾶς δεῖ τὰ μὲν πονεῖν, τὰ δὲ μαλακίζεσθαι, τὰ δὲ ᾅδειν, τά δὲ αὐλεῖν, τὰ δὲ ὀρχεῖσθαι, τὰ δὲ δειπνοποιεῖν, τὰ δὲ κοσμεῖν σοι τὸν οἶκον, τὰς ὁπωσοῦν ἄλλως ταχὺ μαραινομένας μεσολαβούσας χάριτας, ἵνα μᾶλλον ἐξάπτωνται τοῖς διαστήμασι εὐαλούστεραι αὐτῶν αἱ ψυχαὶ, φοβουμένων, μὴ ἄλλο πάλιν γένηται τῆς ἐν τῷ παρόντι τύχης κώλυμα. Ταῦτα δὲ πρὸς μὲν ἑτέρους

my person; but I have not abused your kindness, and I have had intercourse with no one. I will not play the harlot, nor, my Lord, will I lie, as others do; in truth, by Diana! since that time but few have sent me presents, in their awe of the besieger of cities. O my King, Love is swift to come and to fly away: when in hope, he flutters his wings; when in despair, he droops and sheds his feathers. Wherefore it is a favourite trick of courtesans to wheedle their lovers with hopes of ever-deferred enjoyment, although with a man like yourself there is no excuse for delay, since there is no fear of your being sated; we pretend to be ill, to be busily engaged, to be singing, playing the flute, dancing, preparing a supper, or furnishing a house, by such means interrupting the fulfilment of their enjoyment, which, unless we do this, soon becomes insipid. The result is, that the hearts of our lovers are more easily caught and inflamed, since they are afraid that some fresh obstacle may arise in the way of their present fortune. In the case of others,

τάχα ἂν ἐδυνάμην, βασιλεῦ, φυλάττεσθαι καὶ τεχνιτεύειν· πρὸς δὲ σὲ, ὃς οὕτως ἤδη ἔχεις ἐπ' ἐμοὶ, ὡς ἐπιδεικνύναι με καὶ ἀγάλλεσθαι πρὸς τὰς ἄλλας ἑταίρας, ὅτι πασῶν ἐγὼ πρωτεύω, μὰ τὰς φίλας Μούσας, οὐκ ἂν ὑπομείναιμι πλάττεσθαι. Οὐχ οὕτως εἰμὶ λιθίνη. Ὥστε ἀφεῖσα πάντα καὶ τὴν ψυχὴν ἐμαυτῆς εἰς ἀρέσκειάν σου, ὀλίγον ἡγήσομαι δαπανῆσαι. Εὖ οἶδα γὰρ, ὅτι οὐ μόνον ἐν τῇ Θηριππιδίου οἰκίᾳ, ἐν ᾗ μέλλω σοι τὸ τῶν Ἀφροδισίων εὐτρεπίζειν δεῖπνον, ἔσται διαβόητος ἡ παρασκευὴ, ἀλλὰ καὶ ἐν ὅλῃ τῇ Ἀθηναίων πόλει, νὴ τὴν Ἄρτεμιν, καὶ ἐν τῇ Ἑλλάδι πάσῃ. Καὶ μάλιστα οἱ μισητοὶ Λακεδαιμόνιοι, ἵνα δοκῶσιν ἄνδρες εἶναι οἱ ἐν Ἐφέσῳ ἀλώπεκες, οὐ παύσονται τοῖς Ταϋγέτοις ὄρεσι καὶ ταῖς ἐρημίαις ἑαυτῶν διαβάλλοντες ἡμῶν τὰ δεῖπνα, καταλυκουργίζοντες τῆς σῆς ἀνθρωποπαθείας. Ἀλλ' αὐτοὶ μὲν χαιρόντων, δέσποτα· σὺ δὲ ἐμοὶ μέμνησο φυλάξαι τὴν ἡμέραν τοῦ δείπνου, καὶ τὴν ὥραν, ἣν ἂν ἕλῃ· ἀρίστη γὰρ, ἣν βούλει. Ἔρρωσο.

I might perhaps carefully practise these arts; but towards you, who are so devoted to me, that you publicly make a show of me and delight in telling other women that I excel them all, I could not endure to be so deceitful. I am not so silly: if I gave up everything, even my life, to do you pleasure, I should consider the sacrifice a trifling one. For I well know that my preparations will be talked about, not only in Therippidium's house, where I intend to entertain you during the feast of Venus, but throughout Athens; yes, by Artemis, throughout the whole extent of Greece. Above all, the hateful Lacedaemonians, that they, who behaved like foxes at Ephesus, may pretend to be heroes, will not cease to abuse our banquet on the mountains of Taygetus and in their solitary fastnesses, inveighing against your humanity and kindness with the severity of Lycurgus. But think no more of them; remember to observe the day of my banquet, and fix the hour yourself. Whatever time suits you will be the best. Farewell.

II.

Λεόντιον Λαμία.

Οὐδὲν δυσαρεστότερον, ὡς ἔοικεν, ἐστὶ πάλιν μειρακιευομένου πρεσβύτου. Οἷά με Ἐπίκουρος οὗτος διοικεῖ, πάντα λοιδορῶν, πάντα ὑποπτεύων, ἐπιστολὰς ἀδιαλύτους μοι γράφων, ἐκδιώκων ἐκ τοῦ κήπου. Μὰ τὴν Ἀφροδίτην, εἰ Ἄδωνις ἦν ἤδη ἐγγὺς ὀγδοήκοντα γεγονὼς ἔτη, οὐκ ἂν αὐτοῦ ἠνεσχόμην φθειριῶντος καὶ φιλονοσοῦντος, καὶ καταπεπιλημένου εὖ μάλα πόκοις ἀντὶ πίλων. Μέχρι τίνος ὑπομενεῖ τις τὸν φιλόσοφον τοῦτον; ἐχέτω τὰς περὶ φύσεως αὐτοῦ κυρίας δόξας, καὶ τοὺς διεστραμμένους κανόνας· ἐμὲ δὲ ἐφέτω τὴν φυσικῶς κυρίαν ἐμαυτῆς ἀνενόχλητον καὶ ἀνύβριστον. Ὄντως ἐπιπολιορκητὴν ἔχω τοιοῦτον, οὐχ᾽ οἷον σύ, Λάμια, Δημήτριον. Μὴ γάρ ἐστι σωφρονῆσαι διὰ τὸν ἄνθρωπον τοῦτον; Καὶ σωκρατίζειν

II.

LEONTIUM TO LAMIA.

No one is so hard to please, it seems to me, as an old man who plays the youth. How strangely this Epicurus treats me, always finding fault, suspicious of everything, sending me letters that I cannot make out, even threatening to drive me out of his garden. By Venus! if he were an Adonis eighty years old, I could not endure him, full of vermin as he is, and always unwell, wrapped up in garments of raw wool instead of felt. How long can anyone endure a man like this philosopher? Let him stick to his doctrines about nature, and his perverted canons, but let him allow me to enjoy my natural freedom without his insults or annoyance. I have a regular besieger, Lamia, but not one like your Demetrius. How can one be patient with such a man?

καὶ στωμυλεύεσθαι θέλει καὶ εἰρωνεύεσθαι· καὶ Ἀλκιβιάδην τινὰ Πυθοκλέα νομίζει, καὶ Ξανθίππην ἐμὲ οἴεται ποιήσειν. Καὶ πέρας ἀναστᾶσα ὁπήποτε γῆν πρὸ γῆς φεύξομαι μᾶλλον ἢ τὰς ἐπιστολὰς αὐτοῦ τὰς διασπάστους ἀνέξομαι. Ὁ δὲ πάντων δεινότατον ἤδη καὶ ἀφορητότατον ἐτόλμησεν, ὑπὲρ οὗ καὶ γνώμην βουλομένη λαβεῖν, τί μοι ποιητέον, ἐπέσταλκά σοι. Τίμαρχον τὸν καλὸν οἶσθα τὸν Κηφισιάθεν· οὐκ ἀρνοῦμαι πρὸς τὸν νεανίσκον οὐκ οἰκείως ἔχειν ἐκ πολλοῦ (πρὸς σέ μοι τἀληθῆ λέγειν εἰκός, Λάμια), καὶ τὴν πρώτην Ἀφροδίτην ἔμαθον παρ' αὐτοῦ σχεδόν· οὗτος γάρ με διεπαρθένευσεν ἐκ γειτόνων οἰκοῦσαν. Ἐξ ἐκείνου τοῦ χρόνου πάντα μοι τἀγαθὰ πέμπων οὐ διαλέλοιπεν, ἐσθῆτα, χρυσεῖα, θεραπαίνας, θεράποντας, Ἰνδοὺς, Ἰνδάς· τἄλλα σιωπῶ· ἀλλὰ τὰ μικρότατα προλαμβάνει τὰς ὥρας, ἵνα μηδεὶς φθάσῃ με γευσάμενος. Τοιοῦτον νῦν ἐραστὴν

He tries to play the part of Socrates, to imitate him in his mouthing and his irony; he looks upon Pythocles as another Alcibiades, and thinks to make of me his Xantippe. I shall in the end be obliged to remove from here, and will flee from one country to another, rather than put up with his incoherent letters. But about the most monstrous and intolerable thing that he has had the audacity to do, I have written already to ask your advice. You know the handsome Timarchus from Cephisus: I do not deny that I have been intimate with the young man for a long time—it is only right to tell the truth to you, Lamia—it is to him that I owe almost my first acquaintance with the goddess of Love, for he seduced me when I lived in his neighbourhood. Ever since then he has continually sent me all kinds of presents, clothes, money, Indian male and female slaves, and other things, which I need not mention. In the smallest trifles he anticipates the seasons, that no one may taste their delicacies before myself. Yet Epicurus

ἀπόκλεισον, φησι, καὶ μὴ προσίτω σοι, ποίοις δοκεῖς αὐτὸν ἀποκαλῶν ὀνόμασιν, οὔτε ὡς Ἀττικὸς, οὔτε ὡς φιλόσοφος, ἐκ Καππαδοκίας πρῶτος εἰς τὴν Ἑλλάδα ἥκων. Ἐγὼ δὲ, εἰ καὶ ὅλη γένοιτο ἡ Ἀθηναίων πόλις Ἐπικούρων, μὰ τὴν Ἄρτεμιν, οὐ ξυγοστατήσω πάντας αὐτοὺς πρὸς τὸν Τιμάρχου βραχίονα, μᾶλλον δὲ οὐδὲ πρὸς τὸν δάκτυλον. Τί σὺ λέγεις, Λάμια, οὐκ ἀληθῆ ταῦτα, οὐ δίκαια φημί; Καὶ μὴ δὴ, δέομαί σου πρὸς τῆς Ἀφροδίτης, μή σοι ταῦτα ὑπελθέτω· ἀλλὰ φιλόσοφος, ἀλλὰ ἐπιφανὴς, ἀλλὰ πολλοῖς φίλοις κεχρημένος. Λαβέτω, κατεχέτω, διδασκέτω δ' ἄλλους· ἐμὲ δὲ οὐδὲν θάλπει τι δόξα· ἄλλ' ὃν θέλω δὸς Τίμαρχον, Δάματερ. Ἀλλὰ καὶ δι' ἐμὲ πάντα ἠνάγκασται ὁ νεανίσκος καταλιπὼν τὸ Λύκειον, καὶ τὴν ἑαυτοῦ νεότητα καὶ τοὺς συνεφήβους καὶ τὴν ἑταιρίαν, μετ' αὐτοῦ ζῆν καὶ κολακεύειν αὐτὸν, καὶ καθυμνεῖν τὰς ὑπηνέμους αὐτοῦ δόξας. Ὁ Ἀτρεὺς οὗτος, ἔξελθε, φησὶν ἐκ, τῆς ἐμῆς μοναγρίας, καὶ

tells me to shut my door upon him, and
not let him come near me, calling him
by all sorts of names, which you would
not expect to hear from an Athenian or
a philosopher, but from some Cappado-
cian on his first visit to Hellas. But,
if Athens were inhabited entirely by such
as Epicurus, by Diana! they could not,
in my estimation, be compared to Timarchus's arm—no, not even to one of his
fingers. What do you think, Lamia?
Is not what I say just and true? Do
not ever imagine such a thing, I entreat
you by Venus. Yet this Epicurus is a
philosopher, a man of distinction, a man
who has many friends! Let him take
and keep and teach others: reputation
has no charms for me; but, O Ceres!
give me him whom I love—Timarchus.
All through me the youth has been
forced to leave the Lyceum, his youthful
pleasures, and the companionship of his
friends, and to live with Epicurus, to
flatter him, and to praise his windbag
doctrines. "No poaching on my pre-
serves," exclaims this Atreus; "do not go

μὴ πρόσιθι Λεοντίῳ· ὡς οὐ δικαιότερον ἐκείνου ἐροῦντος, σὺ μὲν οὖν μὴ πρόσιθι τῇ ἐμῇ. Καὶ ὁ μὲν, νεανίσκος ὢν, ἀνέχεται τὸν ἕτερον ἀντεραστὴν γέροντα· ὁ δὲ τὸν δικαιότερον οὐχ ὑπομένει. Τί ποιήσω, πρὸς τῶν θεῶν ἱκετεύω σε, Λάμια; Νὴ τὰ μυστήρια, νὴ τὴν τούτων τῶν κακῶν ἀπαλλαγὴν, ὡς ἐνθυμηθεῖσα τοῦ Τιμάρχου τὸν χωρισμὸν, ἄρτι ἀπέψυγμαι καὶ ἰδρῶ τὰ ἄκρα, καὶ ἡ καρδία μου ἀνέστραπται. Δέομαί σου, δέξαι με πρὸς σεαυτὴν ἡμέρας ὀλίγας· καὶ ποιήσω τοῦτον αἰσθάνεσθαι, πηλίκων ἀπήλαυεν ἀγαθῶν, ἔχων ἐν τῇ οἰκίᾳ με. Οὐκ ἔτι φέρει τὸν κόρον, εὖ οἶδα· πρεσβευτὰς εὐθὺς πρὸς ἡμᾶς διαπέμψεται Μητρόδωρον καὶ Ἕρμαχον καὶ Πολύαινον. Ποσάκις οἴει με, Λάμια, πρὸς αὐτὸν ἰδίᾳ παραγενομένην εἰπεῖν τί ποιεῖς Ἐπίκουρε; οὐκ οἶσθα, ὅτι διακωμωδεῖ σε Τιμοκράτης ὁ Μητροδόρου ἐπὶ τούτοις ἐν ταῖς ἐκκλησίαις, ἐν τοῖς θεάτροις, παρὰ τοῖς ἄλλοις σοφισταῖς; Ἀλλὰ τί

near my Leontium"; as if Timarchus had not a far better right to say, " Do you keep your hands off mine." But he, although the younger, submits to an older rival, while the other will not endure him who has the juster claim. What am I to do, Lamia? Tell me, I beseech you, by the gods! By the sacred mysteries, by my hopes of relief from my misery, when I think of being separated from Timarchus, I grow now cold, now hot, in my extremities, and my heart is quite upset. I beseech you, let me come and stay with you for a few days, and I will make him feel what blessings he enjoyed when he had me in his house. I am sure he cannot long endure my contempt; he will soon send me one messenger after another, Metrodorus, Hermachus, and Polyaenus. How often do you think I have said to him privately, " What are you doing, Epicurus? Do you not know that Timocrates, the son of Metrodorus, ridicules you for your conduct in the assemblies, in the theatres, in the company of the other sophists?"

ἐστιν αὐτῷ ποιῆσαι; ἀναίσχυντός ἐστι τὸ ἐρᾶν. Καὶ ἐγὼ ἔσομαι τοίνυν ὁμοίως αὐτῷ ἀναίσχυντος, καὶ οὐκ ἀφήσω τὸν ἐμὸν Τίμαρχον. Ἔρρωσο.

But what can you do with a man like this? He is utterly shameless in his love. I will be equally shameless: I will not desert my Timarchus. Farewell.

III.

Μένανδρος Γλυκέρᾳ.

Ἐγὼ μὰ τὰς Ἐλευσινίας θεὰς, μὰ τὰ μυστήρια αὐτῶν, ἅ σοι καὶ ἐναντίον ὤμοσα πολλάκις, Γλυκέρα, μόνος μόνῃ, ὡς οὐδὲν ἐπαίρω τὰ ἐμά· οὐδὲ βουλόμενός σου χωρίζεσθαι, ταῦτα καὶ λέγω καὶ γράφω. Τί γὰρ ἐμοὶ χωρίς σου γένοιτ' ἂν ἥδιον; τί δ' ἐπαρθῆναι μεῖζον τῆς σῆς φιλίας δυναίμην; εἰ καὶ τὸ ἔσχατον ἡμῶν γῆρας διὰ τοὺς σοὺς τρόπους καὶ ἤθη νεότης ἀεὶ φανεῖταί μοι. Καὶ συννεάσαιμεν ἀλλήλοις καὶ συγγηράσαιμεν, καὶ νὴ τοὺς θεοὺς συναποθάνοιμεν· ἀλλ' αἰσθανόμενοι, Γλυκέρα, ὅτι συναποθνήσκομεν, ἵνα μηδετέρῳ ἡμῶν ἐν ᾅδου συγκαταβαίη τὶς ζῆλος, εἰ τινῶν ἄλλων ὁ σωθεὶς πειράσεται ἀγαθῶν. Μὴ δὲ γένοιτό μοι πειραθῆναι σοῦ μηκέτ' οὔσης· τί γὰρ ἂν ἔτι καταλείποιτο

III.

MENANDER TO GLYCERA.

By the Eleusinian goddesses and their mysteries, by which I have often sworn in your company alone, dear Glycera, I swear that, in making this declaration in writing, I have no wish to exalt myself, or to separate from you. For what pleasure could I enjoy apart from you? in what could I take more pride than in your friendship? Thanks to your manners and disposition, even extreme old age shall seem youth to me. Let us be young and old together, and, by the gods, let us be together in death, understanding that we die together, that jealousy may not go down with either of us to the grave, in case the survivor may enjoy any other blessings. May it never be my misfortune to see you die before me; for then, what enjoyment would be left

ἀγαθόν; "Α δὲ νῦν ἤπειξέ με ἐν Πειραιεῖ μαλακιζόμενον (οἶσθα γάρ μου τὰς συνήθεις ἀσθενείας, ἃς οἱ μὴ φιλοῦντές με τρυφὰς καὶ σαλακωνίας καλεῖν εἰώθασιν) ἐπιστεῖλαί σοι ἐν ἄστει μενούσῃ διὰ τὰ Ἁλῶα τῆς θεοῦ, ταῦτ' ἐστίν. Ἐδεξάμην ἀπὸ Πτολεμαίου τοῦ βασιλέως Αἰγύπτου γράμματα, ἐν οἷς δεῖταί μου πάσας δεήσεις, καὶ προτρέπεται βασιλικῶς ὑπισχνούμενος τὸ δὴ λεγόμενον τοῦτο τὰ τῆς γῆς ἀγαθά, ἐμὲ καὶ Φιλήμονα· καὶ γὰρ ἐκείνῳ γράμματα κεκομίσθαι φασί· καὶ αὐτὸς δὲ ὁ Φιλήμων ἐπέστειλέ μοι τὰ ἴδια δηλῶν, ἐλαφρότερα, καί, ὡς οὐ Μενάνδρῳ γεγραμμένα, ἧττον λαμπρά. Ἀλλ' ὄψεται καὶ βουλεύσεται τὰ ἴδια οὗτος. Ἐγὼ δὲ οὐ περιμενῶ βουλάς· ἀλλὰ σύ μοι, Γλυκέρα, καὶ γνώμη, καὶ Ἀρεοπαγίτις βουλή, καὶ Ἡλιαία, ἅπαντα νὴ τὴν Ἀθηνᾶν ἀεὶ γέγονας, καὶ νῦν ἔσῃ. Τὰς μὲν οὖν ἐπιστολὰς τοῦ βασιλέως σοι διεπεμψάμην, ἵνα μὴ κόπτω σε δὶς καὶ τοῖς ἐμοῖς καὶ τοῖς ἐκείνου γράμμασιν ἐντυγχάνουσαν· ἃ δὲ ἐπιστέλλειν αὐτῷ ἔγνωκα,

for me? I am staying in Piraeus owing to my ill-health; you know my usual ailments, which those who are not fond of me call effeminacy and affectation. The reasons which have induced me to write to you, while you are staying in the city for the sacred festival of Ceres, the Haloa, are the following: I have received a letter from Ptolemy, King of Egypt, in which he entreats me, promising me right royally all the good things of the earth, and invites me to visit him, together with Philemon, to whom also, they say, a letter has been sent. In fact, Philemon has sent it on to me: it is to the same effect as mine, but not so ceremonious or splendid in the promises it holds out, since it is not written to Menander. Let him consider and take counsel what he intends to do; but I will not wait for his advice, for you, my Glycera, are my counsel, my Areopagus, my Heliaea, yea, by Minerva, you have ever been, and shall ever be my all. So then I have sent you the King's letter; but, to spare you the double trouble of reading my letter and his, I wish you also to know

βούλομαί σε εἰδέναι. Πλεῖν μὲν καὶ εἰς Αἴγυπτον ἀπιέναι μακρὰν οὕτω καὶ ἀπῳκισμένην βασιλείαν οὖσαν, μὰ τοὺς δώδεκα θεούς, οὐδὲ ἐνθυμοῦμαι· ἀλλ' οὐδὲ εἰ ἐν Αἰγίνῃ ταύτῃ γε τῇ πλησίον ἔκειτο Αἴγυπτος, οὐδ' οὕτως ἐν νῷ ἂν ἔσχον, ἀφεὶς τὴν ἐμὴν βασιλείαν τῆς σῆς φιλίας, μόνος ἐν τοσούτῳ ὄχλῳ Αἰγυπτίων χωρὶς Γλυκέρας ἐρημίαν πολυάνθρωπον ὁρᾶν. Ἥδιον γὰρ καὶ ἀκινδυνότερον τὰς σὰς θεραπεύω μᾶλλον ἀγκάλας, ἢ τὰς ἁπάντων τῶν σατραπῶν καὶ βασιλέων. Ἐπικίνδυνον μὲν οὖν τὸ ἀνελεύθερον, εὐκαταφρόνητον δὲ τὸ κολακεῦον, ἄπιστον δὲ τὸ εὐτυχοῦν. Ἐγὼ δὲ καὶ τὰς Θηρικλείους, καὶ τὰ καρχήσια, καὶ τὰς χρυσίδας καὶ πάντα τὰ ἐν ταῖς αὐλαῖς ἐπίφθονα παρὰ τούτοις ἀγαθὰ φυόμενα, τῶν κατ' ἔτος Χοῶν καὶ τῶν ἐν τοῖς θεάτροις Ληναίων καὶ τῆς χθιζῆς ὁμιλίας, καὶ τῶν τοῦ Λυκείου γυμνασίων, καὶ τῆς ἱερᾶς Ἀκαδημίας, οὐκ ἀλλάττομαι, μὰ τὸν Διόνυσον καὶ τοὺς Βακχικοὺς αὐτοῦ κισσούς, οἷς στεφανωθῆναι μᾶλλον ἢ τοῖς Πτο-

what answer I have decided to make to it. By the twelve great gods, I could not even think of setting sail for Egypt, a kingdom so far remote from us; but, not even if Egypt were in Aegina, close at hand as it is, I could not even then think of leaving my kingdom of your friendship, and wandering alone in the midst of the crowded inhabitants of Egypt, looking upon a populous desert, as it would seem to me without my Glycera. I prefer your embraces, which are sweeter and less dangerous than the favours of all the kings and satraps. Loss of liberty is loss of security; flattery is contemptible: the favours of Fortune are not to be trusted.

I would not exchange for his Thericlean drinking-cups, his beakers, his golden goblets, and all the envied valuables of his courts, our yearly Choes, the Lenaea in the theatre, a banquet such as we had yesterday, the exercises in the Lyceum and the Sacred Academy —no, I swear it by Bacchus and his ivy-wreaths, with which I would rather be

λεμαίου βούλομαι · διαδήμασιν, όρώσης και καθημένης εν τῷ θεάτρῳ Γλυκέρας. Ποῦ γὰρ ἐν Αἰγύπτῳ ὄψομαι ἐκκλησίαν καὶ ψῆφον ἀναδιδομένην; ποῦ δὲ δημοκρατικὸν ὄχλον οὕτως ἐλευθεριάζοντα; ποῦ δὲ θεσμοθέτας ἐν ταῖς ἱεραῖς κώμαις κεκισσωμένους; ποῖον περισχοίνισμα; ποίαν αἵρεσιν; ποίους Χύτρους; Κεραμικόν, ἀγοράν, δικαστήρια, τὴν καλὴν ἀκρόπολιν, τὰς σεμνὰς θεάς, τὰ μυστήρια, τὴν γειτνιῶσαν Σαλαμῖνα, τὰ στήνια, τὴν Ψυτταλίαν, τὴν Μαραθῶνα, ὅλην ἐν ταῖς Ἀθήναις τὴν Ἑλλάδα, ὅλην τὴν Ἰωνίαν, τὰς Κυκλάδας πάσας; Ἀφεὶς ταῦτα καὶ Γλυκέραν μετ' αὐτῶν, εἰς Αἴγυπτον διέλθω; χρυσὸν λαβεῖν καὶ ἄργυρον καὶ πλοῦτον; ᾧ μετὰ τίνος χρήσομαι; μετὰ Γλυκέρας τοσοῦτον διατεθαλασσευμένης; οὐ πενία δέ μοι ἔσται χωρὶς αὐτῆς ταῦτα; Ἐὰν δὲ ἀκούσω τοὺς σεμνοὺς ἔρωτας εἰς ἄλλον αὐτὴν μετατεθεικέναι, οὐ σποδός μοι πάντες οἱ θησαυροὶ γενήσονται; καὶ ἀποθνήσκων τὰς μὲν λύπας

crowned, in the presence of my Glycera seated in the theatre, than with all the diadems of Ptolemy. For where in Egypt shall I see a public assembly and votes being given ? where shall I see a democracy enjoying liberty ? the legislators in the sacred villages crowned with ivy ? the roped inclosure ? the election of magistrates ? the feast of Pots ? the Ceramicus ? the market-place ? the law-courts ? the beautiful Acropolis ? the dread goddesses ? the mysteries ? the Stenia ? neighbouring Salamis, Psyttalia, Marathon, all Greece in Athens, all Ionia, all the Cyclades ? Shall I leave all these, and Glycera as well, and set out for Egypt ? And for what ? to receive gold and silver and riches ? And with whom am I to enjoy it ? with Glycera separated from me by so wide an expanse of sea ? Will not all this be simple poverty to me without her ? And should I hear that she has transferred her honoured affections to another, will not all these treasures be to me no more than dust and ashes ? and, when I die, shall I not carry away with me my

ἐμαυτῷ συναποίσω, τὰ δὲ χρήματα τοῖς
ἰχνεύουσιν ἀδικεῖν ἐν μέσῳ κείσεται; ἢ μέγα
τὸ συμβιοῦν Πτολεμαίῳ καὶ σατράπαις καὶ
τοιούτοις ψόφοις, ὧν οὔτε τὸ φιλικὸν βέ-
βαιον, οὔτε τὸ διεχθρεῦον ἀκίνδυνον; Ἐὰν
δὲ ὀργισθῇ τί μοι Γλυκέρα, ἅπαξ αὐτὴν
ἁρπάξας κατεφίλησα· ἂν ἔτι ὀργίζεται, μᾶλλον αὐτὴν ἐβιασάμην· κἂν βαρυθύμως ἔχῃ,
δεδάκρυκα· καὶ πρὸς ταῦτ' οὐκ ἔθ' ὑπομείνασα
τὰς ἐμὰς λύπας δεῖται λοιπόν, οὔτε στρατιώ-
τας ἔχουσα οὔτε δορυφόρους οὔτε φύλακας·
ἐγὼ γὰρ αὐτῆς εἰμὶ πάντα. Ἡ μέγα καὶ
θαυμαστὸν ἰδεῖν τὸν καλὸν Νεῖλον; οὐ μέγα
καὶ τὸν Εὐφράτην ἰδεῖν; οὐ μέγα καὶ τὸν
Ἴστρον; οὐ τῶν μεγάλων καὶ ὁ Θερμώδων, ὁ
Τίγρις, ὁ Ἅλυς, ὁ Ῥῆνος; Εἰ μέλλω πάντας
τοὺς ποταμοὺς ὁρᾶν, καταβαπτισθήσεταί μοι
τὸ ζῆν, μὴ βλέποντι Γλυκέραν. Ὁ δὲ Νεῖλος
οὗτος καίπερ ὢν καλός, ἀλλ' ἀποτεθηρίωται·
καὶ οὐκ ἔστιν οὔτε προσελθεῖν αὐτοῦ ταῖς
δίναις ἐλλοχωμένου τοσούτοις κακοῖς. Ἐμοὶ
γένοιτο, βασιλεῦ Πτολεμαῖε, τὸν Ἀττικὸν

sorrows to the grave, and leave my riches a prey to those who are ever on the watch to seize them? Is it so great an honour to live with Ptolemy and his satraps and others with like idle names, whose friendship is not to be trusted, and whose enmity is dangerous? If Glycera is angry with me, I clasp her in my arms and snatch a kiss; if she is still angry, I press her further, and, if she is indignant, I shed tears; then she can no longer resist my grief, but entreats me in her turn; for she has neither soldiers, nor spearmen, nor body-guards, but I am all in all to her. Is it so great and wonderful a thing to see the noble Nile? Are not the Euphrates, the Danube, the Thermodon, the Tigris, the Halys, and the Rhine equally deserving of admiration? If I had to visit all the rivers in the world, my life would be utterly swamped, unless I saw my Glycera. And this Nile, though a beautiful river, is full of savage monsters; and it is impossible to approach its streams, in which so many dangers lie concealed. May it be my lot, King

αἰεὶ στέφεσθαι κισσόν· ἐμοὶ γένοιτο χώματος καὶ τάφου πατρῴου τυχεῖν, καὶ τὸν ἐπ' ἐσχάρας ὑμνῆσαι κατ' ἔτος Διόνυσον τὰς μυστηριώτιδας ἄγειν τελετάς· δραματουργεῖν τι καινὸν ταῖς ἐτησίαις θυμέλαις δρᾶμα, γελῶντα καὶ χαίροντα καὶ ἀγωνιῶντα καὶ φοβούμενον καὶ νικῶντα. Φιλήμων δὲ εὐτυχείτω τἀμὰ ἀγαθὰ, γενόμενος ἐν Αἰγύπτῳ. Οὐκ ἔχει Φιλήμων Γλυκέραν τινά· οὐδὲ ἄξιος ἦν ἴσως τοῦ τοιούτου ἀγαθοῦ. Σὺ δὲ ἐκ τῶν Ἁλώων δέομαι, Γλυκέριον, εὐθὺς πετομένη πρὸς ἡμᾶς ἐπὶ τῆς ἀστράβης φέρου. Μακροτέραν ἑορτὴν οὐδέποτε ἔγνων, οὐδὲ ἀκαιροτέραν. Δήμητερ, ἴλεως γενοῦ.

Ptolemy, ever to be crowned with Attic ivy! to die and be buried in my own native land, and to join every year in the Dionysiac hymns at the altars! to be initiated into the mystic rites, to produce a new play every year upon the stage, now laughing and rejoicing, now in fear and trembling, and now victorious! Let Philemon go to Egypt and enjoy the happiness that is promised to me, for Philemon has no Glycera; perhaps he does not deserve such a blessing. And do you, my dear Glycera, I beseech you, immediately after the Haloan festival, mount your mule and fly to me. I have never known a festival that seemed to last longer, or one more ill-timed. O Ceres, be propitious!

IV.

Γλυκέρα Μενάνδρῳ.

Ὡς διεπέμψω μοι τοῦ βασιλέως τὰς ἐπιστολὰς, εὐθὺς ἀνέγνων. Μὰ τὴν Καλλιγένειαν, ἐν ἧς νῦν εἰμὶ, κατέχαιρον, Μένανδρε, ἐκπαθὴς ὑφ' ἡδονῆς γινομένη, καὶ τὰς παρούσας οὐκ ἐλάνθανον· ἦν δὲ ἥ τε μήτηρ μου καὶ ἡ ἑτέρα ἀδελφὴ Εὐφόριον, καὶ τῶν φίλων ἣν οἶσθα, καὶ παρὰ σοὶ ἐδείπνησε πολλάκις, καὶ ἐπήνεις αὐτῆς τὸν ἐπιχώριον ἀττικισμὸν, ἀλλ' ὡς φοβούμενος αὐτὴν ἐπαινεῖν, ὅτε καὶ μειδιάσασα θερμότερόν σε κατεφίλησα. Οὐ μέμνησαι, Μένανδρε; Θεασάμεναι δέ με παρὰ τὸ εἰωθὸς καὶ τῷ προσώπῳ καὶ τοῖς ὀφθαλμοῖς χαίρουσαν, ὦ Γλυκέριον, ἤροντο, τί σοι τηλικοῦτον γέγονεν ἀγαθὸν, ὅτι καὶ ψυχῇ καὶ σώματι καὶ πᾶσιν ἀλλοιοτέρα νῦν πέφηνας, καὶ τὸ σῶμα γεγάνωσαι

IV.

Glycera to Menander.

As soon as I received the King's letter, I read it. By the glorious Mother, in whose temple I now stand, I rejoiced exceedingly, Menander, being mad with joy, which I could not conceal from my companions. There were with me my mother, my sister Euphorium, and one of my friends whom you know, who has often supped with you, and whose Attic dialect you so commended, but as if you were half afraid to praise her, whenever I smiled and kissed you more warmly. Don't you remember, Menander dear? When they saw my unwonted joy in my face and my eyes, they asked me, "What extraordinary good fortune has happened to you, dear Glycera? You seem altered in mind, in body, in everything. Joy beams over your person; cheerfulness

καὶ διαλάμπεις ἐπίχαρτόν τι καὶ εὐκταῖον. Κἀγὼ, Μένανδρον, ἔφην, τὸν ἐμὸν ὁ Αἰγύπτου βασιλεὺς Πτολεμαῖος ἐπὶ τῷ ἡμίσει τῆς βασιλείας τρόπον τινὰ μεταπέμπεται, μείζονι τῇ φωνῇ φθεγξαμένη καὶ σφοδροτέρᾳ, ὅπως πᾶσαι ἀκούσωσιν αἱ παροῦσαι. Καὶ ταῦτα ἔλεγον ἐγὼ διατινάσσουσα καὶ σοβοῦσα ταῖς χερσὶν ἐμαυτῆς τὴν ἐπιστολὴν σὺν αὐτῇ τῇ βασιλικῇ σφραγῖδι. Χαίροις οὖν ἀπολειπομένη, ἔφρασαν; τὸ δὲ οὐκ ἦν, Μένανδρε. Ἀλλὰ τοῦτο μὲν οὐδενὶ τρόπῳ, μὰ τὰς θεὰς, οὐδ' εἰ βοῦς μοι τὸ λεγόμενον φθέγξαιτο, πεισθείην ἂν, ὅτι βουλήσεταί με ποτὲ ἢ δυνήσεται Μένανδρος, ἀπολιπὼν ἐν Ἀθήναις Γλυκέραν τὴν ἑαυτοῦ, μόνος ἐν Αἰγύπτῳ βασιλεύειν μετὰ πάντων τῶν ἀγαθῶν. Ἀλλὰ καὶ τοῦτό γε δῆλος ἐκ τῶν ἐπιστολῶν, ὧν ἀνέγνων, ἦν ὁ βασιλεὺς τἀμὰ πεπυσμένος, ὡς ἔοικε, περὶ σοῦ καὶ ἀτρέμα δι' ὑπονοιῶν Αἰγυπτίοις θέλων ἀστεϊσμοῖς σε διατωθάζειν. Χαίρω διὰ τοῦτο· ὅτι πεπλεύκασι καὶ εἰς Αἴγυπτον πρὸς αὐτὸν οἱ ἡμέτεροι ἔρωτες, καὶ πείθεται πάντως, ἐξ

and happy contentment pervade your whole being." I told them, raising my voice and speaking louder, that all who were present might hear me: "Ptolemy, King of Egypt, has invited my Menander to visit him, and promised him the half of his kingdom," and, at the same time, in proof of this, I shook triumphantly in the air the missive bearing the royal seal. "Will you be glad if he leaves you?" they asked. Most certainly, dear Menander, that was not the reason, by all the goddesses. Even if an ox were to speak, to use the words of the proverb, I would never believe that Menander would have the heart to leave his Glycera in Athens and reign alone in Egypt, in the midst of such grandeur. It was clear to me, besides, from the King's letter, which I read, that he knew of our relations, and my affection for you. It seemed to me that he meant to banter you in a roundabout way with Egyptian witticisms. I am delighted to think that the report of our love has crossed the sea. The King,

ὧν ἤκουσεν, ἀδύνατον σπουδάζειν, ἐπιθυμῶν Ἀθήνας πρὸς αὐτὸν διαβῆναι. Τί γὰρ Ἀθῆναι χωρὶς Μενάνδρου; τί δὲ Μένανδρος χωρὶς Γλυκέρας; ἥτις αὐτῷ καὶ τὰ προσωπεῖα διασκευάζω, καὶ τὰς ἐσθῆτας ἐνδύω, κἂν τοῖς προσκηνίοις ἕστηκα, τοὺς δακτύλους ἐμαυτῆς πιέζουσα, ἢ ἂν κροταλίσῃ τὸ θέατρον καὶ τρέμουσα τότε νὴ τὴν Ἄρτεμιν ἀναψύχω, καὶ περιβάλλουσά σε τὴν ἱερὰν τῶν δραμάτων ἐκείνην κεφαλὴν ἐναγκαλίζομαι. Ἀλλ᾽ ὅτι ταῖς φίλαις τότε χαίρειν ἔφην, τοῦτ᾽ ἦν, Μένανδρε, ὅτι οὐκ ἄρα Γλυκέρα μόνον, ἀλλὰ καὶ βασιλεῖς ὑπὲρ θάλασσαν ἐρῶσί σου, καὶ διαπόντιοι φῆμαι τὰς σὰς ἀρετὰς κατηγγέλκασι· καὶ Αἴγυπτος καὶ Νεῖλος καὶ Πρωτέως τὰ ἀκρωτήρια, καὶ αἱ Φάριαι σκοπιαί, πάντα μετέωρα νῦν ἐστι βουλόμενα ἰδεῖν Μένανδρον, καὶ ἀκοῦσαι φιλαργύρων, καὶ ἐρώντων, καὶ δεισιδαιμόνων, καὶ ἀπίστων, καὶ πατέρων, καὶ υἱῶν καὶ θεραπόντων, καὶ παντὸς ἐνσκηνοβατου-

from what he has been told, will see the utter uselessness of wishing Athens to be transported to Egypt. For what would Athens be without Menander? What would Menander be without Glycera, who prepares his masks, puts on his costumes for him, and stands at the wings to give the signal for applause in the theatre, and to accompany it with her own? Then, may Diana be my witness! I tremble, then I breathe again, and clasp you in my arms, the sacred fount of comedy. Need I tell you the reason of the joy I exhibited before my friends? It was simply the thought that not Glycera alone, but even distant monarchs love you, and that the fame of your merits has extended across the sea. Egypt, the Nile, the promontory of Proteus, the tower of Pharos, are all full of eager curiosity to behold Menander, and to hear the conversations of the misers, the lovers, the superstitious, the faithless, the fathers, the slaves — in short, all the characters that are introduced upon the stage. They may indeed

μένου· ὧν ἀκούσονται μὲν, οὐκ ὄψονται δὲ Μένανδρον, εἰ μὴ ἐν ἄστει παρὰ Γλυκέρᾳ γένοιντο· καὶ τὴν ἐμὴν εὐδαιμονίαν ἴδοιεν, τὸν πάντη διὰ τὸ κλέος αὐτοῦ Μένανδρον καὶ νύκτωρ καὶ μεθ' ἡμέραν ἐμοὶ περικείμενον. Οὐ μὴν ἀλλ' εἴγε ἄρα πόθος αἱρεῖ σέ τις καὶ τῶν ἐκεῖ ἀγαθῶν, καὶ εἰ μηδενὸς ἄλλου, τῆς γε Αἰγύπτου, χρήματος μεγάλου καὶ τῶν αὐτόθι πυραμίδων, καὶ τῶν περιηχούντων ἀγαλμάτων καὶ τοῦ περιβοήτου λαβυρίνθου, καὶ τῶν ἄλλων, ὅσα ἀπὸ χρόνου ἢ τέχνης παρ' αὐτοῖς τίμια, δέομαί σου, Μένανδρε, μὴ ποιήσῃ με πρόφασιν· μηδέ με 'Αθηναῖοι διὰ ταῦτα μισησάτωσαν, ἤδη τοὺς μεδίμνους ἀριθμοῦντες, οὓς ὁ βασιλεὺς αὐτοῖς πέμψει διὰ σέ· ἀλλ' ἄπιθι πᾶσι θεοῖς, ἀγαθῇ τύχῃ, δεξιοῖς πνεύμασι, Διὶ οὐρίῳ, ἐγὼ γάρ σε οὐκ ἀπολείψω· μὴ τοῦτο δόξῃς με λέγειν, οὐδ' αὐτὴ δύναμαι, κἂν θέλω· ἀλλὰ παρεῖσα τὴν μητέρα καὶ τὰς ἀδελφὰς αὐτὰς ἔσομαι συμπλέουσά σοι, καὶ σφόδρα τῶν εὐθαλασ-

be able to hear your pieces, but those who wish to see the author in person will have to come to Athens to me: here they will be witnesses of my happiness in the possession of a man whose renown fills the universe, and who never quits my side by day or night. However, if the promised happiness which awaits you there has charms for you—at any rate, magnificent Egypt, with its pyramids, its echoing statues, its famous labyrinth, and the other marvels of antiquity and art—I beg you, dear Menander, do not let me stand in the way: this would make me hated by the Athenians, who are already reckoning the bushels of corn which the King, out of regard for you, will bestow upon them. Go, under the protection of the gods and Fortune, with a favourable wind, and may Jupiter be propitious to you! As for me, I will never leave you: do not expect ever to hear me say that; and, even if I desired to do so, it would be impossible for me. I will leave my mother and sisters and join you on board. I feel sure that I

σῶν γεγένημαι εὖ οἶδα, και ἐκκλωμένης κώπης ναυτίας ἐγὼ θεραπεύσω. Θάλψω σου τὸ ἀσθενοῦν τῶν πελαγισμῶν ἄξω δέ σε ἄτερ μίτων Ἀριάδνης εἰς Αἴγυπτον, οὐ Διόνυσον ἀλλὰ Διονύσου θεράποντα καὶ προφήτην· οὐδὲ ἐν Νάξῳ καὶ ἐρημίαις ναυτικαῖς ἀπολειφθήσομαι, τὰς σὰς ἀπιστίας κλαίουσα καὶ ποτνιωμένη. Χαιρέτωσαν οἱ Θησεῖς ἐκεῖνοι καὶ τὰ ἄπιστα τῶν πρεσβυτέρων ἀμπλακήματα· ἡμῖν δὲ βέβαια πάντα, καὶ τὸ ἄστυ, καὶ ὁ Πειραιεύς, καὶ ἡ Αἴγυπτος. Οὐδὲν χωρίον ἡμῶν τοὺς ἔρωτας οὐχὶ δέξεται πλήρεις· κἂν πέτραν οἰκῶμεν, εὖ οἶδα ἀφροδίσιον αὐτὴν τὸ εὔνουν ποιήσει. Πέπεισμαι μήτε χρημάτων σε μήτε περιουσίας μήτε πλούτου τὸ καθάπαξ ἐπιθυμεῖν, ἐν ἐμοὶ καὶ τοῖς δράμασι τὴν εὐδαιμονίαν κατατιθέμενον· ἀλλ' οἱ συγγενεῖς, ἀλλ' ἡ πατρίς, ἀλλ' οἱ φίλοι, σχεδὸν οἶσθα πάντῃ πάντες πολλῶν δέονται, πλουτεῖν θέλουσι καὶ χρηματίζεσθαι. Σὺ μὲν οὐδέποτε περὶ

shall soon turn out to be a good sailor. If the motion of the oars affects you, and the unpleasantness of sea-sickness, I will tend and look after you. Without any thread, I will guide you, like another Ariadne, to Egypt; although you certainly are not Bacchus himself, but his attendant and priest. I have no fear of being abandoned at Naxos, to lament your perfidy in the midst of the solitudes of ocean. What care I for Theseus and the infidelities of the men of ancient times? No place can change our affection, Athens, the Piraeus, or Egypt. There is no country which will not find our love unimpaired: even if we had to live upon a rock, I know that our affection would make it the seat of love. I am convinced that you seek neither money, nor opulence, nor luxury: your happiness consists in the possession of myself and the composition of comedies; but your kinsmen, your country, your friends—all these, you know, have many needs; they all wish to grow rich and to heap up money. Whatever hap-

οὐδενὸς αἰτιάσῃ με οὔτε μικροῦ οὔτε μεγαλου, τοῦτο εὖ οἶδα, πάλαι μὲν ἡττημένος ἐμοῦ πάθεσι καὶ ἔρωτι· νῦν δὲ ἤδη καὶ κρίσιν προστεθεικὼς αὐτοῖς· οἷς μᾶλλον περιέχομαι, Μένανδρε, φοβουμένη τῆς ἐμπαθοῦς φιλίας τὸ ὀλιγοχρόνιον· ἔστι γὰρ ὡς βίαιος ἡ ἐμπαθὴς φιλία, οὕτω καὶ εὐδιάλυτος· οἷς δὲ παραβέβληνται καὶ βουλαί, ἀρραγέστερον ἐν τούτοις ἤδη τὸ ἔργον οὔτε ἀμιγὲς ἡδοναῖς τε καὶ διὰ τὸ πλῆθος, οὔτε περιδεές· λύσεις δὲ τὴν γνώμην, ὥς με πολλάκις περὶ τούτων αὐτὸς νουθετῶν διδάσκεις. Ἀλλ' εἰ καὶ σὺ μήτε μέμψῃ, μήτε αἰτιάσῃ, δέδοικα τοὺς Ἀττικοὺς σφῆκας, οἵτινες ἄρξονται πάντῃ με περιβομβεῖν ἐξιοῦσαν, ὡς αὐτὸν ἀφῃρημένης τῆς Ἀθηναίων πόλεως τὸν πλοῦτον. Ὥστε δέομαί σου, Μένανδρε, ἐπίσχες, μηδέπω τῷ βασιλεῖ μηδὲν ἀντεπιστείλῃς· ἔτι βούλευσαι, περίμεινον ἕως κοινῇ γενώμεθα καὶ μετὰ

pens, you will have nothing to reproach me with, either great or small, of that I am certain; for you have long felt the deepest affection for me, and you have now learnt to judge me aright. This, dearest Menander, is a matter of rejoicing to me, for I always used to fear the brief duration of a love founded upon simple passion. Such a love, however violent it may be, is always easily broken up; but, if it be accompanied by reason, the bonds of affection are drawn tighter, it gains sure possession of its pleasures, and leaves us free from care. Do you, who have often guided me on several occasions, tell me whether I am right in this. But, even if *you* should not reproach me, I should still have great fear of those Athenian wasps, who would be sure to buzz around me on all sides at the moment of my departure, as if I were taking away the wealth of Athens. Wherefore, dear Menander, I beg you, do not be in too great a hurry to reply to the King; think it over a little longer; wait until our meeting and we see our

τῶν φίλων καὶ Θεοφράστου καὶ Επικούρου· τάχα γὰρ ἀλλοιότερα κἀκείνοις καί σοὶ φανεῖται ταῦτα. Μᾶλλον δὲ καὶ θυσώμεθα καὶ ἴδωμεν, τί λέγει τὰ ἱερά, εἴτε λῷον εἰς Αἴγυπτον ἡμᾶς ἀπιέναι, εἴτε μένειν καὶ χρηστηριασθῶμεν εἰς Δελφοὺς πέμψαντες· πάτριος ἡμῶν ἐϛτιν ὁ θεός. Ἀπολογίαν ἕξομεν καὶ πορευόμενοι καὶ μένοντες πρὸς ἀμφότερα, τοὺς θεούς. Μᾶλλον δὲ ἐγὼ τοῦτο ποιήσω· καὶ γὰρ ἔχω τινὰ νεωστὶ γυναῖκα ἀπὸ Φρυγίας ἥκουσαν εὖ μάλα τούτων ἔμπειρον, γαστρομαντεύεσθαι δεινὴν τῇ τῶν σπαρτῶν διατάσει νύκτωρ καὶ τῇ τῶν θεῶν δείξει· καὶ οὐ δεῖ λεγούσῃ πιστεύειν, ἀλλ' ἰδεῖν, ὥς φασι. Διαπέμψομαι πρὸς αὐτήν· καὶ γὰρ, ὡς ἔφη, καὶ κάθαρσίν τινα δεῖ προτελέσαι τὴν γυναῖκα καὶ παρασκευάσαι τινὰ ζῶα ἱερεῦσαι, καὶ λιβανωτὸν ἄῤῥενα καὶ στύρακα μακρὸν καὶ πέμματα σελήνης, καὶ ἄγρια φύλλα ἀνθῶν. Οἶμαι δὲ καὶ σὲ φράσασθαι Πειραιώ-

friends Theophrastus and Epicurus; for perhaps their opinion will be different. Or rather, let us offer sacrifice, and see what the entrails of the victims portend: whether they advise us to set out for Egypt or to stay here; and, since Apollo is the god of our country, let us also send messengers to Delphi, to consult the oracle. Whether we go or whether we stay, we shall always have an excuse —the will of the gods.

I have a better plan still. I know a woman, very clever in all these matters, who has just arrived from Phrygia. She excels in the knowledge of the art of divination, the stretching of the branches of the broom, and the nightly evocation of the shades. As I do not believe merely in words, but require acts as well, I will send to her; for she says she must perform an initiatory lustration and prepare certain animals for the sacrifice, as well as the male frankincense, the tall styrax, the round cakes for the moon, and some leaves of wild flowers. I think that you have decided to come from the Piraeus;

θεν ἐλθεῖν· ἢ δηλῶσαί μοι σαφῶς, μέχρι τίνος οὐ δύνασαι Γλυκέραν ἰδεῖν ἵν' ἐγὼ μὲν καταδράμω πρὸς σέ, τὴν δὲ Φρυγίαν ταύτην ἑτοιμάσωμαι· ἤδη δὲ καταμελετᾶν πειράξεις ἀπὸ ταὐτομάτου τὸν Πειραιᾶ καὶ τὸ ἀγρίδιον καὶ τὴν Μουνυχίαν, καὶ κατ' ὀλίγον ὅπως ἐκπέσωσι τῆς ψυχῆς. Ἐγὼ μὲν δύναμαι πάντα ποιεῖν μὰ τοὺς θεούς· σὺ δὲ οὐ δύνασαι, διαπεπλεγμένος ὅλως ἤδη μοι. Κἂν οἱ βασιλεῖς ἐπιστείλωσι πάντες, ἐγὼ πάντων εἰμὶ παρὰ σοὶ βασιλικωτέρα, καὶ εὐσεβεῖ σοι κέχρημαι ἐραστῇ καὶ ὅρκων ἱερομνήμονι. Ὥστε πειρῶ μᾶλλον, ἐμὴ φιλότης, θᾶσσον εἰς ἄστυ παραγενέσθαι, ὅπως, εἴγε μεταβουλεύσαιο τῆς πρὸς βασιλέα ἀφίξεως, ἔχῃς εὐτρεπισμένα τὰ δράματα ἐξ αὐτῶν, ἃ μάλιστα ὀνῆσαι δύναται Πτολεμαῖον καὶ τὸν αὐτοῦ Διόνυσον, οὐ δημοκρατικὸν ὡς οἶσθα· εἴτε Θαΐδας, εἴτε Μισούμενον, εἴτε Θρασυλέοντα, εἴτε Ἐπιτρέποντας, εἴτε Ῥαπιζομένην, εἴτε Σικύων*** ἀλλ' ὅτι καὶ ἐγὼ θρασεῖα καὶ τολμηρά τις εἰμὶ τὰ Μενάνδρου διακρίνειν

if not, tell me how long you will be able to exist without seeing Glycera, that I may prepare this Phrygian and hasten to you. But perhaps you have already of your own accord considered with yourself how you may gradually forget the Piraeus, your little estate, and Munychia. I indeed can do and endure anything; but you are not equally your own master, since you are entirely wrapped up in me. Even if kings summon you, I am more your queen and mistress than them all, and I consider you as a devoted lover and a most diligent observer of your oath. Therefore, my darling, try all the more to come without delay to the city, so that, in case you change your mind in regard to visiting the King, you may nevertheless have those plays ready which are most likely to please Ptolemy and his Bacchus, no ordinary one, as you know: for instance, either the Thaises, the Misumenos, the Thrasyleon, the Epitrepontes, the Rhapizomene, or the Sicyonian. But how rash and venturesome am I to take upon myself to judge the compositions of

ἰδιῶτις οὖσα· ἀλλὰ σοφὸν ἔχω σου τὸν ἔρωτα, καὶ ταῦτ' εἰδέναι δύνασθαι· σὺ γὰρ μ' ἐδίδαξας εὐφυᾶ γυναῖκα ταχέως παρ' ἐρώντων μανθάνειν, ἀλλ' οἰκονομοῦσιν ἔρωτες σπεύδοντες· αἰδούμεθα τὴν Ἄρτεμιν ἀνάξιοι ὑμῶν εἶναι μὴ θᾶττον μανθάνουσαι. Πάντως δέομαι Μένανδρε, κἀκεῖνο παρασκευάσασθαι τὸ δρᾶμα, ἐν ᾧ μὲ γέγραφας, ἵνα κἂν μὴ παραγένωμαι σὺν σοι, δι' ἄλλου πλεύσω πρὸς Πτολεμαῖον, κἂν μᾶλλον αἴσθηται ὁ βασιλεὺς, ὅσον ἰσχύει καὶ παρὰ σοὶ γεγραμμένους φέρειν ἑαυτοῦ τοὺς ἔρωτας, ἀφεὶς ἐν ἄστει τοὺς ἀληθινούς. Ἀλλ' οὐδὲ τούτους ἀφήσεις, εὖ ἴσθι· κυβερνᾶν ἢ πρωρατεύειν ἕως δεῦρο παραγίνῃ πρὸς ἡμᾶς Πειραιόθεν μυηθήσομαι, ἵνα σε ταῖς ἐμαῖς

Menander—I, a woman who knows nothing about such matters! But I have a clever master in your affection, which has taught me to understand even them; you have shown me that any woman, who possesses natural ability, quickly learns from those she loves, and that love acts without delay. I should be ashamed, by Diana, if I were to show myself unworthy of such a master by being slow to learn. Anyhow, dear Menander, I entreat you also to get ready that play in which you have described myself, so that, even if not present in person, I may sail by proxy to the court of Ptolemy; so the King will more clearly understand how strong your love must be, since you take with you at least the written history of the same, although you leave behind you in the city the living object of your affections. But you shall not even leave that behind; you may rest assured that I shall practise myself in the mysteries of guiding the helm and keeping look-out, until you come to me from the Piraeus, that I may safely guide you over the waves

χερσὶν ἀκύμονα ναυστολήσω, πλέουσα, εἰ τοῦτο ἄμεινον εἶναι φαίνοιτο· φανείη δὲ, ὦ θεοὶ πάντες, ὃ κοινῇ λυσιτελὲς ᾖ, καὶ μαντεύσαιτο ἡ Φρυγία τὰ συμφέροντα κρεῖσσον τῆς θεοφορήτου σου κόρης. Ἔρρωσο.

with my own hands, if you think it best to go. I pray to all the gods that what may be to the advantage of us both may be disclosed, and that the Phrygian may prophesy what is to our interest even better than your damsel inspired with divine frenzy. Farewell.

LIBER TERTIUS.

I.

Γλαυκίππη Χαρώπῃ.

Οὐκέτ' εἰμὶ ἐν ἐμαυτῇ, ὦ μῆτερ, οὐδ' ἀνέχομαι γήμασθαι, ᾧ με κατ' ἐγγύησιν ἐπηγγείλατο ἔναγχος ὁ πατὴρ, τῷ Μηθυμναίῳ μειρακίῳ τῷ παιδὶ τοῦ κυβερνήτου, ἐξ ὅτου τὸν ἀστικὸν ἔφηβον ἐθεασάμην τὸν ὠσχοφόρον, ὅτε με ἄστυδε προὔτρεψας ἀφικέσθαι, ὠσχοφορίων ὄντων. Καλὸς μὲν γάρ ἐστι, καλὸς, ὦ μῆτερ, καὶ ἥδιστος, καὶ βοστρύχους ἔχει βρύων οὐλοτέρους, καὶ μειδιᾷ τῆς θαλάσσης γαληνιώσης χαριέστερον, καὶ τὰς βολὰς τῶν ὀφθαλμῶν ἐστι κυαναυγὴς, οἷος τὸ πρῶτον ὑπὸ τῶν ἀκτίνων τῶν ἡλιακῶν ὁ πόντος καταλαμπόμενος φαίνεται· τὸ δὲ ὅλον πρόσωπον αὐταῖς ἐνορχεῖσθαι ταῖς παρειαῖς εἴποις ἂν τὰς Χάριτας τὸν Ὀρχομενὸν ἀπολι-

BOOK III.

I.

GLAUCIPPE TO CHAROPE.

O MOTHER, I am quite beside myself! It is impossible for me to wed the young Methymnaean, the pilot's son, to whom my father lately betrothed me, since I have seen the young man from the city, who carried the holy palm branch, when you gave me permission to go to Athens for the festival of the Oschophoria. Ah, mother, how beautiful he is! how charming! His locks are curlier than moss; he laughs more pleasantly than the sea in a calm; his eyes are azure, like the ocean, when the first beams of the rising sun glitter upon it. And his whole countenance? You would say that the

πούσας καὶ τῆς Γαργαφίας κρήνης ἀπονιψαμένας, τὼ χείλη δὲ, τὰ ῥόδα τῆς Ἀφροδίτης ἀποσυλήσας τῶν κόλπων, διήνθισται, ἐπὶ τῶν ἄκρων ἐπιθέμενος. Ἢ τούτῳ μιγήσομαι, ἢ τὴν Λεσβίαν μιμησαμένη Σαπφὼ, οὐκ ἀπὸ τῆς Λευκάδος πέτρας, ἀλλ' ἀπὸ τῶν Πειραϊκῶν προβόλων ἐμαυτὴν εἰς τὸ κλυδώνιον ὤσω.

Graces, having abandoned Orchomenus, after bathing in the fountain of Gargaphia, had come to frolic around his cheeks. On his lips bloom roses, which he seems to have plucked from Cytherea's bosom to adorn them. He must either be mine or, following the example of the Lesbian Sappho, I will throw myself, not from the Leucadian rocks, but from the crags of Piraeus, into the waves.

II.

Χαρώπη Γλαυκίππῃ.

Μέμηνας, ὦ θυγάτριον, καὶ ἀληθῶς ἐξέστης. Ἑλλεβόρου δεῖ σοι, καὶ οὐ τοῦ κοινοῦ, τοῦ δὲ ἀπὸ τῆς Φωκίδος Ἀντικύρας, ἥτις, δέον αἰσχύνεσθαι κορικῶς, ἀπέξεσας τὴν αἰδῶ τοῦ προσώπου. Ἔχε ἀτρέμα, καὶ κατὰ σεαυτὴν ῥίπιζε τὸ κακὸν ἐξωθοῦσα τῆς διανοίας. Εἰ γάρ τι τούτων ὁ σὸς πατὴρ πύθοιτο, οὐδὲν διασκεψάμενος, οὐδὲ μελλήσας, τοῖς ἐναλίοις βορὰν παραρρίψει σε θηρίοις.

II.

CHAROPE TO GLAUCIPPE.

SILLY child, you are surely mad, without a spark of reason. You really need a dose of hellebore, not the ordinary kind, but that which comes from Anticyra, in Phocis, since you have lost all maiden modesty. Keep quiet, calm yourself, banish such extravagance from your thoughts and return to your right mind. If your father should hear anything of it, he would certainly throw you, without more ado, into the sea, as a dainty morsel for the monsters of the deep.

III.

Εὔαγρος Φιλοθήρῳ.

Εὐοψία μὲν ἦν καὶ πλῆθος ἰχθύων· ἐγὼ δὲ τὴν σαγήνην ἀπολέσας ἠπόρουν ὅ τι πράξαιμι. Ἔδοξεν οὖν Σισύφειόν τι μοι βουλευσαμένῳ βούλευμα ἐλθεῖν παρὰ τὸν δανειστὴν Χρέμητα, καὶ ὑποθήκην αὐτῷ καθομολογήσαντι τὸ σκάφος λαβεῖν χρυσίνους τέσσαρας, ἐξ ὧν αὖθις καινουργῆσαί μοι τὴν σαγήνην ὑπάρξειε, καὶ δῆτα τοῦτο λόγου θᾶττον ἐγένετο. Καὶ ὁ Χρέμης ὁ κατεσκληκώς, ὁ κατεσπακὼς τὰς ὀφρῦς ὁ ταυρηδὸν πάντας ὑποβλέπων, ἴσως ἔρωτι τῆς ἀκάτου, χαλάσας τὸ βαρὺ καὶ ἀμειδές, ἀνεὶς τὰς ὄψεις, ὑπεμειδία πρός με, καὶ οἷος εἶναι ὑπουργεῖν πάντα ἔφασκεν. Εὐθὺς μὲν οὖν ἔκδηλος ἦν οὕτως ἀθρόως τὸ σκυθρωπὸν λύσας οὐκ

III.

EVAGRUS TO PHILOTHERUS.

RECENTLY there was an abundant supply of fish; but, since my nets were quite spoilt, I did not know what to do. An inspiration came to me, which I thought worthy of Sisyphus. I resolved to go to the money-lender Chremes, and to offer my boat to him as security for four pieces of gold, that I might be able to repair my nets. No sooner said than done. Chremes, that skinny old wretch, as a rule knits his brows and looks savagely at everybody. Perhaps it was the hope of getting possession of my boat which caused him suddenly to relax his severity. The wrinkles on his brow cleared; he even smiled at me, and assured me that he was ready to render me any service that lay in his power. So prompt an alteration made his friendliness suspicious, and clearly showed that

ἀγαθόν τι διανοούμενος, ἀλλ' ὕπουλον ἔχωι τὸ φιλάνθρωπον ὡς δὲ ἐνστάντος τοῦ καιροῦ πρὸς τῷ ἀρχαίῳ καὶ τὸν τόκον ἀπῄτει, οὐδὲ εἰς ὥραν ἐνδιδοὺς, ἐπέγνων τοῦτον ἐκεῖνον, ὃν ἠπιστάμην πρὸς τῇ Διομήτιδι πύλῃ καθήμενον, τὸν τὴν καμπύλην ἔχοντα, τὸν ἐχθρὰ πᾶσι φρονοῦντα Χρέμητα τὸν Φλοιέα, καὶ γὰρ ἕτοιμος ἦν ἐπιλήψεσθαι τοῦ σκάφους. Ἰδὼν οὖν, εἰς ὅσον ἀμηχανίας ἐληλάκειν, οἴκαδε ἀποτρέχω, καὶ τὸ χρυσοῦν ἁλύσιον, ὅπερ ποτὲ εὐπορῶν τῇ γαμετῇ κόσμον εἶναι περιαυχένιον ἐπεποιήκειν, ἀποσπάσας τοῦ τραχήλου, ὡς Πασέωνα τὸν τραπεζίτην ἐλθὼν, ἀπημπόλησα, καὶ συναγαγὼν τὰ νομίσματα σὺν αὐτοῖς τόκοις φέρων ἀπέδωκα, καὶ ὤμοσα κατ' ἐμαυτοῦ, μήποτε ὑπομεῖναι παρά τινα τῶν ἐν πόλει δανειστῶν ἐλθεῖν, μηδ' ἂν φθάνοιμι λιμῷ κατασκλῆναι. Ἄμεινον γὰρ εὐπρεπῶς ἀποθανεῖν, ἢ ζῆν ὑποκείμενον δημοτικῷ καὶ φιλοκερδεῖ πρεσβύτῃ.

his intentions were anything but good; alas! his kindness was only skinned over, for, when the money became due, he claimed the interest with the capital, and refused to grant me so much as an hour's grace. Then I recognised the real Chremes of Phoela, the common enemy of mankind, who may usually be found before the Diometian Gate, armed with a crooked stick. He was actually making preparations to seize my boat. Then I perceived in what a cruel plight I was. I ran home with all speed, took from my wife's neck the golden necklace which I had given her in my more prosperous days, and sold it to the money-changer Paseon. With the money I got I paid both the capital and the interest, and I took an oath to myself that in future I would rather die of hunger than ever apply again to a city money-lender. It is better to die honourably than to live at the mercy of a low and avaricious old man.

IV.

Τρεχέδειπνος Λοπαδεκθάμβῳ.

Ὁ γνώμων οὔπω σκιάζει τὴν ἕκτην· ἐγὼ δὲ ἀποσκλῆναι κινδυνεύω, τῷ λιμῷ κεντούμενος. Εἶεν, ὥρα σοι βουλεύματος, Λοπαδέκθαμβε, μᾶλλον δὲ μοχλοῦ καὶ καλωδίου ἀπάγξασθαι. Εἰ γὰρ καὶ ὅλην καταβαλοῦμεν τὴν κίονα τὴν τὸ πικρὸν τοῦτο ὡρολόγιον ἀνέχουσαν, ἢ τὸν γνώμονα τρέψομεν ἐκεῖσε νεύειν, οὗ τάχιον δυνήσεται τὰς ὥρας ἀποσημαίνειν, ἔσται τὸ βούλευμα Παλαμήδειον· ὡς νῦν ἐγώ σοι αὖος ὑπὸ λιμοῦ καὶ αὐχμηρός. Θεοχάρης δὲ οὐ πρότερον καταλαμβάνει τὴν στιβάδα, πρὶν αὐτῷ τὸν οἰκεῖον δραμόντα φράσαι τὴν ἕκτην ἑστάναι. Δεῖ οὖν ἡμῖν τοιούτου σκέμματος, ὃ κατασοφίσασθαι καὶ παραλογίσασθαι τὴν Θεοχάρους εὐταξίαν δυνήσεται. Τραφεὶς γὰρ ὑπὸ παιδαγωγῷ βαρεῖ

IV.

TRECHEDEIPNUS TO LOPADECTHAMBUS.

THE sun-dial does not yet mark the sixth hour, and I am in danger of wasting away under the pinch of hunger. Come, it is time to take counsel, Lopadecthambus, or rather, let us get a beam and a rope and hang ourselves. But I have an idea. If we were to throw down the whole column which supports that confounded dial, or turn the index so that it may make the hours seem to have gone faster, it will be a device worthy of Palamedes. I am exhausted and parched with hunger. Theochares never takes his seat at table until the servant runs to let him know that it is the sixth hour. We therefore need some plan to outwit and overreach the regularity of Theochares. For, as he has been brought up under the care of a stern and morose tutor, his

καὶ ὠφρυωμένῳ οὐδὲν φρονεῖ νεώτερον, ἀλλ' οἷά τις Λάχης ἢ 'Αποληξίας αὐστηρός ἐστι τοῖς τρόποις, καὶ οὐκ ἐπιτρέπει τῇ γαστρὶ πρὸ τῆς ὥρας ἢ ἐκείνης τοῦ πίμπλασθαι. Ἔρρωσο.

ideas are not those of a young man, but he is as austere in his manners as Laches or Apolexias, and he will not allow his belly to satisfy its needs before that hour. Farewell.

V.

Ἑκτοδιώκτης Μανδιλοκολάπτῃ.

Χθὲς δείλης ὀψίας Γοργίας ὁ Ἐτεοβουδάτης συμβαλών μοι κατὰ τύχην χρηστῶς ἠσπάσατο καὶ κατεμέμφετο, ὅτι μὴ θαμίζοιμι παρ' αὐτόν. Καὶ μικρὰ προσπαίξας, ἴθι, πρὸς Διὸς, εἶπεν, ὦ βέλτιστε, καὶ μετὰ βραχὺ λουσάμενος ἧκε, Ἀηδόνιον ἡμῖν τὴν ἑταίραν ἄγων· ἔστι δέ μοι συνήθης ἐπιεικῶς, καὶ μένει πάντως, ὡς οὐκ ἀγνοεῖς, μικρὸν ἄποθεν τοῦ Λεωκορίου. Δεῖπνον δὲ ἡμῖν ηὐτρέπισται γεννικὸν, ἰχθύες τεμαχίται, καὶ σταμνία τοῦ Μενδησίου, νέκταρος εἴποι τις ἂν, πεπληρωμένα. Καὶ ὁ μὲν ταῦτα εἰπὼν ᾤχετο· ἐγὼ δὲ παρὰ τὴν Ἀηδόνιον δραμὼν, καὶ φράσας, παρ' ὅτου ἐκαλεῖτο, ἐδέησα κινδύνῳ περιπεσεῖν· ἀγνώμονος γὰρ, ὡς ἔοικε, πειραθεῖσα τοῦ Γοργίου, καὶ μικροπρεποῦς

V.

HECTODIOCTES TO MANDILOCOLAPTES.

YESTERDAY, late in the evening, Gorgias, of the family of the Eteobudatae, meeting me by chance, greeted me courteously, and reproached me for not going to see him more frequently. Then, after a few playful words, he said to me, "Go, by Jupiter, my good friend, have a bath and come back to me without delay. Do not forget to bring Aedonium, with whom I am very intimate, and who, as you know, is always to be found near the Leocorium. I have prepared a noble supper, slices of fish, and jars of wine from Mendos, which you would say was the nectar of the gods." With these words, he left me. I ran in all haste to Aedonium ; and when I told her by whom she had been invited, I nearly got into trouble. For, as it seems, she

πρὸς τὰς ἀντιδόσεις, τὴν ὀργὴν ἔναυλον ἐγκειμένην ἔχουσα, πλήρη τὴν κακάβην ἀνασπάσασα τῶν χυτροπόδων, ἐδέησέ μου κατὰ τοῦ βρέχματος καταχέοντος τοῦ ὕδατος, εἰ μὴ φθάσας ἀπεπήδησα, παρὰ βραχὺ φυγὼν τὸν κίνδυνον. Οὕτως ἡμεῖς ἐλπίσιν ἀπατηλαῖς βουκολούμενοι πλείους τῶν ἡδονῶν τοὺς προπηλακισμοὺς ὑπομένομεν.

had found Gorgias ungrateful and mean in the matter of presents in return for her favours. In her anger, which is ever rankling in her breast, she snatched a full kettle from the stove, and, unless I had avoided the danger by quickly starting back, she would have poured all its contents over the top of my head. Thus, after feeding ourselves on idle hopes, do we gain a greater share of humiliation than of pleasure.

VI.

Ἀρτεπίθυμος Κνισοζώμῳ.

Ἀγχόνης μοι δεῖ, καὶ ὄψει με οὐ μετὰ μακρὸν ἐν βρόχῳ τὸν τράχηλον ἔχοντα· οὔτε γὰρ ῥαπίσματα οἷός τε εἰμὶ φέρειν, καὶ τὴν ἄλλην παροινίαν τῶν κάκιστα ἀπολουμένων ἐρανιστῶν, οὔτε τῆς μιαρᾶς καὶ ἀδηφάγου γαστρὸς κρατεῖν· ἡ μὲν γὰρ αἰτεῖ, καὶ οὐ πρὸς κόρον μόνον, ἀλλ' εἰς τρυφήν· τὸ πρόσωπον δὲ τὰς ἐπαλλήλους πληγὰς οὐκ ἀνέχεται, καὶ κινδυνεύω τοῖν ὀφθαλμοῖν τὸν ἕτερον συσταλῆναι ὑπὸ τῶν ῥαπισμάτων ἐνοχλούμενος. Ἰοὺ, ἰοὺ τῶν κακῶν, οἷα ὑπομένειν ἡμᾶς ἀναγκάζει ἡ παμφάγος αὕτη καὶ παμβορωτάτη γαστήρ. Ἔκρινα οὖν πολυτελοῦς τραπέζης ἀπολαύσας ἀποπτύσαι τὸ ζῆν, ὀδυνηροῦ βίου κρείττω τὸν καθ' ἡδονὴν θάνατον ἡγησάμενος.

VI.

ARTEPITHYMUS TO CNISOZOMUS.

I WANT a rope : you will soon see me with my neck in a noose. For I cannot endure slaps in the face, and all the drunken insults of these cursed diners; and yet I cannot control my confounded and gluttonous stomach. It is always asking for more; it is not satisfied with being filled, but clamours for luxuries. But my face cannot stand blows one after the other, and I am in danger of having one of my eyes bunged up by their slaps. Alas, alas! what misery does our greedy and ravenous stomach force us to endure! I have therefore made up my mind to have one more good dinner and to put an end to my life in disgust, since, in my opinion, a voluntary death is preferable to a painful life.

VII.

Ἐτοιμόκορος Ζωμεκπνέοντι.

Ἰαταταιὰξ, τίς ἦν ἡ χθὲς ἡμέρα, ἢ τίς δαίμων, ἢ θεὸς ἀπὸ μηχανῆς ἐρρύσατό με ἀκαρῆ μέλλοντα παρὰ τοὺς πλείονας ἰέναι. Εἰ μὴ γὰρ ἀναξεύξαντά με τοῦ συμποσίου κατά τινα ἀγαθὴν τύχην Ἀκεσίλαος ὁ ἰατρὸς ἡμιθνῆτα, μᾶλλον δὲ αὐτονεκρὸν θεασάμενος, ἕνα τῶν κάτω, μαθηταῖς ἐπιτάττων φοράδην ἀνελὼν, ἤγαγεν ὡς ἑαυτὸν οἴκαδε, καὶ ἀπερᾶν ἀπηνάγκασεν, ἔπειτα διατεμὼν φλέβα, ῥυῆναι τὸ πολὺ τοῦ αἵματος ἐποίησεν, οὐδὲν ἂν ἐκώλυσεν ἀνεπαισθήτῳ με τῷ θανάτῳ διαφθαρέντα ἀπολωλέναι. Οἷα γὰρ, οἷα (πάσχει τὰ δίκαια) λακκόπλουτοι εἰργάσαντό με, ἄλλος ἄλλοθεν περιττὰ πίνειν, καὶ πλείονα ἢ κατὰ τὸ κύτος τῆς γαστρὸς ἐσθίειν ἀναγκά-

VII.

HETOEMOCORUS TO ZOMECPNEON.

OH, Lord! oh, Lord! what a day I had yesterday! What spirit or god interfered, unexpectedly interfered, to save me, just as I was on the point of going to join the majority? For, as I was returning from the banquet, had not Acesilaus the physician, by good luck, seen me, half-dead, or rather a corpse, an inhabitant of the nether world, and ordered his pupils to pick me up and carry me home, and, after administering an emetic to me, bled me till the blood flowed plentifully, nothing could have saved me from dying before I had regained consciousness. How these wealthy people treated me—and serve him right[1]—one making me drink to excess, and another forcing me to eat more

[1] Apparently a marginal note by an enemy of parasites in general.

ζοντες. Ὁ μὲν γὰρ ἀλλᾶντα ἐνέσαττεν, ὁ δὲ κόπαιον εὐμέγεθες παρώθει ταῖς γνάθοις, ὁ δὲ κρᾶμα, οὐκ οἶνον, ἀλλὰ νάπυ καὶ γάρον καὶ ὄξος ἐργασάμενος, καθάπερ εἰς πίθον ἐνέχει, ἅτινα, λέβητας, πιθάκνας, ἀμίδας ἐμημεκὼς ἀπεπλήρωσα· ὥστε αὐτὸν τὸν Ἀκεσίλαον θαυμάζειν, ποῦ καὶ τίνα τρόπον ἐχώρησε τοσοῦτος ὁ τῶν βρωμάτων φορυτός. Ἀλλ' ἐπειδὴ θεοὶ σωτῆρες καὶ ἀλεξίκακοι προὔπτου με κινδύνου φανερῶς ἐξείλοντο, ἐπ' ἐργασίαν τρέψομαι, καὶ Πειραιεῖ βαδιοῦμαι τὰ ἐκ τῶν νεῶν φορτία ἐπὶ τὰς ἀποθήκας μισθοῦ μετατιθείς. Ἄμεινον γὰρ ἐπὶ θύμοις καὶ ἀλφίτοις διαβόσκειν τὴν γαστέρα, ὁμολογουμένην ἔχοντα τὴν τοῦ ζῆν ἀσφάλειαν, ἢ πεμμάτων ἀπολαύοντα καὶ φασιανῶν ὀρνίθων, τὸν ἄδηλον ὁσημέραι θάνατον ἀπεκδέχεσθαι.

than the skin of my belly could hold. One stuffed me with sausages, another rammed a great hunk of bread down my throat, while another made me drink a mixture, not wine, but mustard, fish-sauce, and vinegar, just as if he were pouring it into a cask. What a number of pots, pans, and pails I filled, when I brought all this up! Acesilaus was utterly astonished, and could not make out where and how I had managed to stow away such a mish-mash of food. But now that the protecting and tutelary gods have visibly preserved me from a great danger, I will in future work. I will go down to the Piraeus, and carry luggage for hire from the vessels to the warehouses. For it is better to feed one's stomach with thyme and barley-porridge, and enjoy a certain amount of security, than to feast upon cakes and pheasants, with the uncertain prospect of death before one's eyes every day.

VIII.

Οἰνοπήκτης Κοτυλοβροχθίσῳ.

Ἴθι λαβὼν τὴν σύριγγα καὶ τὰ κύμβαλα ἧκε περὶ πρώτην φυλακὴν τῆς νυκτὸς ἐπὶ τὸν χρυσοῦν στενωπὸν τὸν ἐπὶ τὴν ἄγνον, ἔνθα συμβαλεῖν ἡμῖν ἀλλήλοις ἔξεσται, καὶ τὸ ἐντεῦθεν, ἀπὸ Σκίρου λαβοῦσι Κλυμένην τὴν ἑταῖραν ἄγειν παρὰ τὸν νεόπλουτον, τὸν Θηριππίδην τὸν Αἰξωνέα. Διακαῶς δὲ αὐτῆς οὗτος ἐρᾷ, πολὺς ἐξ οὗ χρόνος, καὶ δαπανᾶται οὐκ ὀλίγα μάτην. Ἠισθημένη γὰρ τὸν ἔρωτα ἐκκεκαυμένον τοῦ μειρακίου, θρύπτεται καὶ συνεχῶς ἀκκίζεται· καὶ πλείονα ἐπὶ πλείοσιν ἀποφερομένη, οὔ φησιν ἑαυτὴν ἐπιδώσειν, εἰ μὴ τὸ χωρίον πρὸς τοῖς ἀργυρίοις λάβοι. Ὥρα οὖν καὶ βίᾳ ταύτην εἰ συνήθως ἀντιτεί-

VIII.

OENOPECTES TO COTYLOBROCHTHISUS.

Go, fetch your flute and cymbals; and, towards the first watch of the night, come to the Golden Alley near Agnus, where we shall be able to meet. We can make arrangements to carry off Clymene from the Scyrian quarter and take her to Therippides of the deme of Aexona, who has just come into a fortune. For some time he has been madly in love with her, and has spent considerable sums upon her, but all to no purpose. For she, seeing the ardour of his passion, plays the coquette and shows herself affected and indifferent; and, although he has loaded her with presents, she refuses to let him enjoy her favours unless he adds landed property in the neighbourhood of the silver mines. I think it is time to put an end to this, and to

νυιτο ἡμῖν, ἀποσπᾶν· δύω δὲ ὄντε καὶ ἐρρω-
μένω τάχιστα αὐτὴν ἀπάξαιμεν. Θηριππίδης
δὲ εἰ τοῦτο αἴσθοιτο, καὶ τοὔργον ἐπιγνοίη
τῆς ἡμετέρας ἀγρυπνίας κατόρθωμα, ληψό-
μεθα χρυσοῦς τοῦ νέου σκέμματος οὐκ ὀλίγους, καὶ λαμπρὰν ἐσθῆτα, καὶ προσέτι τὴν
οἰκίαν εἰσιέναι ἐπ' ἀδείας ἕξομεν, καὶ τὸ χρῆσθαι τὸ λοιπὸν ἀνεπικωλύτως. Τάχα δὲ οὐδὲ
παρασίτους ἡμᾶς, ἀλλὰ φίλους ἡγήσεται· οἱ
γὰρ παράκλησιν εἰς εὐποιΐαν μὴ ἀναμείναντες, οὐκέτι κόλακες, ἀλλὰ φίλοι λογίζονται.

carry her off by force, in case she still offers resistance : two stout fellows like ourselves ought to have no difficulty in getting possession of the charmer. When Therippides learns that this happy result is the fruit of our watching, we shall certainly get some money or clothes for our cleverness : he will give us free entry into his house; we shall henceforth enjoy every pleasure, without any hindrance, by way of reward. Perhaps he will even no longer treat us as parasites, but look upon us as friends ; for those who know how to anticipate the wishes of others are not considered to be flatterers, but friends.

IX.

* * * — * * *

Ἀποπειρώμενος τῶν σκυλακίων εἰ λοιπὸν ἐπιτήδεια κατὰ δρόμον, λαγωὸν ἔν τινι θάμνῳ διαστροβήσας ἐξαίφνης ἀνέστησα, τὰ δὲ σκυλάκια οἱ ἐμοὶ υἱεῖς τῶν ἱμαντίων ἀπέλυσαν. Καὶ τὰ μὲν ἐθορύβει, καὶ ἐγγὺς ἦν ἑλεῖν τὸ θηρίον· ὁ λαγωὸς δὲ τοῦ κινδύνου φυγῇ ὑπερβὰς τὸ σιμὸν, φωλεοῦ τινος κατάδυσιν εὕρετο. Μία δὲ ἡ προθυμοτέρα τῶν κυνῶν, ἤδη κεχηνυῖα καὶ ψαῦσαι προσδοκῶσα τῷ δήγματι, συγκατῆλθεν εἰς τὴν ὀπὴν τῆς γῆς, ἐντεῦθεν ἀνελκύσαι βιαζομένη τὸ λαγώδιον, καὶ θραύει τοῖν προσθίοιν ποδοῖν τὸν ἕτερον. Καὶ ἀνειλόμην χωλεύουσαν σκύλακα ἀγαθὴν, καὶ τὸ ζῶον ἡμίβρωτον· καὶ γέγονέ μοι κέρδους ἐφιεμένῳ λυπροῦ ζημίαν μεγάλην ἀπενέγκασθαι.

IX.

[THIS LETTER HAS NO ADDRESS.]

WHILE I was trying my young dogs, to see if they were fit for coursing, I suddenly started a hare which was concealed in the brushwood. My sons unleashed the dogs; they rushed on and were on the point of catching the hare, when, in its efforts to escape, it ran up a hill and took refuge in a warren. The most eager of the pack, which was already snapping at it with open mouth and thought to seize it with its teeth, followed it into the hole, and, in the attempt to pull it out, broke one of its fore-legs. All I could do was to pull out a lame dog and a half-eaten hare. I was only trying to gain a trifling success, but, instead, I experienced a severe loss.

X.

Ιοφῶν Ἐράστονι.

Ἐπιτριβείη καὶ κακὸς κακῶς ἀπόλοιτο ὁ κάκιστος ἀλεκτρυὼν καὶ μιαρώτατος, ὅς με, ἡδὺν ὄνειρον θεώμενον, ἀναβοήσας ἐξήγειρεν. Ἐδόκουν γὰρ, ὦ φίλτατε γειτόνων, λαμπρός τις εἶναι καὶ βαθύπλουτος· εἶτα οἰκετῶν ἐφέπεσθαί μοι στίφος, οὓς οἰκονόμους καὶ διοικητὰς ἐνόμιζον ἔχειν. Ἐῴκειν δὲ καὶ τὼ χεῖρε δακτυλίων πεπληρῶσθαι, καὶ πολυταλάντους λίθους περιφέρειν· καὶ ἦσαν οἱ δάκτυλοί μου μαλακοὶ, καὶ ἥκιστα τῆς δικέλλης ἐμέμνηντο. Ἐφαίνοντο δὲ καὶ οἱ κόλακες ἐγγύθεν, Γρυλλίωνα εἴποις ἂν καὶ Παταικίωνα παρεστάναι. Ἐν τούτῳ δὴ καὶ ὁ δῆμος Ἀθηναίων εἰς τὸ θέατρον προελθόντες, ἐβόων προχειρίσασθαί με στρατηγόν· μεσούσης δὲ τῆς χειροτονίας, ὁ παμπόνηρος ἀλεκτρυὼν ἀνεβόησε, καὶ τὸ φάσμα ἠφανίσθη.

X.

Iophon to Eraston.

Cursed be the detestable cock, which woke me up with its crowing, when I was enjoying a most delightful dream. I thought, my dear neighbour, that I was a person of wealth and distinction. I was attended by a number of slaves, stewards, and treasurers. My hands were loaded with rings and precious stones of great value; my fingers were soft and delicate, free from hardness, and showed no traces of the use of the mattock. I was surrounded by flatterers, such as Gryllion and Pataecion. At the same time, the people of Athens, assembled in the theatre, cried out for my appointment as general. But, while they were busily engaged in voting, the confounded cock crowed, and the vision disappeared. However, on

"Ομως ἀνεγρόμενος περιχαρὴς ἦν ἐγώ· ἐνθύμιον δὲ ποιησάμενος, τοὺς φυλλοχόους ἑστάναι μῆνας, ἔγνων εἶναι τὰ ἐνύπνια ψευδέστατα.

my first awaking, I was still full of joy. But, when I reflected that we were in the month of the fall of the leaves, I remembered that then dreams are always most false, and I said good-bye to my illusions.

XI.

Δρυαντίδας Χρονίῳ.

Οὐκέτι σοι μέλει οὔτε τῆς εὐνῆς ἡμῶν, οὔτε τῶν κοινῶν παίδων, οὔτε μὴν τῆς κατ' ἀγρὸν διατριβῆς· ὅλη δὲ εἶ τοῦ ἄστεος. Πανὶ μὲν καὶ Νύμφαις ἀπεχθομένη, ἃς Ἐπιμηλίδας ἐκάλεις, καὶ Δρυάδας, καὶ Ναΐδας, καινοὺς δὲ ἡμῖν ἐπεισάγουσα θεοὺς πρὸς πολλοῖς τοῖς προϋπάρχουσι. Ποῦ γὰρ ἐγὼ κατ' ἀγρὸν ἱδρύσω Κωλιάδας ἢ Γενετυλλίδας; οἶδα ἀκούσας ἄλλα τινα δαιμόνων ὀνόματα, ὧν διὰ τὸ πλῆθος ἀπώλισθέ μοι τῆς μνήμης τὰ πλείονα. Οὐ σωφρονεῖς, ὡς ἔοικεν, ὦ γύναι, οὐδὲ ὑγιές τι διανοῇ, ἀλλὰ ἁμιλλᾶσαι ταῖς ἀστικαῖς ταυταισὶ ταῖς ὑπὸ τρυφῆς διαρρεούσαις, ὧν καὶ τὸ πρόσωπον ἐπίπλαστον, καὶ ὁ τρόπος μοχθηρίας ὑπεργέμων· φύκει γὰρ καὶ ψιμυθίῳ

XI.

DRYANTIDAS TO CHRONIUM.

You have forgotten our marriage bed, our children, our country life. The city has taken complete hold of you. Pan and the Nymphs, whom you used to invoke under the name of Dryads, Epimelides, and Naiads, are now hated by you, and, in addition to the numerous deities already in existence, you are introducing fresh ones. Where shall I be able to find room in the country for the Coliades or Genetyllides? I think I also heard some other divinities mentioned, but, owing to their number, the names of most of them have slipped my memory. Foolish woman that you are, you must have lost your reason! You wish to try and rival those women of Athens who, plunged in luxury, have made-up faces, and whose morals are of the worst.

ΑΛΚΙΦΡΟΝΟΣ ΡΗΤΟΡΟΣ

καὶ παιδέρωτι δευσοποιοῦσι τὰς παρειὰς ὑπὲρ τοὺς δεινοὺς τῶν ζωγράφων. Σὺ δέ, ἢν ὑγιαίνῃς, ὁποίαν σε τὸ ὕδωρ ἢ τὸ ῥύμμα τὸ πρὶν ἐκάθηρεν, τοιαύτη διαμενεῖς.

They paint their cheeks with dyes, ceruse, and vermilion, more skilfully than the cleverest artist. But you, if you are sensible, will not imitate them. Remain as you are; pure water and soap are enough for a respectable woman.

XII.

Πρατίνας Ἐπιγόνῳ.

Μεσημβρίας οὔσης σταθηρᾶς, φιλήνεμόν τινα ἐπιλεξάμενος πίτυν, καὶ πρὸς τὰς αὔρας ἐκκειμένην, ὑπὸ ταύτῃ τὸ καῦμα ἐσκίαζον καί μοι ψυχάζοντι μάλ' ἡδέως, ἐπῆλθέ τι καὶ μουσικῆς ἐφάψασθαι, καὶ λαβὼν τὴν σύριγγα ἐπέτρεχον τῇ γλώττῃ στενὸν τὸ πνεῦμα μετὰ τῶν χειλῶν ἐπισύρων, καί μοι ἡδύ τι καὶ νόμιον ἐξηκούετο μέλος. Ἐν τούτῳ δὲ οὐκ οἶδ' ὅπως ὑπὸ τῆς ἡδυφωνίας θελγόμεναι πᾶσαί μοι πανταχόθεν αἱ αἶγες περιεχύθησαν, καὶ ἀφεῖσαι νέμεσθαι τοὺς κομάρους καὶ τὸν ἀνθερικὸν, ὅλαι τοῦ μέλους ἐγένοντο. Ἐγὼ δὲ ἐν μέσοις τοῖς Ἡδωνοῖς ἐμιμούμην τὸν παῖδα τῆς Καλλιόπης. Ταῦτά

XII.

PRATINAS TO EPIGONUS.

WHEN the noonday heat was at its height, I selected a pine-tree, which was swept by the wind and exposed to the breeze, and threw myself beneath its shade to escape from the sweltering heat. While I was cooling myself very comfortably, the idea came into my head to try a little music. I took my pipe; I gently moved my tongue up and down its reeds, and played a sweet pastoral melody. Meanwhile, all my goats collected round me from all directions, enchanted, I know not why, by the sweet strains. They forgot to browse upon the arbutus and asphodel, and gave no thought to anything but the music. At that time I was like the son of Calliope in the midst of the Edonians. My only object in communicating to you

σε οὖν εὐαγγελίζομαι, φίλον ἄνδρα συνειδέναι βουλόμενος, ὅτι μοι μουσικόν ἐστιν ἔχειν τὸ αἰπόλιον.

this pleasant story is to let a friend know that I have a flock of goats which is exceedingly fond of music and knows how to appreciate it.

XIII.

Καλλικράτης Αἴγωνι.

Ἐγὼ μὲν, ἥκοντος τοῦ καιροῦ, γύρους περισκάψας καὶ ἐμβαθύνας βόθρον, οἷός τε ἤμην ἐλάδια ἐμφυτεύειν, καὶ ἐπάγειν αὐτοῖς ναματιαῖον ὕδωρ, ὅ μοι ἐκ τῆς πλησίον φάραγγος ἐποχετεύεται· ἐπελθὼν δὲ ὄμβρος ἐς τρεῖς ἡμέρας καὶ νύκτας ἴσας, ποταμοὺς ἄνωθεν ἐκ τῆς ἀκρωρείας τῶν ὀρῶν ἐγέννησεν, οἳ ῥύμῃ κατασυρόμενοι ἰλὺν ἐπεσπάσαντο, καὶ τοὺς βόθρους κατέχωσαν, ὥστε εἶναι πάντα ἰσόπεδα, καὶ οὐδὲ δοκεῖν ὅλως εἰργασμένα. Οὕτως ἠφάνισταί μοι τὰ πονήματα, καὶ εἰς μίαν ὄψιν ἄτοπον κατέστη. Τίς ἂν οὖν ἔτι πονοίη, μάτην ἀδήλους ἐλπίδας ἐκ γεωργίας καραδοκῶν; Μετιτέον μοι ἐφ' ἕτερον βίον· φασὶ γὰρ ἅμα ταῖς τῶν ἐπιτηδευμάτων ἀλλαγαῖς καὶ τὰς τύχας μετασχηματίζεσθαι.

XIII.

CALLICRATES TO AEGON.

WHEN the season for planting came, I was on the point of setting some young olive-trees, and watering them with water from the spring, which was brought to me from the neighbouring valley. I had already marked out the holes and dug trenches. Unfortunately, a storm of rain came on, which, for three days and as many nights, drove down from the summit of the mountains regular rivers, which, in their impetuous course, have filled the trenches with mud. All my fields have the same level; there is no trace of cultivation; all my labour is lost. The whole place has assumed a uniform and strange appearance. Who in future will work any more and flatter himself in vain with idle hopes in return for all his labour? I must try another trade. It is said that Fortune changes when we change our occupation.

XIV.

Σιτάλκης Οἰνοπίωνι.

Εἰ πατρώζεις, ὦ παῖ, καὶ τἀμὰ φρονεῖς, χαίρειν τοὺς ἀλαζόνας ἐκείνους τοὺς ἀνυποδήτους καὶ ὠχριῶντας, οἳ περὶ τὴν 'Ακαδημίαν ἀλινδοῦνται, βιωφελὲς μὲν οὐδὲν οὐδὲ πράττειν δυνάμενοι, οὐδὲ εἰδότες, τὰ μετέωρα δὲ πολυπραγμονεῖν ἐπιτηδεύοντες, ἐάσας, ἔχου τῶν κατ' ἀγρὸν ἔργων, ἀφ' ὧν σοι διαπονοῦντι μεστὴ μὲν ἡ σιπύη πανσπερμίας, οἱ δὲ ἀμφορεῖς οἴνου γέμοντες, πλεῖα δὲ ἀγαθῶν τὰ σύμπαντα.

XIV.

SITALCES TO OENOPION.

MY son, if you wish to imitate your father and follow his advice, do not listen to those charlatans whom you see wandering, barefooted and with pale faces, in the neighbourhood of the Academy. They can neither do nor teach anything useful on this earth; they only pore over heavenly things, which they profess to understand. Leave these people, work, cultivate your land; this will fill your meal-sack with corn, your jars with wine, and your house with wealth.

XV.

Κότινος Τρυγοδώρῳ.

Ὁ τρυγητὴς ἐγγὺς, καὶ ἀρρίχων ἔστι μοι χρεία· δάνεισον οὖν μοι τούτων τοὺς περιττοὺς, ὅσον οὐκ εἰς μακρὸν ἀποδώσοντι. Ἔχω οὖν κἀγὼ πιθάκια πλείονα· εἰ οὖν δέοιο, προθύμως λάμβανε, τὰ γὰρ κοινὰ τῶν φίλων οὐχ ἥκιστα τοῖς ἀγροῖς ἐμφιλοχωρεῖν ἐθέλει.

XV.

Cotinus to Trygodorus.

THE vintage is close at hand; I want some baskets; lend me some, if you have any to spare; I will return them to you soon. I have several little casks; if you want any, take them without ceremony. The rule, that friends should share what they have in common, holds good in the country more than anywhere else.

XVI.

Φυλλὶς Θρασωνίδῃ.

Εἰ γεωργεῖν ἐβούλου, καὶ νοῦν ἔχειν, ὦ Θρασωνίδη, καὶ τῷ πατρὶ πείθεσθαι, ἔφερες ἂν καὶ τοῖς θεοῖς κιττὸν καὶ δάφνας, καὶ μυρίνην, καὶ ἄνθη ὅσα σύγκαιρα· καὶ ἡμῖν τοῖς γονεῦσιν πυροὺς ἐκθερίσας, καὶ οἶνον ἐκ βοτρύων ἀποθλίψας, καὶ βδάλας τὰ αἰγίδια, τὸν γαυλὸν πληρώσας γάλακτος. Νῦν δὲ ἀγρὸν καὶ γεωργίαν ἀπαναίνῃ, κράνους δὲ ἐπαινεῖς τριλοφίαν, καὶ ἀσπίδος ἐρᾷς, ὥσπερ Ἀκαρνὰν ἢ Μηλιεὺς μισθοφόρος. Μὴ σύγε, ὦ παιδίον, ἀλλ' ἐπάνιθι ὡς ἡμᾶς, καὶ τὸν ἐν ἡσυχίᾳ βίον ἀσπάζου (καὶ γὰρ ἀσφαλὴς καὶ ἀκίνδυνος ἡ γεωργία, οὐ λόχους, οὐκ ἐνέδρας, οὐ φάλαγγας ἔχουσα, ἡμῖν τε ὁ γηροκόμος ἐγγύς) ἀντὶ τῆς ἐν ἀμφιβόλῳ ζωῆς τὴν ὁμολογουμένην ἑλόμενος σωτηρίαν.

XVI.

Phyllis to Thrasonides.

IF you will be sensible, Thrasonides, listen to your father, and devote yourself to agriculture. You would present to the gods, ivy, laurels, myrtles, and flowers in season; to us, your parents, you would bring the wheat you have reaped, the wine you have pressed, and the pail full of milk from your goats. But, as it is, you despise the country and agriculture, and all your affection is devoted to a helmet surmounted with triple crest or a shield, just as if you were a Melian or Acarnanian mercenary. Give up such ideas, my boy; come back to us and lead a peaceful life; the fields offer greater security. There one is out of reach of danger, without having to fear cohorts, phalanxes, or ambuscades. Be the stay of our approaching old age: a life free from danger is better than a career full of perils.

XVII.

Χαιρέστρατος Ληρίῳ.

Ἐπιτριβείης, ὦ Λήριον, κακὴ κακῶς, ὅτι με τῇ μέθῃ καὶ τοῖς αὐλοῖς κατακηλήσασα, βραδὺν ἀπέφηνας τοῖς ἐκ τῶν ἀγρῶν ἀποπέμψασιν. Οἱ μὲν γὰρ ἕωθεν προσεδόκων με φέροντα αὐτοῖς τὰ κεράμια (σκεύη) ὧν ἕνεκα ἀφικόμην· ἐγὼ δὲ ὁ χρυσοῦς πάννυχος καταυλούμενος εἰς ἡμέραν ἐκάθευδον. Ἀλλ' ἄπιθι, ὦ τάλαινα, καὶ τοὺς ἀθλίους τουτουσὶ θέλγε τοῖς γοητεύμασιν· ἐμοὶ δὲ ἢν ἔτι ἐνοχλοίης, κακόν τι παμμέγεθες προσλαβοῦσα ἀπελεύσῃ.

XVII.

Chaerestratus to Lerium.

May ill-luck attend you, Lerium! may you come to a bad end, for having intoxicated me with wine and music, so that I was late in getting back to the people who had sent me from the country! The first thing in the morning they expected me with the wine jars which I had come to fetch for them; but I, like a nice fellow that I was, amused myself with you all night, and, charmed by the sound of your flute, slept until daybreak. Away with you, worthless woman! tempt city young men with your fascinations; if you molest me any more, you shall pay dearly for it.

XVIII.

Εὔσταχυς Πιθακίωνι.

Τοῦ ἐμοῦ παιδὸς γενέσια ἑορτάζων, ἥκειν σε ἐπὶ τὴν πανδαισίαν, ὦ Πιθακίων, παρακαλῶ· ἥκειν δὲ οὐ μόνον, ἀλλ' ἐπαγόμενον τὴν γυναῖκα, καὶ τὰ παιδία, καὶ τὸν συνέργαστρον· εἰ βούλοιο δὲ, καὶ τὴν κύνα, ἀγαθὴν οὖσαν φύλακα, καὶ τῷ βάρει τῆς ὑλακῆς ἀποσοβοῦσαν τοὺς ἐπιβουλεύοντας τοῖς ποιμνίοις· ἡ τοιαύτη οὐκ ἂν ἀτιμάζοι τὸ δαιτυμὼν εἶναι σὺν ἡμῖν. Ἑορτάσομεν δὲ μάλ ἡδέως, καὶ πιόμεθα εἰς μέθην, καὶ μετὰ τὸν κόρον ᾀσόμεθα· καὶ ὅστις ἐπιτήδειος κορδακίζειν, εἰς μέσους παρελθὼν, τὸ κοινὸν ψυχαγωγήσει. Μὴ μέλλε οὖν, ὦ φίλτατε, καλὸν γὰρ ἐν ταῖς κατ' εὐχὴν ἑορταῖς ἐξ ἑωθινοῦ συντάττειν τὰ συμπόσια.

XVIII.

EUSTACHYS TO PITHACION.

As I am keeping my son's birthday, I invite you to the feast. Bring your wife, your children, your servant, and even the dog, if you like. He is a trusty protector, and his loud barking will scare away those who have evil designs upon our flocks: I am sure he will not disdain to make one of the party. We will spend the day in joviality; we will drink till we are drunk; and, when we have had enough, we will take to singing. If there is any one of us who knows how to dance the Cordax, he can step out into the middle, and delight the company. Answer me at once, for, on festive occasions, one must begin to make all preparations in the morning.

XIX.

Πιθακίων Εὐστάχυϊ.

Κοινωνικὸς ὢν καὶ φιλέταιρος ὄναιο σαυτοῦ, καὶ τῆς γυναικὸς, καὶ τῶν παιδίων, ὦ Εὔσταχυ· ἐγὼ δὲ τὸν κλῶπα φωράσας, ἐφ᾽ ᾧ πάλαι ἤσχαλλον, τὴν ἐχέτλην ὑφελομένῳ καὶ δύο δρεπάνας, ἔχω παρ᾽ ἐμαυτῷ, τοὺς κωμήτας ἀναμένων ἐπικούρους. Νῦν γὰρ οὐκ ἐδοκίμαζον, ἀσθενέστερος ὢν καὶ μόνος, τὼ χεῖρε ἐπιβάλλειν αὐτῷ· ὁ μὲν γὰρ δριμὺ βλέπει, καὶ τοξοποιεῖ τὰς ὀφρῦς, καὶ σφριγῶντας ἔχει τοὺς ὤμους, καὶ ἁδρὰν τὴν ἐπιγουνίδα φαίνει· ἐγὼ δὲ ὑπὸ τῶν πόνων, καὶ τῆς δικέλλης κατέσκληκα, καὶ τύλους μὲν ἐν ταῖς χερσὶν ἔχω, λεπτότερον δέ μοι τὸ δέρμα λεβηρίδος. Ἡ μὲν οὖν γυνὴ καὶ τὰ παιδία εἴσω βαδιοῦνται, καὶ τῆς εὐωχίας μεθέξουσιν· ὁ δὲ σύργαστρος μαλακῶς ἔχει τὰ νῦν· ἐγὼ δὲ καὶ ἡ κύων τὸν μιαρὸν οἴκοι φυλάξομεν.

XIX.
PITHACION TO EUSTACHYS.

MY best wishes to you and your wife and children, my dear Eustachys, for being so ready to share your pleasures with your friends. I have caught the thief, who caused me such annoyance by stealing a plough-handle and two sickles. I have got him safe under lock and key, and am waiting for the neighbours to come and help me. For, being alone and infirm, I have not ventured to lay hands upon him myself. He has a savage look and arches his brows, his shoulders are stalwart, his legs are stout and strong; whereas I am exhausted by labour and handling the mattock, my hands are horny, my skin is as thin as the slough of a serpent. My wife and children will come to do honour to your feast. My servant is ill, so I cannot leave the house: I must stay at home with the dog and mount guard over the prisoner.

XX.

Ναπαῖος Κρηνιάδῃ.

Οἶσθά με ἐπισάξαντα τὴν ὄνον σῦκα καὶ παλάθας; καταγαγόντα οὖν, ἕως οὗ ταῦτα ἀπεδόμην τῶν τινὶ γνωρίμων, ἄγει μέ τις λαβὼν εἰς τὸ θέατρον, καὶ καθίσας ἐν καλῷ, διαφόροις ἐψυχαγώγει θεωρίαις. Τὰς μὲν οὖν ἄλλας οὐ συνέχω τῇ μνήμῃ, εἰμὶ γὰρ τὰ τοιαῦτα καὶ εἰδέναι καὶ ἀπαγγέλλειν κακός· ἓν δὲ ἰδών, ἀχανὴς ἐγώ σοι καὶ μικροῦ δεῖν ἄναυδος. Εἷς γάρ τις εἰς μέσους παρελθών, καὶ στήσας τρίποδα, τρεῖς μικρὰς παρετίθει παροψίδας, εἶτα ὑπὸ ταύταις ἔσκεπε μικρά τινα καὶ λευκὰ καὶ στρογγύλα λιθίδια, οἷα ἡμεῖς ἐπὶ ταῖς ὄχθαις τῶν χειμάρρων ἀνευρίσκομεν· ταῦτα ποτὲ μὲν κατὰ μίαν ἔσκεπε παροψίδα, ποτὲ

XX.

NAPAEUS TO CRENIADES.

You remember the day when I had loaded my ass with green and dried figs? After I had taken him to the stable, and sold the figs to one of my friends, someone took me to the theatre, where he put me into a good place, and gave me a treat of all kinds of spectacles. Although I forgot what else I saw—since I am not at all clever at understanding or giving an account of such things—I remember one thing, which struck me dumb with astonishment. A man came forward with a three-legged table. On this he placed three little cups, under which he hid some little round white pebbles, such as we find on the bank of a torrent. At one time he put them separately, one under each cup; at another time he showed them, all together, under one cup;

δὲ, οὐκ οἶδ' ὅπως, ὑπὸ τῇ μιᾷ ἐδείκνυ, ποτὲ δὲ παντελῶς ἀπὸ τῶν παροψίδων ἠφάνιζε, καὶ ἐπὶ τοῦ στόματος ἔφαινεν· εἶτα καταβροχθίσας, τοὺς πλησίον ἑστῶτας ἄγων εἰς μέσον, τὴν μὲν ἐκ ῥινὸς τινὸς, τὴν δὲ ἐξ ὠτίου, τὴν δὲ ἐκ κεφαλῆς ἀνῃρεῖτο· καὶ πάλιν ἀνελόμενος ἐξ ὀφθαλμῶν ἐποίει. Κλεπτίστατος ἄνθρωπος, ὑπὲρ ὃν ἀκούομεν Εὐρυβάτην τὸν Οἰχαλιέα. Μὴ γένοιτο κατ' ἀγρὸν τοιοῦτο θηρίον, οὐ γὰρ ἁλώσεται ὑπ' οὐδενὸς, καὶ πάντα ὑφαιρούμενος τὰ ἔνδον, φροῦδά μοι τὰ κατ' ἀγρὸν ἀπεργάσεται.

then he made them disappear from the cups, I don't know how, and showed them, the next moment, in his mouth. After this he swallowed them, called some of the spectators on to the platform, and pulled out of their nose, head, and ears the pebbles which he ended by juggling away altogether. What a clever thief the man must be, far sharper than Eurybates of Oechalia, of whom we have often heard. I am sure I don't want to see him in the country; since nobody would be able to catch him in the act, he would plunder the house without being noticed. What then would become of the fruit of my labours?

XXI.

Εὐνάπη Γλαύκῃ.

Ὁ μὲν ἀνὴρ ἀπόδημός ἐστί μοι, τρίτην ταύτην ἡμέραν ἔχων ἐν ἄστει· ὁ δὲ θητεύων παρ' ἡμῖν Παρμένων, ζημία καθαρά, ῥάθυμος ἄνθρωπος, καὶ τὰ πολλὰ καταπίπτων εἰς ὕπνον. Ὁ δὲ λύκος ἀργαλέος πάροικος, καὶ βλέπων φονῶδές τι καὶ ὠμοβόρον, Χιόνην τὴν καλλίστην τῶν αἰγῶν ἐκ τοῦ φελλέως ἁρπάσας οἴχεται· καὶ ὁ μὲν δειπνεῖ ἀγαθὴν αἶγα καὶ εὐγάλακτον, ἐγὼ δὲ δάκρυα τῶν ὀφθαλμῶν ἀπολείβω. Πέπυσται δὲ τούτων οὐδὲν ὁ ἀνήρ· εἰ δὲ μάθῃ, κρεμήσεται μὲν ἐκ τῆς πλησίον πίτυος ὁ μισθωτός· αὐτὸς δὲ οὐ πρότερον ἀνήσει πάντα μηχανώμενος, πρὶν τὰς παρὰ τοῦ λύκου δίκας εἰσπράξασθαι.

XXI.

EUNAPE TO GLAUCE.

My husband has been in town for three days, and Parmeno, our servant, does nothing but damage; he is so careless, and spends all his time in sleeping. We have in our neighbourhood a wolf, whose savage appearance indicates his ferocious instincts. He has carried off Chione, the finest of our goats, from the stony field. Now he is making a meal of the poor creature, which gave us milk in such abundance, and I am left to lament her loss. My husband knows nothing about it as yet. When he hears of it, he will hang up the hireling on the nearest pine-tree, and will not be satisfied until he has done everything in his power to wreak vengeance upon the wolf.

XXII.

Πολύαλσος Εὐσταφύλῳ.

Πάγην ἔστησα ἐπὶ τὰς μιαρὰς ἀλώπεκας, κρεάδιον τῆς σκανδάλας ἀφάψας. Ἐπεὶ γὰρ ἐπολέμουν τὰς σταφυλὰς, καὶ οὐ μόνον τὰς ῥᾶγας ἔκοπτον, ἀλλ' ἤδη καὶ ὁλοκλήρους ἀπέτεμνον τῶν οἰνάρων τοὺς βότρυς, ὁ δεσπότης δὲ ἐπιστήσεσθαι κατηγγέλλετο· (ἀργαλέος ἄνθρωπος καὶ δριμὺς, γνωμίδια καὶ προβουλευμάτια συνεχῶς ἐπὶ τῆς πνυκὸς Ἀθηναίοις εἰσηγούμενος, καὶ πολλοὺς ἤδη διὰ σκαιότητα τρόπου καὶ δεινότητα ῥημάτων ἐπὶ τοὺς Ἕνδεκα ἀγαγών) δείσας, μή τι πάθοιμι κἀγὼ, καὶ ταῦτα τοιούτου δεσπότου ὄντος, τὴν κλέπτην ἀλώπεκα συλλαβὼν ἐβουλόμην παραδοῦναι. Ἀλλ' ἡ μὲν οὐχ ἧκε· Πλαγγὼν δὲ, τὸ Μελιταῖον κυνίδιον, ὃ τρέφομεν ἄθυρμα τῇ δεσποίνῃ προσηνὲς, ὑπὸ

XXII.

POLYALSUS TO EUSTAPHYLUS.

I SET a trap for those confounded foxes, and hung some pieces of meat on the trap. They ravaged my vines, and, not content with picking a few grapes, carried off whole bunches and pulled up the plants. The news came that our master would soon be here; he has the reputation of being harsh and bitter, a man who, at Athens, is always worrying the assembly with all sorts of proposals, not to mention that his spitefulness and violent speeches have brought many to the Eleven. With such a man, how could I help being afraid of the same lot? That is the reason why I was so anxious to hand over to him the thief who stole his grapes. Alas! no fox appeared; but Plangon, the little Maltese dog, which is kept for our mistress's amusement, smelt

τῆς ἄγαν λιχνείας ἐπὶ τὸ κρέας ὁρμῆσαν, κεῖταί σοι τρίτην ταύτην ἡμέραν ἐκτάδην, νεκρὸν, ἤδη μυδῆσαν. Ἔλαθον οὖν ἐπὶ κακῷ κακὸν ἀναρρίπίσας. Καὶ τίς παρ' ἀνθρώπῳ σκυθρωπῷ τῶν τοιούτων συγγνώμη; Φευξόμεθα ᾖ ποδῶν ἔχομεν, χαιρέτω δὲ ὁ ἀγρὸς καὶ τἀμὰ πάντα· ὥρα γὰρ σώζειν ἐμαυτὸν, καὶ μὴ παθεῖν ἀναμένειν, ἀλλὰ πρὸ τοῦ παθεῖν φυλάξασθαι.

the bait and flung himself upon it, for he is a terrible glutton. For three days he has been stretched on his back, lifeless, almost in a state of putrefaction. Without thinking, I have brought one misfortune upon another. How can I hope for pardon from a man of such cruel disposition as our master? No, I will run away as fast as my legs can carry me. Good-bye to country life and all that I possess. It is high time to save myself, and not to wait for misfortune, but to look after myself before it comes.

XXIII.

Θάλλος Πιτυίστῳ.

Πάντα φιλῶ τρυγᾶν, ἔστι γὰρ τὸ καρπῶν ἀποδρέπεσθαι πόνων ἀμοιβὴ δίκαιος· ἐξαιρέτως δὲ ἐθέλω βλίττειν τὰ σμήνη. Ἔχων οὖν, σίμβλους ὑπὸ τῇ πέτρᾳ ἀποκλάσας, κηρία νεογενῆ, πρῶτον μὲν οὖν τοῖς θεοῖς ἀπηρξάμην, ἔπειτα δὲ τοῖς φίλοις ὑμῖν ἀπάρχομαι. Ἔστι δὲ λευκὰ ἰδεῖν, καὶ ἀποστάζοντα λιβάδας Ἀττικοῦ μέλιτος, οἷον αἱ Βριλησίαι λαγόνες ἐξανθοῦσι. Καὶ νῦν μὲν ταῦτα πέμπομεν, καὶ εἰς νέωτα δὲ δέχοιο παρ᾽ ἡμῶν μείζω τούτων καὶ ἡδίονα.

XXIII.

Thallus to Pityistus.

I LOVE to cull the fruits of the earth, of whatever kind they are; for the gathering-in of the harvest is a fitting reward of our labours; but what I am particularly fond of is to rob the hives of their honey. I have just paid a visit to some hives which I found amongst the rocks. They have provided me with some honeycombs, quite fresh. I offered the firstfruits of them to the gods; you, my friends, must now have a share of what is left. They are white in colour, and distil drops of Attic honey, such as is found in the caverns of Brilessus. For the moment, I send you this as a present; next year you shall have something bigger and more agreeable.

XXIV.

Φιλοποίμην Μοσχίωνι.

Λύκον ἔοικα τρέφειν. Τὸ μιαρὸν ἀνδράποδον ἐμπεσὼν εἰς τὰς αἶγας, οὐκ ἔστιν ἥντινα οὐκ ἀπολώλεκε, τὰς μὲν ἀποδόμενος, τὰς δὲ καταθύων. Καὶ τῷ μὲν ἡ γαστὴρ τῆς κραιπάλης ἐμπίμπλαται, καὶ τὰ λοιπὰ τῇ τενθείᾳ δαπανᾶται, καὶ ψάλλεται, καὶ καταυλεῖται, καὶ πρὸς τοῖς μυροπωλείοις φιληδεῖ· τὰ δὲ αὔλια ἔρημα, αἶγες δὲ ἐκεῖναι αἱ πρότερον οἴχονται. Τέως μὲν οὖν ἡσυχίαν ἄγω, μὴ προαισθόμενος ψύττα κατατείνας φύγῃ· εἰ δὲ ἀνυπόπτως λαβοίμην αὐτοῦ καὶ ἐγκρατὴς γενοίμην, δεδήσεται τὼ χεῖρε, χοίνικας παχείας ἐπισύρων· καὶ τῇ σκαπάνῃ προςανέχων, ὑπὸ τῇ δικέλλῃ καὶ τῇ σμινύῃ τῆς μὲν τρυφῆς ἐπιλήσεται, παθὼν δὲ, οἷόν ἐστι γνώσεται τὸ τὴν ἄγροικον σωφροσύνην ἀσπάζεσθαι.

XXIV.

Philopoemen to Moschion.

It seems to me that I am keeping a wolf in my house. My confounded slave falls upon my goats and does not spare a single one; he has sold some, and sacrificed others. His belly is swollen with gorging, and he spends what he has left on his gluttony. He amuses himself with pipe and flute-players, and delights in the perfumers' shops. In the meantime the stalls are deserted, and the flocks of goats which I once had have disappeared. However, I keep quite quiet, that he may not get suspicious and take to flight. In this manner I hope to surprise him. If I catch hold of him, he shall have his hands bound, and he shall be made to drag heavy chains along with him. Then, the rake, the pick, and the hoe shall help him to forget his luxurious habits; he shall learn to his sorrow what it means to choose the temperate life of a countryman.

XXV.

Ὕλη Νομίῳ.

Θαμίζεις εἰς τὸ ἄστυ κατιών, ὦ Νόμιε, καὶ τὸν ἀγρὸν οὐδὲ ἀκαρῆ θέλεις ὁρᾶν. Ἀργεῖ δὲ ἡ γῆ χηρεύουσα τῶν ἐμπονούντων· ἐγὼ δὲ οἰκουρῶ μόνη, μετὰ τῆς Σύρας ἀγαπητῶς τὰ παιδία βουκολοῦσα. Σὺ δὲ ἡμῖν αὐτόχρημα μεσαιπόλιος ἄνθρωπος, μειράκιον ἀστικὸν ἀνεφάνης· ἀκούω γάρ σε τὰ πολλὰ ἐπὶ Σκίρου καὶ Κεραμεικοῦ διατρίβειν, οὗ φασὶ τοὺς ἐξωλεστάτους σχολῇ καὶ ῥᾳστώνῃ τὸν βίον καταναλίσκειν.

XXV.

HYLE TO NOMIUS.

You are too fond of visiting the city, Nomius, and do not condescend to look at the country for a moment. Our deserted fields no longer produce any crops, for want of someone to attend to them. I am obliged to remain at home with Syra, and do the best I can to support the children. And you, an old man with grey hairs, play the young Athenian dandy. I am told that you spend the greater part of your time in Scirus and the Ceramicus, which is said to be the meeting-place of worthless persons, who go there to spend their time in idleness and sloth.

XXVI.

Ληναῖος Κορύδωνι.

Ἄρτι μοι τὴν ἄλω διακαθήραντι, καὶ τὸ πτύον ἀποτιθεμένῳ ὁ δεσπότης ἐπέστη· καὶ ἰδών, ἐφίλει τὴν φιλεργίαν· Ἐφάνη δέ μοι ποθὲν ὁ Κωρύκειος δαίμων, Στρόμβιχος ὁ παμπόνηρος· ἰδὼν γάρ με ἐφεπόμενον τῷ δεσπότῃ, κειμένην τὴν σισύραν, ἣν ἀποθέμενος εἰργαζόμην, ὑπὸ μάλης ᾤχετο φέρων, ὡς ὁμοῦ ζημίαν, καὶ τὸν ἀπὸ τῶν ὁμοδούλων προσοφλῆσαι γέλωτα.

XXVI.

LENAEUS TO CORYDON.

JUST now, after I had cleaned the threshing-floor, and was laying down the winnowing - fan, the master came up, looked ρn, and praised my industry. But that rascal Strombichus, like a cunning and malicious sprite, seeing that I was following my master, took my goatskin which I had taken off during my work, and carried it away under his arm. I was obliged to put up with the loss, and, in addition, the laughter of my comrades.

XXVII.

Γέμελλος Σαλμωνίδι.

Τί ταῦτα, ὦ Σαλμωνὶς, ὑπερηφανεῖς, τάλαινα; οὐκ ἐγώ σε εἰς τοὐργαστήριον καθημένην παρὰ τὸν ἀκέστην τὸν ἑτερόποδα ἀνειλόμην; καὶ ταῦτα λαθραίως τῆς μητρός; καὶ καθάπερ τινὰ ἐπίκληρον ἐγγυητὴν ἀγαγόμενος ἔχω; Σὺ δὲ φρυάττῃ, παιδισκάριον εὐτελὲς, καὶ κιχλίζουσα καὶ μωκωμένη με διατελεῖς. Οὐ παύσῃ τάλαινα τῆς ἀγερωχίας; ἐγώ σοι τὸν ἐραστὴν δείξω δεσπότην, καὶ κάχρυς ἐπὶ τῶν ἀγρῶν φρύγειν ἀναπείσω· καὶ τότε εἴσῃ μαθοῦσα, οἵων κακῶν σεαυτὴν ἔνδον ἔθηκας.

XXVII.

GEMELLUS TO SALMONIS.

UNHAPPY Salmonis! what means this haughty behaviour towards your master? You seem to forget that I rescued you from the lame botcher's shop, without letting my mother know anything about it. Did I not after that instal you in my house as my lawful wife, who will inherit all my property? And yet, you worthless hussy, you put on these airs, laugh in my face, and always treat me with contempt. Wretch, leave off this insolent behaviour, or I will show you that your lover is your master. I will send you to roast barley in the country, and then you will understand, to your cost, to what unhappiness you have brought yourself.

XXVIII.

Σαλμωνὶς Γεμέλλῳ.

Πάντα ὑπομένειν οἷα τε εἰμὶ, πλὴν τοῦ σοι συγκαθεύδειν, δέσποτα. Καὶ τὴν νύκτα οὐκ ἔφυγον οὐδὲ ἐπὶ τοῖς θάμνοις ἐκρυπτόμην, ὡς ἐδόκεις, ἀλλὰ τὴν κάρδοπον ὑπεισελθοῦσα ἐκείμην, ἀμφιθεμένη τὸ κοῖλον τοῦ σκεύους εἰς κάλυμμα. Ἐπειδὴ δὲ κέκρικα βρόχῳ τὸν βίον ἐκλιπεῖν, ἄκουε, λέγω σοι ἀναφανδὸν (πάντα γάρ μου περιαιρεῖ φόβον ἡ πρὸς τὸ τελευτᾶν ὁρμή), ἐγώ σε, ὦ Γέμελλε, στυγῶ, τοῦτο μὲν βδελυττομένη τὸ βάρος τοῦ σώματος, καὶ ὥσπερ τι κίναδος ἐκτρεπομένη· τοῦτο δέ, τὴν δυσχέρειαν τοῦ στόματος, ἐκ τοῦ μυχαιτάτου τῆς φάρυγγος τὴν δυσοσμίαν ἐκπέμποντος. Κακὸς κακῶς ἀπόλοιο τοιοῦτος ὤν. Βάδιζε παρά τινα λημῶσαν ἄγροικον γραῦν ἐπὶ ἑνὶ γομφίῳ σαλεύουσαν, ἀληλιμμένην τῷ τῆς πίττης ἐλαίῳ.

XXVIII.

SALMONIS TO GEMELLUS.

I AM ready to suffer anything, master, rather than sleep with you. Last night I did not run away, or hide myself in the bushes, as you imagined; I was lying under the kneading-trough, with which I covered myself. And now, since I have made up my mind to hang myself, I am not afraid to speak frankly to you, Gemellus, for my resolution to die removes all my fear. Hear then what I have to say. I hate you; I loathe your unwieldy person; your manners, like those of a wild beast, frighten me; the smell from your mouth is like poison. Wretch that you are, may you perish wretchedly! Meanwhile, go and look for some bleareyed old woman, who has only one tooth left, and is anointed with rancid oil.

XXIX.

"Ο ρ ι ο ς 'Ανθοφορίωνι.

Ἠπιστάμην σε, ὦ 'Ανθοφορίων, ἁπλοϊκὸν εἶναι ἄνθρωπον, καὶ αὐτόχρημα τὸν ἀπὸ τῆς ἀγροικίας ἄγροικον, ὄζοντα στεμφύλων καὶ κόνιν πνέοντα· ἠγνόουν δὲ, ὅτι δεινὸς εἶ ῥήτωρ, ὑπὲρ τοὺς ἐν Μητιχείῳ τῶν ἀλλοτρίων ἕνεκεν ἀδικομαχοῦντας. Κινήσας γὰρ ἀπὸ τοῦ κωμάρχου δίκας ἔναγχος, οὐκ ἔστιν ἥντινα οὐχὶ νικήσας ἀπηλλάγης. Μακάριε τῆς γλώσσης, καὶ λαλίστερε τρυγόνος. Ἐγὼ δὲ ἑρμαίῳ σοι χρῶμαι, τὸ τοῦ λόγου· ἔκκειμαι γὰρ τοῖς βουλομένοις τἀμὰ σφετερίζεσθαι, καὶ ἀγαπῶ τὴν ἡσυχίαν, καὶ ταῦτα εἰδὼς, ὅτι μοι πολλὰ ἐκ τῆς ἀπραγμοσύνης φύεται πράγματα.

XXIX.

ORIUS TO ANTHOPHORION.

UNTIL now I always believed that you were a quiet, simple fellow, who had become a regular countryman, smelling of pressed olives and reeking with dust; but I did not know that you were a clever speaker, superior even to those who plead in foreign commercial cases in the Meticheum. It seems that you have taken to pleading causes before the village magistrates, and that, since then, you have always gained the day. Good luck to you! with your tongue you will become a greater chatterer than a turtle-dove. As the proverb says, I shall make use of you as a windfall. I am daily exposed to the greed of certain persons who have designs upon my property; you shall defend me. I love peace and quietness, but I know that my carelessness and inactivity often cause me trouble and annoyance.

XXX.

Ἀμπελίων Εὐέργῳ.

Πολὺς ὁ χειμὼν τὸ τῆτες, καὶ οὐδενὶ ἐξιτητόν. Πάντα ἡ χιὼν κατείληφε, καὶ λευκανθίζουσιν οὐχ οἱ λόφοι μόνον, ἀλλὰ καὶ τὰ κοῖλα τῆς γῆς· ἀπορία δὲ ἔργων, ἀργὸν δὲ καθίζειν ὄνειδος. Προκύψας δῆτα τῆς καλύβης, οὐκ ἔφθην παρανοίξας τὸ θυρίον, καὶ ὁρῶ σὺν τῷ νιφετῷ δῆμον ὅλον ὀρνέων φερόμενον, καὶ κοψίχους καὶ κίχλας. Εὐθέως οὖν ἀπὸ τῆς λεκάνης ἀνασπάσας ἰξὸν ἐπαλείφω τῶν ἀχράδων τοὺς κλάδους· καὶ ὅσον οὔπω τὸ νέφος ἐπέστη τῶν στρουθίων, καὶ πᾶσαι ἐκ τῶν ὀροδάμνων ἐκρέμαντο, θέαμα ἡδὺ, πτερῶν ἐχόμεναι, καὶ κεφαλῆς καὶ ποδῶν εἰλημμέναι. Ἐκ τούτων λάχος σοι τὰς πίονας καὶ εὐσάρκους ἀπέσταλκα πέντε εἴκοσιν. Κοινὸν γὰρ ἀγαθὸν τοῖς ἀγαθοῖς· φθονούντων δὲ οἱ πονηροὶ τῶν γειτόνων.

XXX.

AMPELION TO EVERGUS.

THE winter is very severe this year, and no one is able to go out. The snow has not only covered the earth, it has also whitened the hills and valleys. One must give up all idea of work, although it is disgraceful to remain idle. To amuse myself, I tried to look out. No sooner was my door opened than I saw, together with the falling snow, a regular flock of blackbirds and thrushes. I had some birdlime all ready prepared in a jar, and quickly smeared it over some wild pear-tree branches. The birds flung themselves upon it in swarms, and then found themselves caught by the branches. It was a treat to see them—some hanging by their wings, others by the head or claws. I picked out a couple of dozen of the fattest and plumpest amongst them, and I send them to you. Honest people ought to share one another's luck; let my ill-disposed neighbours be jealous if they please!

XXXI.

Φιλόκωμος Θεστύλλῳ.

Οὐπώποτε εἰς ἄστυ καταβὰς, οὐδὲ εἰδὼς τί ποτέ ἐστιν ἡ λεγομένη πόλις, ποθῶ τὸ καινὸν τοῦτο θέαμα ἰδεῖν, ὑφ' ἑνὶ περιβόλῳ κατοικοῦντας ἀνθρώπους, καὶ τὰ ἄλλα ὅσα διαφέρει πόλις ἀγροικίας μαθεῖν. Εἰ οὖν σοι πρόφασις ὁδοῦ ἄστυδε γένηται, ἧκε ἀπάξων νῦν κἀμέ· καὶ γὰρ ἐγὼ δεῖν οἶμαι τοῦ πλεῖόν τι μαθεῖν, ἤδη μοι βρύειν θριξὶ τῆς ὑπήνης ἀρχομένης. Τίς οὖν δή με κἀκεῖ μυσταγωγεῖν ἐπιτήδειος, ἢ σύ, ὁ τὰ πολλὰ εἴσω πυλῶν ἀλινδούμενος;

XXXI.

Philocomus to Thestyllus.

SINCE I have never yet been in Athens, and do not know what kind of a thing that is which is called a city, I am curious to see that fresh sight—people confined within the same inclosure—and to learn the difference between the inhabitants of town and country. If, therefore, you have any occasion to go to the city, come and fetch me; we will go together. I think I ought to try and increase my knowledge, now that my beard is beginning to sprout. And who could initiate me into the mysteries of the city better than yourself? You have entered its gates often enough.

XXXII.

Σκοπιάδης Σκοτίωνι.

Βάλλ' ἐς μακαρίαν. Οἷον κακόν ἐστιν ὦ Σκοτίων ἡ μέθη. Ἐμπεσὼν γὰρ εἰς συμπόσιον κακοδαιμόνων ἀνθρώπων (οἰνόφλυγες δὲ πάντες ἦσαν, καὶ οὐδεὶς τῷ μέτρῳ τὸ πιεῖν ἔστεργε· συνεχῶς δὲ περιφερομένης τῆς κύλικος, ἦν τοῖς ἀρνουμένοις τοὐπιτίμιον, δεῖν αὐτοὺς καὶ εἰς τὴν ὑστεραίαν ἑστιᾶν)· πιὼν οὖν, ὅσον οὔπω πρότερον ἐν ἀσκῷ βαστάσας οἶδα, τρίτην ταύτην ἡμέραν ἔχω· καὶ ἔτι σοι καρηβαρῶ, καὶ τὴν κραιπάλην ἀπερυγγάνω

XXXII.

SCOPIADES TO SCOTION.

CONFOUND it! what a curse is drunkenness, my friend! I found it out, when I recently fell in with a company of dissipated fellows: they were all heavy drinkers, and not one of them knew how to take a glass in moderation. The cup went round continually, and I was obliged to drink, for there was a penalty attached to those who refused: they were obliged to give a banquet at their own expense the following day. Being obliged to do as the rest, I must have swallowed more than a whole skin. This is the third day I have had a fearful headache, and I am still very bilious.

XXXIII.

Ἄνθυλλα Κορίσκῳ.

Ἔοικε καὶ τὰ νάματα εἰς τὰ ἄνω ῥυήσεσθαι εἴγε οὕτως, ὦ Κορίσκε, ἀφηλικέστερος γεγονώς, ὅτε ἤδη λοιπὸν υἱδοὺς καὶ θυγατριδοὺς ἔχομεν, ἐρᾷς κιθαρῳδοῦ γυναικὸς, κἀμὲ κνίζεις ἄχρι τοῦ καὶ αὐτὴν ἐκρινῆσαι τὴν καρδίαν. Ἐγὼ μὲν γὰρ ἀτιμάζομαι, τριακοστὸν ἔτος ἤδη συνοῦσά σοι· παρθένιον δὲ ἡ ἱππόπορνος μεθ' ὑποκορισμῶν ἐκθεραπεύεται, ὅλον σε αὐτοῖς ἀγροῖς καταπιοῦσα. Γελῶσι δὲ οἱ νέοι, καὶ σὺ τοῦ γέλωτος ἀναισθήτως ἔχεις. Ὦ γῆρας ἑταίρας παίγνιον.

XXXIII.

ANTHYLLA TO CORISCUS.

IT seems as if rivers could flow upwards to their source, to see you, in spite of your years and the grandchildren that we have, madly in love with a flute-player; it grieves me enough to wear away my heart. You are disgracing me, who have now been your wife for thirty years; and you bestow all your affection upon a girl, a well-known street-walker, who has already eaten up your money and land. The young fellows laugh at you, but you don't seem to mind it. Poor old man, the plaything of a prostitute!

XXXIV.

Γνάθων Καλλικωμίδῃ.

Τίμωνα οἶσθα, ὦ Καλλικωμίδη, τὸν Ἐχεκρατίδου τὸν Κολλυτέα, ὃς ἐκ πλουσίου, σπαθήσας τὴν οὐσίαν εἰς ἡμᾶς τοὺς παρασίτους καὶ τὰς ἑταίρας, εἰς ἀπορίαν συνηλάθη· εἶτ' ἐκ φιλανθρώπου μισάνθρωπος ἐγένετο, καὶ τὴν Ἀπημάντου ἐμιμήσατο στύγα; Καταλαβὼν γὰρ τὴν ἐσχατιὰν, ταῖς βώλοις τοὺς παριόντας βάλλει, προμηθούμενος μηδένα αὐτῷ καθάπαξ ἀνθρώπων ἐντυγχάνειν· οὕτως τὴν κοινὴν φύσιν ἀπέστραπται. Οἱ δὲ λοιποὶ τῶν Ἀθήνῃσι νεοπλούτων Φείδωνός τε εἰσὶ καὶ Γνίφωνος μικροπρεπέστεροι. Ὥρα μοι μετανίστασθαι, καὶ πονοῦντι ζῆν. Δέχου δὴ οὖν με μισθωτὸν κατ' ἀγρὸν, πάντα ὑπομένειν ἀνεχόμενον ὑπὲρ τοῦ τὴν ἀπλήρωτον ἐμπλῆσαι γαστέρα.

XXXIV.

GNATHO TO CALLICOMIDES.

You know Timon, the son of Echecratides, of the borough of Colyttus? He was once rich; to-day he is in a state of abject poverty, to which he has brought himself by wasting his fortune on prostitutes and parasites, like ourselves. His misfortunes have altered his opinion of mankind, and he has become as great a misanthrope as Apemantus. He has retired to a field a long way off, where he throws clods of earth at the passers-by, or hides himself, to avoid meeting anyone, so great is his abhorrence of his fellow-men. On the other hand, the other Athenians, who have lately come into money, are meaner than Phidon or Gniphon. How is one to live? I think I shall leave the city and try and earn my living by hard work. Take me as a hired labourer on your farm. I will put up with anything, if only I can satisfy my insatiable maw.

XXXV.

Θαλλίσκος Πετραίῳ.

Αὐχμὸς τὰ νῦν· οὐδαμοῦ νέφος ὑπὲρ γῆς αἴρεται, δεῖ δὲ ἐπομβρίας· διψῆν γὰρ τὰς ἀρούρας αὐτὰς τὸ κατάξηρον τῆς βώλου δείκνυσι. Μάταια ἡμῖν, ὡς ἔοικε, καὶ ἀνήκοα τέθυται τῷ Ὑετίῳ· καίτοι γε ἐξ ἁμίλλης ἐκαλλιερήσαμεν πάντες οἱ τῆς κώμης οἰκήτορες, καὶ ὡς ἕκαστος δυνάμεως ἢ περιουσίας εἶχε, συνεισενέγκατο, ὁ μὲν κριὸν, ὁ δὲ τράγον, ὁ δὲ καπρὸν, ὁ πένης πόπανον, ὁ δὲ ἔτι πενέστερος λιβανωτοῦ χόνδρους εὖ μάλα εὐρωτιῶντας, ταῦρον δὲ οὐδείς· οὐ γὰρ εὐπορία βοσκημάτων ἡμῖν, τὴν λεπτόγειον τῆς Ἀττικῆς κατοικοῦσιν. Ἀλλ' οὐδὲν ὄφελος τῶν δαπανημάτων· ἔοικε γὰρ πρὸς ἑτέροις ἔθνεσιν ὁ Ζεὺς ὢν τῶν τῇδε ἀμελεῖν.

XXXV.

THALLISCUS TO PETRAEUS.

A VERY great drought prevails just now; there is not a cloud in the sky. We want rain; the soil is so dry that our land is parched. In vain have we offered sacrifice to Jupiter God of Rain. All we inhabitants of the village have done our best to appease him with our gifts, according to our means. One contributed a ram, another a goat; those who were not so well off gave a sacrificial cake; those whose means were even less, a few mouldy grains of incense. It is true that no one sacrificed a bull; but we have no large cattle, since we live on the poor soil of Attica. All our expenses have been useless; it seems as if Jupiter devoted his care to other countries, to the neglect of ours.

XXXVI.

Πρατίνος Μεγαλοτελεῖ.

Χαλεπὸς ἦν ἡμῖν ὁ στρατιώτης, χαλεπός. Ἐπεὶ γὰρ ἧκε δείλης ὀψίας καὶ κατήχθη οὐ κατὰ τύχην ἀγαθὴν εἰς ἡμᾶς, οὐκ ἐπαύσατο ἐνοχλῶν τοῖς διηγήμασι, δεκάδας τινὰς καὶ φάλαγγας ὀνομάζων, εἶτα σαρίσσας καὶ καταπέλτας καὶ γέρρας· καὶ νῦν ὡς ἀνέτρεψε τοὺς Θρᾶκας, τὸν προηγεμόνα βαλὼν μεσαγκύλῳ, νῦν δὲ ὡς κοντῷ διαπείρας τὸν Ἀρμένιον ἀπώλεσεν· ἐπὶ πᾶσί τε αἰχμαλώτους παρῆγε καὶ ἐδείκνυ γυναῖκας, ἃς ἔλεγεν ἐκ τῆς λείας ὑπὸ τῶν στρατηγῶν ἀριστείας αὐτῷ γέρας δεδόσθαι. Τῷ δὲ ἐγκανάξας κύλικα εὐμεγέθη, φλυαρίας φάρμακον ὤρεγον· ὁ δὲ καὶ ταύτην καὶ πλείονας ἐπὶ ταύτῃ καὶ ἁδροτέρας ἐκπιών, οὐκ ἐπαύσατο ἀδολεσχίας.

XXXVI.

PRATINUS TO MEGALOTELES.

AH! what trouble the soldier brought upon us! After his arrival in the evening, when, in an ill-starred moment, he took up his quarters with us, he never ceased to din into our ears stories about decuries, phalanxes, pikes, shields, and cross-bows. Then he told us how he had routed the Thracians and run their captain through with his lance; and, after that, how he pierced an Armenian through and through. Finally, he produced his prisoners, and exhibited the women, whom, he declares, he received from different generals as the reward of his gallantry. I poured out a large cup of wine, hoping to cure his chattering; he swallowed it, and several larger ones after it, but it did not stop him; he still went on chattering.

XXXVII.

Ἐπιφυλλὶς Ἀμαρακίνῃ.

Εἰρεσιώνην ἐξ ἀνθῶν πλέξασα, ᾔειν ἐς Ἑρμαφροδίτου, τῷ Ἀλωπεκῆθεν ταύτην ἀναθήσουσα. Εἶτά μοι λόχος ἐξαίφνης ἀναφαίνεται νέων ἀγερώχων, ἐπ' ἐμὲ συντεταγμένων· ὁ λόχος δὲ Μοσχίωνι συνέπραττεν. Ἐπεὶ γὰρ τὸν μακαρίτην ἀπέβαλον Φαιδρίαν, οὐκ ἐπαύσατό μοι πράγματα παρέχων, καὶ γαμησείων· ἐγὼ δὲ ἀνηνάμην, ἅμα μὲν τὰ νεογνὰ παιδία κατοικτείρουσα, ἅμα δὲ τὸν ἥρω Φαιδρίαν ἐν ὀφθαλμοῖς τιθεμένη. Ἐλάνθανον δὲ ὑβριστὴν ὑμέναιον ἀναμένουσα, καὶ θάλαμον νάπην εὑρίσκουσα. Εἰς γὰρ τὸ συνηρεφὲς ἀγαγὼν, οὗ τὸ πύκνωμα συνεχὲς ἦν τῶν δένδρων, αὐτοῦ που κατὰ τῶν ἀνθῶν καὶ τῆς φυλλάδος, αἰδοῦμαι εἰπεῖν, ὦ φιλτάτη, τί παθεῖν ἐπηνάγκασε. Καὶ ἔχω τὸν

XXXVII.

Epiphyllis to Amaricine.

HAVING woven a garland of flowers, I was going to the temple of Hermaphroditus, intending to offer it in honour of him of Alopece.[1] Suddenly a party of insolent young men came in sight, ready to attack me, led by Moschion, who, as soon as I lost my dear husband, incessantly worried me to marry him, but I refused, partly out of pity for my little ones, and partly because I could not forget the deceased Phaedrias. But I unwittingly kept myself for a disgraceful amour, and found a nuptial chamber in a grove. He took me into a shady part of the forest, where the trees grew thickly together, and there, on the top of the flowers and leaves, he compelled me to endure—I am ashamed to say what, my dear. I have gained a

[1] Her late husband.

ἐξ ὕβρεως ἄνδρα· οὐχ ἑκοῦσα μὲν, ὅμως δὲ ἔχω. Καλὸν μὲν γὰρ ἀπείραστον εἶναι τῶν ἀβουλήτων· ὅτῳ δὲ οὐχ ὑπάρχει τοῦτο κρύπτειν τὴν συμφορὰν ἀναγκαῖον.

husband by the insult I have suffered—not of my own free will, but still it is true. It is a good thing not to experience what is disagreeable; but when this is impossible, we must at least conceal our misfortune.

XXXVIII.

Εὔδικος Πασίωνι.

Φρύγα οἰκέτην ἔχω πονηρὸν, ὃς ἀπέβη τοιοῦτος ἐπὶ τῶν ἀγρῶν. Ὡς γὰρ τῇ ἔνῃ καὶ νέᾳ κατ' ἐκλογὴν τοῦτον ἐπριάμην, Νουμήνιον μὲν εὐθὺς ἐθέμην καλεῖσθαι· δόξαντα δὲ εἶναι ῥωμαλέον, καὶ ἐγρηγόρως βλέποντα, μετὰ περιχαρίας ἦγον, ὡς ἐπὶ τῆς ἐσχατιᾶς μοι ἐσόμενον. Ἦν δὲ οὗτος ἅμα λαμπρὰ ζημία· ἐσθίει μὲν γὰρ τεσσάρων σκαπανέων σιτία· ὑπνοῖ δὲ, ὅσον ἤκουσα τετυφωμένου σοφιστοῦ λέγοντος, Ἐπιμενίδην τινὰ Κρῆτα κεκοιμῆσθαι, ἢ ὡς ἀκούομεν τὴν Ἡρακλέους τριέσπερον. Τί ἂν οὖν ποιοίμην, ὦ φίλτατε ἑταίρων καὶ συνεργῶν, ἴθι φράσον, ἐπὶ τοιούτῳ θηρίῳ καταβαλὼν ἀργυρίδιον;

XXXVIII.

EUDICUS TO PASION.

I HAVE a good-for-nothing slave, a Phrygian, who has turned out so in the country. Since I picked him out of a number of others and bought him on the last day of the month, I immediately determined to call him Numenius.[1] As he seemed to be strong and looked sharp, I was glad to take him away to help me on my farm in the country. But he has turned out a sheer loss to me; he eats as much food as four diggers, and he sleeps, as I heard a crazy sophist say, like Epimenides the Cretan, or for three successive nights, as when Hercules was born. Whatever am I to do, my dear friend and fellow-labourer, now that I have thrown away my money on the purchase of such a monster?

[1] Connected with the new moon.

XXXIX.

Εὐθύδικος Ἐπιφανίῳ.

Πρὸς θεῶν καὶ δαιμόνων, ὦ μῆτερ, πρὸς ὀλίγον καταλιποῦσα τοὺς σκοπέλους καὶ τὴν ἀγροικίαν, θέασαι πρὸ τῆς τελευταίας ἡμέρας τὰ κατ' ἄστυ καλά. Οἷα γάρ, οἷά σε λανθάνει, Ἀλῶα καὶ Ἀπατούρια καὶ Διονύσια, καὶ ἡ νῦν ἑστῶσα σεμνοτάτη τῶν Θεσμοφορίων ἑορτή. Ἡ μὲν γὰρ ἄνοδος κατὰ τὴν πρώτην γέγονεν ἡμέραν, ἡ νηστεία δέ τὸ τήμερον εἶναι παρ' Ἀθηναίοις ἑορτάζεται, τὰ Καλλιγένεια δὲ εἰς τὴν ἐπιοῦσαν θύουσιν. Εἰ οὖν ἐπειχθείης, ἔρχῃ ἔωθεν πρὸ τοῦ τὸν ἑωσφόρον ἐξελθεῖν· συνθύεις ταῖς Ἀθηναίων γυναιξὶν αὔριον. Ἧκε οὖν, μὴ μέλλε, καὶ πρὸς ἐμῆς καὶ τῶν αὐταδέλφων τῶν ἐμῶν σωτηρίας· τὸ γὰρ ἄγευστον πόλεως καταλῦσαι τὸν βίον, ἀποτρόπαιον, ὡς

XXXIX.

EUTHYDICUS TO EPIPHANIUM.

By the Gods and Deities, mother, leave the rocks and country for a little while, and come and see the beauties of the city before you die. You don't know what you are missing: the Haloa, the Apaturia, and the Dionysia, and the most holy festival of the Thesmophoria, which we are now celebrating. The Ascent took place on the first day, to-day the fast is being solemnly kept, and the sacrifice to Calligeneia takes place to-morrow. If you make haste, and start early before the morning star rises, you will be able to join in the sacrifice with the Athenian women. Come, then, don't waste time, I beseech you, as I wish well to my brothers and myself; for to end your days without having had a taste of the city would be abominable, beastly,

ὃν θηριῶδες καὶ δύστροπον. Ἀνέχου δέ, ὦ μῆτερ, τῆς ἐπὶ τῷ συμφέροντι παρρησίας. Καλὸν ἅπασιν ἀνθρώποις ἀνυποστόλως ὁμιλεῖν· οὐχ ἥκιστα δὲ ἀναγκαῖον τὸ πρὸς τοὺς οἰκείους ἀληθίζεσθαι.

and ill-mannered. You must excuse my freedom, mother, it is for your benefit. It is right that all should speak frankly; but above all it is necessary to be sincere with one's own relations.

XL.

Φιλομήτωρ Φιλίσῳ.

Ἐγὼ μὲν τὸν παῖδα ἀποδόσθαι εἰς ἄστυ ξύλα καὶ κριθὰς ἀπέπεμψα, ἐπανήκειν τὴν αὐτὴν τὰ κέρματα κομίζοντα παρεγγυῶν· χόλος δὲ ἐμπεσών, ἐξ ὅτου δαιμόνων εἰς αὐτόν, οὐκ ἔχω λέγειν, ὅλον παρήμειψε, καὶ φρενῶν ἔξω κατέστησε. Θεασάμενος γὰρ ἕνα τουτωνὶ τῶν μεμηνότων, οὓς διὰ τὸ μανιῶδες πάθος κύνας ἀποκαλεῖν εἰώθασιν, ὑπερέβαλε τῇ μιμήσει τῶν κακῶν τὸν ἀρχηγέτην. Καὶ ἔστιν ἰδεῖν θέαμα ἀποτρόπαιον καὶ φοβερόν, κόμην αὐχμηρὰν ἀνασείων, τὸ βλέμμα ἰταμός, ἡμίγυμνος ἐν τριβωνίῳ, πηρίδιον ἐξηρτημένος, καὶ ῥόπαλον ἐξ ἀχράδος πεποιημένον μετὰ χεῖρας ἔχων, ἀνυπόδητος, ῥυπῶν, ἄπρακτος· τὸν ἀγρὸν καὶ ἡμᾶς οὐκ εἰδὼς τοὺς

XL.

Philometor to Philisus.

I SENT my son to the city to sell wood and barley, and gave him strict orders to come back the same day with the money; but the wrath of some Deity or other overtook him, drove him out of his mind, and changed him altogether. For, having seen one of those lunatics, who are nicknamed " Dogs " from their mad behaviour, he outdid his master in imitating his extravagances. He is a fearful and disgusting sight : he shakes his unkempt hair, he looks wild, goes about half-naked in a threadbare cloak, with a little wallet slung over his shoulders, and a staff of wild pear-tree wood in his hands. He is unshod and filthy, and no one can do anything with him ; he declares he does not know his parents or the farm either: he says that

γονεῖς, ἀλλ' ἀρνούμενος, φύσει λέγων γεγονέναι τὰ πάντα, καὶ τὴν τῶν στοιχείων σύγκρασιν αἰτίαν εἶναι γενέσεως, οὐχὶ τοὺς πατέρας. Εὔδηλον δέ ἐστι καὶ χρημάτων περιορᾶν, καὶ γεωργίαν στυγεῖν· ἀλλὰ καὶ αἰσχύνης αὐτῷ μέλει οὐδέν, καὶ τὴν αἰδὼ τοῦ προσώπου ἀπέξυσται. Οἴμοι οἷόν σε, ὦ γεωργία, τὸ τῶν ἀπατεώνων τουτωνὶ φροντιστήριον ἐξετραχήλισε. Μέμφομαι τῷ Σόλωνι καὶ τῷ Δράκοντι, οἳ τοὺς μὲν κλέπτοντας σταφυλὰς θανάτῳ ζημιοῦν ἐδικαίωσαν· τοὺς δὲ ἀνδραποδίζοντας ἀπὸ τοῦ φρονεῖν τοὺς νέους, ἀθῴους εἶναι τιμωρίας ἀπέλιπον.

everything is produced by nature, and that the mixture of the elements, not our parents, is the cause of generation. It is evident that he despises money, and hates agriculture; he is lost to all sense of shame, and all trace of modesty is banished from his countenance. O Agriculture! what utter ruin this thinking-shop of impostors has brought upon you! I blame Draco and Solon; for, while they thought fit to punish with death those who stole grapes, they allowed those who made slaves of young men's understandings to go scot-free.

XLI.

Δρυάδης Μηλίωνι.

Ἐπεμψά σοι, τῶν Δεκελεάσι προβάτων ἀποκείρας τὰ ῥωμαλέα, τοὺς πόκους· ὅσα γὰρ ψώρας ὑπόπλεα, ταῦτα τῷ ποιμένι Πυρρίᾳ παρέδωκα χρῆσθαι ἐς ὅ, τι ἂν θέλῃ, πρὶν φθάσαι διαφθαρῆναι παντελῶς ὑπὸ τῆς νόσου. Ἔχουσα οὖν ἀφθονίαν ἐρίων, ἐξύφηνον ἡμῖν ἐσθήματα πρόσφορα ταῖς ὥραις, ὡς εἶναι τὰ μὲν τῷ θέρει προσαρμόζοντα λεπτοϋφῆ, τὰ δὲ χειμέρια ἐχέτω περιττῶς τῆς κρόκης, καὶ πεπαχύνθω πλέον· ἵνα τὰ μὲν τῇ μανότητι σκιάζῃ μόνον, καὶ μὴ καταθάλπῃ τὰ σώματα· τὰ δὲ τῇ βαρύτητι ἀπείργῃ τὸν κρυμὸν, καὶ ἀλεξάνεμα τυγχάνῃ. Καὶ ἡ παρθένος δὲ ἡ παῖς, ἣν ἔχομεν ἐν ὥρᾳ γάμου, συλλαμβανέτω τῆς ἱστουργίας ταῖς θεραπαινίσιν, ἵνα εἰς

XLI.

DRYADES TO MELION.

I HAVE sent you the fleeces of some sheep shorn at Decelea. I only picked out those that were healthy; those that were full of the scab I gave to my shepherd Pyrrhias, to do what he liked with them, before they were entirely destroyed by the disease. Since you have abundance of wool, make me some clothes suitable for the different seasons; let those for summer wear be finely woven; those for winter should have plenty of nap, and be thicker; the former should rather shade than heat the body by their thinness, while the latter should keep the cold from it, and screen it from the wind by their thickness. Let our maiden daughter, who is now of an age to marry, assist the handmaids in weaving, so that, when she leaves us for a

ἀνδρὸς ἐλθοῦσα μὴ καταισχύνῃ τοὺς πατέρας ἡμᾶς. Καὶ ἄλλως δὲ εἰδέναι σε χρὴ, ὡς αἱ ταλασίαν ἀγαπῶσαι, καὶ τὴν Ἐργάνην θεραπεύουσαι, κόσμῳ βίου καὶ σωφροσύνῃ σχολάζουσι.

husband, she may not disgrace her parents. Besides, you must know that those who are fond of spinning wool, and are the handmaids of the goddess of labour, devote themselves to an orderly and chaste life.

XLII.

Ραγηστράγγισος Σταφυλοδαίμονι.

Ἄρδην ἀπόλωλά σοι· ὁ γὰρ χθὲς εὐπάρυφος, πιναροῖς, ὡς ὁρᾷς, καὶ τριχίνοις ῥάκεσι καλύπτω τὴν αἰδῶ. Ἀπέδυσε γάρ με Παταικίων ὁ παμπόνηρος, ὃς τὰ κέρματά μου (εἶχον δὲ, ὡς οἶσθα, ὑπόσυχνον ἀργύριον), δεξιαῖς χρώμενος ταῖς καλινδήσεσι τῶν κύβων, ἄχρι δραχμῶν καὶ ὀβολῶν ἀπεσύλησεν. Ἐξὸν δέ μοι παριδεῖν, ὅσον ἐξημιώθην, εἶτα ἀθώῳ γενέσθαι τοῦ πλείονος, ἐκ τῆς κατ' ὀργὴν ἔριδος τὴν εἰς τοὔσχατον ὑπέμεινα βλάβην· καθ' ἓν γὰρ ἕκαστον τῶν ἱματίων ἐκ προκλήσεως ἀποτιθεὶς, τέλος ἁπάντων ἐψιλώθην τῶν ἐνδυμάτων. Ποῖ δὴ οὖν βαδιστέον; χαλεπῶς γὰρ καὶ λάβρως ἐπαιγίζων ὁ βορρᾶς δίεισί μου τῶν πλευρῶν ὥσπερ βέλος. Ἐς Κυνόσαργες ἴσως οἰχητέον· ἢ γάρ τις τῶν ἐκεῖ

XLII.

RHAGESTRANGISUS TO STAPHYLODAEMON.

I AM utterly ruined. I, who but yesterday was clad in fine garments, am now obliged to cover my nakedness with filthy rags made of hair. That accursed villain Pataecion has stripped me bare; with his lucky throws of the dice he has cleaned me out of my money, with which as you know I was well supplied, even to the last drachma[1] and obol.[2] And when it was in my power, by ignoring the loss I had sustained, to escape a still greater one, in my anger and quarrelsomeness, I went on to the bitter end; I staked each of my articles of clothing as I was challenged, and, at last, was stripped naked. Where am I to go? for the north wind, blowing with cruel violence, goes through my sides like a knife. Perhaps to the Cynosarges; either one of the young men there will

[1] About 9¾d. [2] About 1½d.

νεανίσκων, ἐποικτείρας ἀμφιέσει με ἱματίοις, ἢ καταλήψομαι τὰς ἐγγύθεν καμίνους, καὶ τῷ πυρὶ ὁ δύστηνος θάλψομαι· τοῖς γὰρ γυμνοῖς σισύρα καὶ ἐφεστρὶς ἡ φλόξ, καὶ τὸ ἐκ τῆς ἕλης θέρεσθαι.

out of pity give me some clothes to cover me, or I shall be able to get near the stoves and warm my wretched self by the fire; for to the naked, fire and warmth take the place of both outer and inner garments.

XLIII.

Ψιχοκλαύστης Βουκίωνι.

Τῇ προτεραίᾳ ξυράμενοι τὰς κεφαλὰς, ἐγὼ καὶ Στρουθίων καὶ Κύναιδος οἱ παράσιτοι, λουσάμενοι εἰς τὸ ἐν Σηραγγίῳ βαλανεῖον ἀμφὶ πέμπτην ὥραν δρόμον ἀφέντες, εἰς τὸ προάστειον τὸ 'Αγκύλης τὸ Χαρικλέους τοῦ μειρακίσκου ᾠχόμεθα. Ἔνθα αὐτός τε ἀσμένως ὑπεδέξατο, φιλόγελώς τε ὢν καὶ φιλαναλωτής· ἡμεῖς τε διατριβὴν αὐτῷ τε καὶ τοῖς συμπόταις παρέσχομεν, παρὰ μέρος ἀλλήλους ἐπιρραπίζοντες, καὶ ἀνάπαιστα εὔκροτα ἐπιλέγοντες αὐτοσκομμάτων ἀστικῶν καὶ αὐτοχαρίτων Ἀττικῶν καὶ αἱμυλίας γέμοντα. Ἐν τούτῳ δι' ἱλαρότητος καὶ εὐφροσύνης διακειμένου τοῦ συμποσίου, ἐπέστη ποθὲν Σμικρίνης ὁ δύστροπος καὶ δύσκολος, εἵπετο δὲ αὐτῷ πλῆθος οἰκετῶν, οἳ δραμόντες ἐφ' ἡμᾶς ὥρμησαν. Αὐτὸς δὲ ὁ Σμικρίνης,

XLIII.

Psichoclaustes to Bucion.

THE day before yesterday, the parasites Struthion and Cynaedus and myself shaved our heads, took a bath at Serangium, and, about the fifth hour, hurried as fast as we could to the suburb of Ancyle, where young Charicles has an estate. He made us very welcome, being generous and fond of merriment; and, on our part, we afforded amusement to him and his guests, slapping one another in turns to the accompaniment of sonorous anapaests, full of genuine town witticisms and Attic grace and liveliness. In the meantime, while cheerfulness and merriment prevailed, that cross-grained, sulky Smicrines came on the scene from somewhere, followed by a crowd of servants, who rushed upon us from all directions. Smicrines first smote Charicles on the

πρῶτα μὲν τῇ καμπύλῃ παίει τὸν νῶτον τοῦ Χαρικλέους, ἔπειτα δὲ ἐπὶ κόρρης πατάξας, ἦγεν ὡς ἔσχατον ἀνδράποδον· ἡμεῖς δὲ νεύματι μόνῳ τοῦ πρεσβύτου εἰς τοὐπίσω τὰς χεῖρας ἐστρεβλούμεθα· τὰ δὲ μετὰ ταῦτα ξήνας ἡμᾶς ὑστριχίδι, οὐκ ὀλίγαις οὐδ' εὐαριθμήτοις μάστιξι, τέλος ἀγαγὼν εἰς τὸ δεσμωτήριον ἀπέθετο ὁ ἄγριος γέρων. Καὶ εἰ μὴ συνήθης ὢν καὶ πολλὰ καθηδυπαθήσας μεθ' ἡμῶν ὁ χαρίεις Εὔδημος, ἀνὴρ ἐν τοῖς πρώτοις τοῦ συμποσίου τῶν Ἀρεοπαγιτῶν, ἀνέῳξεν ἡμῖν τὸ δεσμωτήριον, τάχα ἂν καὶ τῷ δημίῳ παρεδόθημεν. Οὕτως ὁ δριμὺς γέρων καὶ πικρὸς ἐπίμπρατο καθ' ἡμῶν, καὶ πάντα ἔπραττεν ὡς ἂν τὴν ἐπὶ θανάτῳ, ἴσα τοῖς ἀνδροφόνοις καὶ ἱεροσύλοις ὑπαχθείημεν.

back with a crooked stick, and then, hitting him on the face, carried him off like the meanest slave; at a nod from the old man, our hands were tied behind our backs, after which we were flogged severely with a whip of hog's bristles: the blows inflicted upon us were more than we could count; and, at last, the cruel old man ordered us to be dragged off to prison; and, had not that good fellow Eudemus, one of the chief members of the council of Areopagus, an old acquaintance of ours, who had spent many a pleasant hour with us, opened the prison door for us, we should most likely have been handed over to the executioner, so furious against us was that harsh and cruel old man; and he did everything he could to get us led away to death, as if we had been murderers and temple robbers.

XLIV.

Γνάθων Λειχοπίνακι.

Ἡμῶν ὡς Μεγαρέων ἢ Αἰγιέων οὐδεὶς λόγος, εὐδοκιμεῖ δὲ τανῦν Γρυλλίων μόνος καὶ κατάρχει τοῦ ἄστεος, καὶ πᾶσα αὐτῷ καθάπερ Κράτητι τῷ Θήβηθεν κυνὶ ἀνέῳγεν ἡ οἰκία. Ἐμοὶ δοκεῖν, Θετταλίδα τινὰ γραῦν ἢ Ἀκαρνανίδα φαρμακεύτριαν πεπορισμένος καταγοητεύει τοὺς ἀθλίους νεανίσκους. Τί γὰρ καὶ στωμύλον ἔχει; τί δὲ ὁμιλητικὸν καὶ ἡδὺ φέρει; Ἀλλ' ἴσως εὐμενεστέροις ὄμμασιν ἐκεῖνον εἶδον αἱ Χάριτες· ὡς τοὺς μὲν ἀπομάττεσθαι πρὸς αὐτοῦ, ἡμᾶς δὲ ἀγαπᾶν, εἰ τὰς ἀπομαγδαλίας ὡς κυσί τις παραρρίψειε. Τάχα δὲ οὐ γόης, ἀλλὰ τύχῃ κέχρηται δεξιᾷ. Τύχη γὰρ παρὰ πάντα

XLIV.

GNATHON TO LEICHOPINAX.

WE are thought no more of than Megareans or Aegieans; at the present time Gryllion alone is in good repute, and holds sway over the city: every house is open to him, as if he were Crates the Cynic from Thebes. It seems to me that he has got hold of some Thessalian or Acarnanian sorceress, with whose assistance he bewitches the unhappy youths of our city. What a fund of talk he possesses! how delightful is his conversation! But perhaps the Graces have looked upon him with favourable eyes, so that, while others have the inside of the loaf, we must be content if anyone throws us the leavings, like dogs, after he has wiped his hands upon it.[1] But perhaps he is no magician, but only very fortunate; for it is fortune that pre-

---

[1] The meaning of this passage is greatly disputed.

ἐστὶ τὰ τῶν ἀνθρώπων πράγματα· οὐδὲν γὰρ ἐν ἀνθρώποις γνώμη, πάντα δὲ τύχη· καὶ ταύτης ὁ τυχὼν ἡδύς ἐστι καὶ νομίζεται.

vails beyond everything in human affairs. Prudence counts for nothing, fortune is everything; the man who is fortunate is pleasant, and has the reputation of being so.

XLV.

Τραπεζολείχων Ψιχοδιαλέκτῃ.

Ἤλγησα, ὦ καλὲ Ψιχίων, ἀκούσας τὴν συμβᾶσάν σοι περὶ τὸ πρόσωπον συμφοράν. Εἰ δὲ καὶ τοῦτον ἐγένετο τὸν τρόπον, ὃν διηγήσατο ἡμῖν ἐπανελθοῦσα τοῦ συμποσίου Λειριόνη (λέγω δὲ τὴν παιδίσκην Φυλλίδος τῆς ψαλτρίας), πόλεμον ὑπέστης καὶ πόρθησιν ἱκανὴν ἄνευ μηχανῆς καὶ ἑλεπόλεως· ἀκούω γὰρ καὶ τὸν καταπύγονα καὶ θηλυδρίαν περικατεάξαι σοι τὴν φιάλην, ὡς τὰ θραύσματα λωβήσασθαί σοι τὴν ῥῖνα καὶ τὴν δεξιὰν σιαγόνα, καὶ τοῦ αἵματος ἀναχθῆναι κρουνούς, οἵους ὕδατος ἐν Γερανίᾳ πέτραι σταλάσσουσι. Τίς ἔτι ἀνέξεται τῶν κακοδαιμόνων τούτων, εἰ, τοσούτου τὸ γαστρίζεσθαι πωλούντων, ὠνούμεθα κινδύνῳ τὸ ζῆν, καὶ τὸν ἐκ λιμοῦ θάνατον δεδιότες, τὴν μετὰ κινδύνου πλησμονὴν ἀσπαζόμεθα;

XLV.

TRAPEZOLEICHON TO PSICHODIALECTES.

I WAS much grieved, my dear Psichion, when I heard of the accident to your face. If it happened as Leirione—I mean the servant of Phyllis the harpist—told us on her return from the banquet, you have indeed been in the wars and exposed to destruction, without any engines of war being brought against you. I hear that the disgusting and effeminate wretch broke a goblet over your head with such violence that the pieces injured your nose and your right cheek, and streams of blood spirted up from the wound, like the drippings from the rocks of Gerania. Who will be able to endure such wretches much longer ? They ask so high a price for filling our bellies that we have to pay for it with the peril of our lives ; and, in our fear of being starved to death, we welcome the chance of getting a good meal, even if we have to pay dearly for it.

XLVI.

Στεμφυλοχαίρων Τραπεζοχάροντι.

Ὡς εὐτυχῶς, ὡς μακαρίως πέπραγα. Ἴσως ἐρήσῃ με, τίνα τρόπον, ὦ Τραπεζόχαρον. Ἐγὼ δή σοι φράσω καὶ πρὶν ἔρεσθαι. Ἦγε μὲν ἡ πόλις, ὡς οἶσθα, τὴν Κουρεῶτιν ἡμέραν· ἐγὼ δὲ παραληφθεὶς ἐπὶ δεῖπνον τέρπειν, ὠρχούμην τὸν κόρδακα. Οἱ δαιτύμονες δὲ ἐκ φιλονεικίας ἔπινον, ἕως, τῆς ἁμίλλης εἰς ἄπειρον προχωρούσης, κῶμος κατέσχε τὸ συμπόσιον, καὶ πάντας ὕπνος ὑπείληφει νυστακτής, ἄχρι καὶ αὐτῶν τῶν οἰκετῶν. Ἐγὼ δὲ περιέβλεπον μὲν, εἴ τι τῶν ἀργυρῶν σκευῶν ὑφελέσθαι δυναίμην· ὡς δὲ ταῦτα, ἔτι νηφόντων, ἐξ ὀφθαλμῶν ἐγεγόνει, καὶ ἦν ἐν ἀσφαλεῖ, τὸ χειρόμακτρον ὑπὸ μάλης λαβὼν ἐξηλλόμην, ὡς ἐν τῇ φυγῇ τῶν διαβάθρων ἅτερον ἀποβαλεῖν. Ὅρα δὲ ὡς ἐστι

XLVI.

STEMPHYLOCHAERON TO TRAPEZOCHARON.

WHAT a stroke of luck I have had! Perhaps you will ask me how. Well, I will tell you, and you will have no need to inquire. The city, as you know, was celebrating the Cureotis, and I, having been invited to the feast to amuse the guests, was dancing the cordax. The banqueters vied with one another in drinking, and the contest went on without stopping, until drunkenness overcame them all, and at length they became drowsy and fell asleep, even the servants. I looked round to see if I could filch some of the plate; but since this had been put away out of sight, in a place of safety, while they were still sober, I took a napkin under my arm and ran away in such a hurry that, during my flight, I lost one of my slippers. Look what ex-

πολυτελὲς, ὀθόνης Αἰγυπτίας καὶ ἀλουργοῦ πορφύρας τῆς Ἑρμιονίτιδος λεπτὸν ἐς ὑπερβολὴν καὶ πολύτιμον ὕφασμα. Εἰ τοῦτο ἀδεῶς ἀπεμπολήσαιμι, γαστριῶ σε ἀγαγὼν εἰς τὸν πανδοκέα Πιθαλίωνα· πολλὰς γὰρ ὁμοῦ πολλάκις παροινίας ἀνέπλημεν· καὶ χρή σε, τὸν κοινωνὸν τῶν δυστυχημάτων, μερίτην γενεσθαι καὶ τῆς εὐτυχούσης ἡμέρας.

pensive material it is made of—Egyptian linen and purple from Hermione : the texture is exceedingly fine and very valuable. If I can safely dispose of it, I will treat you to a good feed at Pinacion's inn. For, since we have often had to put up with many drunken insults together, it is only fair that you, who have been the partner of my misfortunes, should share my good luck.

XLVII.

Ὡρολόγιος Λαχανοθαυμάσῳ.

Ἑρμῆ κερδῷε, καὶ ἀλεξίκακε Ἡράκλεις, ἀπεσώθην· οὐδὲν δεινὸν γένοιτο ἔτι. Προχόην ὑφελόμενος ἀργυρᾶν Φανίου τοῦ πλουσίου, δρόμῳ δοὺς φέρεσθαι, ἦν γὰρ ἀωρία νυκτὸς μεσούσης, ἠπειγόμην σώζειν ἐμαυτόν. Κύνες δὲ ἐξαίφνης οἰκουροὶ περιχυθέντες ἄλλος ἄλλοθεν χαλεποὶ καὶ βαρεῖς τὴν ὑλακὴν ἐπῄεσαν, Μολοττοὶ καὶ Κνώσιοι, ὑφ' ὧν οὐδὲν ἐκώλυέ με ὡς ἠδικηκότα τὴν Ἄρτεμιν διασπᾶσθαι μέσον, ὡς μηδὲ τὰ ἀκρωτήρια εἰς τὴν ὑστεραίαν περιλειφθῆναι πρὸς ταφὴν τοῖς ἑτοίμοις εἰς ἔλεον καὶ συμπάθειαν. Εὑρὼν οὖν ὑδορρόον ἀνεῳγότα οὐκ εἰς βάθος ἀλλ' ἐπιπολῆς, καὶ ὑποδὺς εἰς τοῦτον, κατεκρύβην. Ἔτι σοι ταῦτα τρέμων καὶ παλλόμενος λέγω.

XLVII.

HOROLOGIUS TO LACHANOTHAUMASUS.

O MERCURY, god of gain, and Hercules, averter of evil! I am saved. May I never be in such straits again. I had filched a silver pitcher from the wealthy Phanius, and had taken to flight; it was the dead of night, and I made all haste to get safely away. Suddenly the house-dogs, of Molossian and Cnosian breed, rushed upon me from all sides, and, barking loudly and fiercely, attacked me. I barely escaped being torn to pieces by them, as if I had offended Diana, so that not even my extremities would have remained for burial the next day, if any kind people had wanted to show their pity and sympathy. Finding, by good luck, an open watercourse of no great depth, I jumped into it and concealed myself. It makes me shake and tremble

Ἑωσφόρου δὲ ἀνασχόντος, τῶν μὲν οὐκ ᾐσθόμην οὐκ ἔθ᾽ ὑλακτούντων (οἴκοι γὰρ πάντες ἐδέδεντο)· αὐτὸς δὲ εἰς Πειραιᾶ δραμών, νηῒ Σικελικῇ λύειν μελλούσῃ τὰ πρυμνήσια περιτυχών, ἀπεδόμην τῷ ναυκλήρῳ τὴν προχόην. Καὶ νῦν τὸ τίμημα ἔχων νένασμαι τοῖς κέρμασι, καὶ νεόπλουτος ἐπανελήλυθα, καὶ τοσοῦτον ῥιπίζομαι ταῖς ἐλπίσιν, ὡς ἐπιθυμεῖν κόλακας τρέφειν, καὶ κεχρῆσθαι παρασίτοις, οὐ παρασιτεῖν αὐτός. Ἀλλ᾽ ἢν τουτὶ τὸ πορισθὲν ἀργύριον ἀναλώσω, πάλιν ἐπὶ τὴν ἀρχαίαν ἐπιτήδευσιν τρέψομαι· οὐδὲ γὰρ κύων σκυτοτραγεῖν μαθοῦσα τῆς τέχνης ἐπιλήσεται.

even now to tell you. As soon as it was daybreak, I heard their barking no more, for they had all been tied up in the house. I immediately hurried down to the Piraeus, and, finding a Sicilian vessel just about to set sail, I sold my pitcher to the skipper, so that I now have my pockets full of money. I have returned, newly enriched, and I am in such a flutter of expectation that I am eager to support some flatterers, and to keep parasites of my own, instead of being one myself. When I have spent the money I have just gained, I shall return to my old profession. A dog who has once become accustomed to gnaw leather will never forget the habit.

XLVIII.

Φλοιογλύπτης Μαππαφασίῳ.

Κακὸς κακῶς ἀπόλοιτο καὶ ἄφωνος εἴη Λικύμνιος ὁ τῆς τραγῳδίας. Ὡς γὰρ ἐνίκα τοὺς ἀντιτέχνους Κριτίαν τὸν Κλεωναῖον, καὶ Ἵππασον τὸν Ἀμβρακιώτην τοὺς Αἰσχύλου Προπόμπους, τορῷ τινι καὶ γεγωνοτέρῳ φωνήματι χρησάμενος, γαῦρος ἦν, καὶ κιττοστεφὴς ἦγε συμπόσιον· ἔνθα παραληφθεὶς, φεῦ τῶν κακῶν οἷα ὑπέμεινα. Τοῦτο μὲν πιττούμενος τὴν κεφαλήν, καὶ γάρῳ τοὺς ὀφθαλμοὺς ῥαινόμενος· τοῦτο δὲ, ἀντὶ πλακοῦντος, τῶν ἄλλων ἄμητας ἐσθιόντων καὶ σησαμοῦντας, αὐτὸς μέλιτι δεδευμένους λίθους ἀπέτραγον. Ἡ πασῶν δὲ ἰταμωτάτη, τὸ ἐκ Κεραμεικοῦ πορνίδιον, ἡ μέτοικος, ἡ Φενεᾶτις

XLVIII.

PHLOIOGLYPTES TO MAPPAPHASIUS.

CURSED be Licymnius the tragedian! may he be struck dumb! He had gained the victory over his competitors, Critias of Cleonae and Hippasus of Ambracia in the recital of the Propompi of Aeschylus; and, although he owed his success only to the shrill and penetrating tone of his voice, he went mad over it, crowned his head with ivy, and gave a banquet. To my misfortune, I was invited: what insults did I not have to put up with! Some amused themselves with smearing my head with pitch, or dabbing fish-sauce in my eyes; others rammed down my throat stones moistened with honey, while they were eating cakes of milk and Indian corn. But the most mischievous of all was the little courtesan who has just taken up her quarters in the Cerami-

Ὑακινθὶς, κύστιν αἵματος πληρώσασα, καταφέρει μου τῆς κεφαλῆς· καὶ ὁμοῦ τῷ κτύπῳ λελούμην τῷ αἵματι. Καὶ τῶν μὲν εὐωχουμένων πολὺς καὶ καπυρὸς ἐξεχύθη γέλως· ἐγὼ δὲ ὧν ἔπαθον μισθὸν οὐκ ἀπηνεγκάμην ἄξιον, ἀλλά μοι γέγονε τῶν ὕβρεων ἀμοιβὴ τὸ μέτρον τῆς γαστρὸς, πέρα δὲ οὐδέν. Μήτε οὖν εἰς νέωτα εἴη, μήτε μὴν βιῴη ὁ θεοῖς ἐχθρὸς Λικύμνιος, ὃν ἐγὼ τῆς ἀχαρίστου φωνῆς ἕνεκα ὀρθοκόρυζον καλεῖσθαι πρὸς ἡμῶν καὶ τοῦ χοροῦ τῶν Διονυσοκολάκων ἔκρινα. Ἔρρωσο.

cus, Hyacinthis from Phenea; she filled a bladder with blood, and amused herself by beating me over the head with it; besides the noise this made, I was bathed in blood; and all the guests burst out into most immoderate shouts of laughter. And what adequate recompense did I receive for all I suffered? The only compensation for my insults was—that I got a bellyful, and that was all. May that enemy of the gods never live to see the new year! His voice is so disagreeable that I have determined that he shall be called by us and his fellow-actors—the prince of squallers.

XLIX.

Καπνοσφράντης Ἀριστομάχῳ.

Ὦ δαῖμον, ὅς με κεκλήρωσαι καὶ εἴληχας, ὡς πονηρὸς εἶ, καὶ λυπεῖς ἀεὶ τῇ πενίᾳ συνδέων. Ἢν γὰρ ἀπορία τοῦ καλοῦντος γένηται, ἀνάγκη με σκάνδικας ἐσθίειν καὶ γήθυα, ἢ πόας ἀναλέγειν, καὶ τῆς Ἐννεακρούνου πίνοντα πίμπλασθαι τὴν γαστέρα. Εἶτα, ἕως μὲν τὰς ὕβρεις τὸ σῶμα ὑπέμενε, καὶ ἦν ἐν ὥρᾳ τοῦ πάσχειν νεότητι καὶ ἀκμῇ νευρούμενον, φορητὸς ἡ ὕβρις. Ἐπειδὴ δὲ τὸ λοιπὸν ἐγώ σοι μεσαιπόλιος, καὶ τὸ λειπόμενον τοῦ βίου πρὸς γῆρας ὁρᾷ, τίς ἴασις τῶν κακῶν; Ἁλιαρτίου σχοινίου χρεία, καὶ κρεμήσομαι πρὸ τοῦ Διπύλου, ἢν μή τι δεξιὸν ἡ τύχη βουλεύσηται. Εἰ δὲ καὶ τοῖς αὐτοῖς ἐπιμείνειεν, οὐ πρότερον

XLIX.

CAPNOSPHRANTES TO ARISTOMACHUS.

O FATAL presiding genius of my destiny, how cruel thou art! how long wilt thou torture me, condemning me to all the horrors of poverty? For, if no one invites me to a meal, I shall be obliged to eat chervil and leeks, to pick herbs, and to quench my thirst with the water of Enneacrunus. As long as my frame was able to endure ill-treatment and was full of youthful vigour, I managed to put up with it; but now that my hair is beginning to turn grey, and all of life that is left to me is advancing towards old age, what remedy is there for my woes? Nothing is left for me but a rope from Haliartus, that I may go and hang myself in front of the Dipylum, unless it please Fortune to improve my lot. And, even if things remain as they

στραγγαλίσω τὸν τράχηλον, πρὶν τραπέζης ἀπολαῦσαι πολυτελοῦς. Οὐκ εἰς μακρὸν δὲ ὁ περίβλεπτος οὗτος καὶ ἀοίδιμος γάμος Χαριτοῦς καὶ Λεωκράτους μετὰ τὴν ἔνην καὶ νέαν τοῦ Πυανεψιῶνος, εἰς ὃν πάντως ἢ παρὰ τὴν πρώτην ἡμέραν, ἢ τοῖς ἐπαυλίοις κεκλήσομαι. Δεῖ γὰρ θυμηδίας καὶ παρασίτων τοῖς γάμοις, καὶ ἄνευ ἡμῶν ἀνέορτα πάντα, καὶ συῶν οὐκ ἀνθρώπων πανήγυρις.

are, at least, I won't throttle myself until I have had a regular good meal. In a short time, after the new moon of the month Pyanepsion, the famous and much-talked of wedding of Charito and Leocrates will take place; I shall be invited for the first, or, at any rate, for the second day. Marriage feasts need the presence of parasites to amuse the company: without us there is not the same air of enjoyment : the guests are more like pigs than an assembly of human beings.

L.

Βουκοπνίκτης Ἀντοπίκτῃ.

Οὐκ ἀνέχομαι ὁρῶν Ζευξίππην τὴν ἱππόπορνον ἀπηνῶς τῷ μειρακίῳ χρωμένην· οὐ γὰρ δαπανᾶται εἰς αὐτὴν χρυσίον μόνον καὶ ἀργύριον, ἀλλ' ἤδη καὶ συνοικίας καὶ ἀγρούς. Ἡ δὲ ἐπὶ πλέον ἐκτύφεσθαι τὸν ἔρωτα τούτῳ μηχανωμένη, τοῦ Εὐβοέως ἐρᾶν προςποιεῖται τοῦ νεανίσκου, ἵνα καὶ τὰ τούτου σπαθήσασα, ἐπ' ἄλλον τρέψῃ τὸν ἔρωτα. Ἐγὼ δὲ ὀδυνῶμαι τὴν καρδίαν, ὁρῶν ὑποῤῥέοντα τοσοῦτον πλοῦτον, ὃν οἱ μακαρῖται αὐτῷ Λυσίας καὶ Φανοστράτη κατέλιπον. Ἃ γὰρ ἐκεῖνοι κατ' ὀβολὸν συνήγαγον, ἀθρόως ἀναλοῖ τὸ πολύκοινον τοῦτο καὶ αἰσχρότατον γύναιον. Πάσχω μὲν οὖν τι

L.

BUCOPNICTES TO ANTOPICTES.

I CANNOT endure to see Zeuxippe, the most infamous of all our courtesans, treat that young man so cruelly. He has not only spent all his money upon her, but, at the rate he is going, he will soon have parted with his houses and land. In order to keep his passion alive, she pretends to be in love with a young Euboean; by her artifices she will succeed in ruining them both; after which she will turn her attention to a fresh lover. But my heart is torn with grief, when I see the splendid inheritance which Lysias and Phanostrata, of blessed memory, have left to their heir, being squandered so rapidly. What they painfully amassed obol by obol will be swallowed up in one moment at the caprice of the commonest and most disgusting woman in Athens.

καὶ ἐπὶ τῷ μειρακίῳ· κύριος γὰρ γενόμενος τῆς οὐσίας, πολλὴν τὴν εἰς ἡμᾶς φιλανθρωπίαν ἀνεδείξατο. Ὁρῶ δὲ καὶ τὰ ἡμέτερα σκάζοντα· εἰ γὰρ εἰς ταύτην ἅπαντα τεθείη τὰ προσόντα τούτῳ τῷ βελτίστῳ, καλῶς, ὦ θεοί, καλῶς ἀπολαύσομεν τῆς πλησμονῆς. Ἔστι γὰρ, ὡς οἶσθα, ἁπλοϊκὸς ὁ Φίληβος, καὶ πρὸς ἡμᾶς τοὺς παρασίτους ἐπιεικὴς καὶ μέτριος τὸν τρόπον, ᾠδαῖς μᾶλλον καὶ γέλωτι ἢ ταῖς εἰς ἡμᾶς ὕβρεσι θελγόμενος.

I feel compassion for the youth, for, as soon as he became his own master, he showed great kindness to us; it will be a great misfortune for us, if he is ruined. If this excellent young man's entire fortune makes its way into this woman's hands, good Heavens! what a charming feast we shall have! Philebus, as you know, is a simple fellow; he has always been gentle and kind to us parasites; he takes more pleasure in our witticisms and songs than in insulting us.

LI.

Λαιμοκύκλῳ Ψικλεολόβῃ.

Ἰδοὺ μετὰ τὸν Εὐρώταν καὶ τὸ Λερναῖον ὕδωρ καὶ τὰ Πειρήνης νάματα, ἐρῶν τῆς Καλλιρρόης, ἐκ Κορίνθου πάλιν Ἀθήναζε κατεπείγομαι· οὐ γάρ με τῶν τρυφημάτων τῶν ἐν τούτοις οὐδὲν ἤρεσεν· ἀλλ' ἕτοιμος ἐνθένδε ἀποσοβεῖν, καὶ σπεύδειν ὡς ὑμᾶς. Ἀχάριστοι γὰρ ὤφθησαν οἵδε καὶ ἥκιστα συμποτικοί· καὶ πλείους παρ' αὐτοῖς αἱ παροινίαι τῶν ἀπολαύσεων. Ὡς ἄμεινον ἐμοὶ ὀλύνθους ἢ παλάθας ἐπιμασᾶσθαι τῶν Ἀττικῶν, ἢ διὰ τὸ παρὰ τούτοις χρυσίον ἀποδρύπτεσθαι. Οἷα γὰρ οἷα νεουργεῖν ἐπιχειροῦσιν, ἀναγκάζοντες ἀσκωλιάζοντας πίνειν

LI.

PSICLEOLOBE TO LAEMOCYCLUS.

I HAVE travelled over the countries watered by the Eurotas and Lerna's marsh; I have seen the streams of Pirene; now I eagerly leave Corinth for Athens, and return with renewed affection to the fountain of Callirhoe. The luxury and festivities of those places have no charms for me; I abandon them without regret, and hasten back to you.

The inhabitants of Peloponnesus appeared to me ill-mannered and by no means pleasant table-companions; at their drinking parties, one finds more insults than pleasure. For this reason, I prefer to content myself with the figs and raisins of Attica, rather than run the risk of growing thin for the gold of Corinth. They are always inventing new tortures; they make us drink while dancing on

διάπυρόν τε οἶνον καὶ θερμὸν ἄνευ τοῦ πρὸς ὕδωρ κράματος καταχέοντες· εἶτ' ὀστέα, κῶλά τε καὶ ἀστραγάλους, καθάπερ τοῖς κυσὶ παραρριπτοῦντες, καὶ νάρθηκας ἐπιρρηγνύντες, καὶ σκύτεσι καὶ τοῖς ἄλλοις ἱμᾶσιν ἀντὶ παιδιᾶς πλήττοντες. Ἐμοὶ γένοιτο, πρόμαχε Ἀθηνᾶ καὶ πολιοῦχε τοῦ ἄστεος, Ἀθήνησι καὶ ζῆσαι καὶ τὸν βίον ἀπολιπεῖν. Ἄμεινον γὰρ πρὸ τῆς Διομηίδος πύλης ἢ πρὸ τῶν Ἱππάδων ἐκτάδην πατεῖσθαι νεκρὸν τύμβου περιχυθέντος, ἢ τῆς Πελοποννήσου εὐδαιμονίας ἀνέχεσθαι.

one leg; they pour down our throats hot, fiery wine without water; then they throw us the bones and feet from the joints as if we were dogs, break their canes over our backs, and, by way of amusing themselves, flog us with whips and thongs. O Minerva, guardian and defender of the city, may it be my lot to live and die at Athens! It is better to be stretched lifeless in front of the Diomeian or Knights' gates, to be trampled under the feet of the passers-by, with the bare earth around me for a grave, than to put up with the pleasures of Peloponnesus.

LII.

Κοπαδίων Εὐηνίσσῳ.

Οὔ μοι μέλει· ποιούντων ὅσα καὶ βούλονται ῥιψοκίνδυνοι Γρόνθων καὶ Σαρδανάπαλος· ἐμὲ γὰρ κοινωνῆσαι τῆς ἀτόπου πράξεως ἀδύνατον, οὐδὲ εἰ μάντευμά μοι ἐκ τῆς Δωδωναίας δρυὸς ἐπιτρέποι τὴν πρᾶξιν, ὡς ἔστιν ἐργάζεσθαι χρηστή· φύεται γὰρ σπανίως καὶ ἐν παισὶ τὸ χρηστὸν καὶ πιστὸν ἦθος καὶ ὑγιές. Πάντως οὖν ἀφεκτέον· ὑποπειρῶσι γὰρ τὴν παλλακὴν τοῦ τῆς οἰκίας δεσπότου, καὶ ἤδη αὐτοῖς ἡ πρᾶξις εἰς τὴν ἀκμὴν προκεχώρηκε. Καὶ οὐκ ἀρκοῦνται τῇ τῶν ἀφροδισίων ἀθέσμῳ πλησμονῇ, ἀλλὰ γὰρ τὰ ἐκ τῆς οἰκίας σκεύη καθ' ἓν ὥσπερ φώρια λαμβάνουσι. Καὶ ἴσως μὲν ἄχρι τινὸς λήσεται τοὔργον πραττόμενον· πάντως δέ ποτε ἢ λάλος γείτων ἢ ψίθυρος οἰκέτης ἀγορεύσει

LII.

COPADION TO EVENISSUS.

I WILL have nothing to do with it! Let Gronthon and Sardanapalus do what they please. They are regular mad-caps, and they shall never persuade me to take part in so disgraceful a deed. I will do nothing of the sort, even though the oracle of Dodona were to recommend it as an honourable act. It is a rare thing to find in slaves either prudence, faithfulness, or honour. The whole affair is by all means to be avoided. You must know they are trying to seduce the mistress of the head of a household, and have already succeeded in the attempt; and, not satisfied with having got all they wanted, they are carrying off the furniture, one article after the other.

Perhaps their thefts will escape notice for a while; but, sooner or later, the neighbours will talk, the servants will

τὸ πρᾶγμα εἰς τοὐμφανές· καὶ ἀνάγκη μετὰ πῦρ καὶ σίδηρον καὶ τὰς πολλὰς βασάνους τέλος αὐτοῖς γενέσθαι τὸ κώνειον ἢ τὸ βάραθρον· ἀφειδῶς γὰρ χρώμενοι τῷ τολμήματι ἰσόρροπον τῇ πράξει τὴν τιμωρίαν ἐκτίσουσι.

whisper, and the whole affair will be found out; and the end of it all will be, that the criminals will be condemned to drink hemlock, or thrown into the pit after they have suffered torture, imprisonment, and other punishments. Those who aid and abet such a crime without any shame will certainly suffer punishment in proportion to their misdeeds.

LIII.

Ἀκρατολύμας Χωνεικράτῳ.

Χθὲς Καρίωνος περὶ τὸ φρέαρ ἀσχολουμένου εἰσέφρησα εἰς τοὐπτάνιον· εἶτα εὑρὼν λοπάδα εὖ μάλα κεκαρυκευμένην, καὶ ἀλεκτρυόνα ὀπτὸν, καὶ χύτραν μεμβράδας ἔχουσαν, καὶ ἀφύας Μεγαρικὰς, ἐξήρπασα· καὶ ἀποπηδήσας, ποῖ καταχθείην ἐζήτουν, καὶ εὐκαίρως μόνος ἂν φάγοιμι. Ἀπορίᾳ δὲ τόπου δραμὼν ἐπὶ τὴν Ποικίλην (καὶ γὰρ οὐκ ἠνόχλει ταύτην οὐδὲ εἷς τῶν ἀδολέσχων τουτωνὶ φιλοσόφων), κεῖθι τῶν πόνων ἀπήλαυον. Ἀνανεύσας δὲ τῆς λοπάδος, ὁρῶ προσιόντα τῶν ἀπὸ τῆς τηλίας τινὰ νεανίσκων, καὶ δείσας, τὰ μὲν βρώματα ὄπισθεν ἀπεθέμην, αὐτὸς δὲ εἰς τοὖδαφος ἐκείμην κρύπτων τὰ κλέμματα· καὶ

LIII.

ACRATOLYMAS TO CHONEICRATUS.

YESTERDAY, while Charion was busy at the well, I slipped into the kitchen. There I saw a large dish filled with exquisite dainties, a roast fowl, and a pot containing anchovies and sardines from Megara. I seized hold of it, and, hastily retiring, looked about for a convenient spot whither I might betake myself to have a comfortable meal. As I could not find any place handy, I ran to the Painted Porch, and, as it just happened to be the time when it was not infested by any chattering philosophers, I began to enjoy the fruit of my labours. But, looking up from my dish, I saw approaching one of those young men from the gaming-table, and, seized with alarm, I threw what I was eating behind me, and flung myself on the ground, intend-

ηὐχόμην τοῖς ἀποτροπαίοις παρελθεῖν τὸ νέφος, ὑποσχόμενος λιβανωτοῦ χόνδρους, οὓς οἴκοι ἀναλεξάμενος τῶν ἱερῶν ἔχω, εὖ μάλα εὐρωτιῶντας, καὶ οὐκ ἠστόχησα· οἱ θεοὶ γὰρ αὐτὸν ἄλλην ὁδὸν ἔτρεψαν· κἀγὼ σπουδῇ καταβροχθίσας πάνθ' ὅσα ἐνέκειτο τοῖς σκεύεσι, φίλῳ πανδοκεῖ τὴν λοπάδα καὶ τὸ χυτρίδιον, τὰ λείψανα τῶν κλεμμάτων, χάρισμα δοὺς, ἀπεχώρησα, ἐπιεικής τις καὶ μέτριος ἐκ τῶν δωρημάτων ἀναφανείς.

ing to conceal my theft. I prayed to the averting gods that the storm might pass by, promising them some grains of incense, which I had picked up at the sacrifices and keep at home, although they are quite mouldy. My prayers were heard; for the gods made him turn in another direction. Having hurriedly gulped down all that was in the dishes, I gave the plate, the pot, and the fragments of what I had stolen to a friendly tavern-keeper, and departed, having thus gained a reputation for liberality and generosity.

LIV.

Χυτρολείκτης Πατελλοχάροντι.

Τί δακρύεις; ἴσως ἐρήσῃ με, ἢ πόθεν κατέαγα τὸ κρανίον, ἢ πῶς τὸ ἀνθηρὸν τοῦτο εἰς μέρη κατερρωγὸς ἱμάτιον φορῶ; Ἐνίκησα κυβεύων, ὡς μή ποτ' ὤφελον. Τί γὰρ ἔδει με ἀσθενέστερον ὄντα ῥωμαλέοις συνεξετάζεσθαι νεανίαις; Ἐπεὶ γὰρ εἰς ἐμαυτὸν ὅλας τὰς ἐκθέσεις συνελεξάμην, ἀπορία δὲ ἦν αὐτοῖς παντελὴς ἀργυρίου, ἐπ' ἐμὲ πάντες ὥρμησαν· καὶ οἱ μὲν πὺξ ἔπαιον, ἄλλοι δὲ λίθοις ἐχρῶντο, οἱ δὲ διέσχιζον τὸ ἱμάτιον. Ἐγὼ δὲ ἀπρὶξ εἰχόμην τῶν κερμάτων, ἀποθανεῖν πρότερον ἢ προέσθαι τι ἐκείνοις τῶν ἐμοὶ πεπορισμένων αἱρούμενος· καὶ δὴ μέχρι τινὸς ἀντέστην γενναίως, καὶ τὰς φορὰς τῶν πληγῶν ὑπομένων, καὶ τὰς ἐκστροφὰς τῶν δακτύλων ἀνεχόμενος, καὶ ἤμην οἷά τις Σπαρτιάτης ἀνὴρ ἐπὶ τοῦ βωμοῦ τῆς Ὀρθίας τυπτόμενος. Ἀλλ' οὐκ ἦν Λακεδαίμων, ἐν ᾗ ταῦτα ὑπέμενον,

LIV.

CHYTROLEICTES TO PATELLOCHARON.

PERHAPS you will ask me why I am weeping, how I got my skull broken, and why I am wearing this fine coat torn to rags. I won some money—would to Heaven I never had! What right had I, weak as I was, to pit myself against stalwart young men? When I had swept in all the stakes, and they were entirely cleaned out, they all fell upon me; some beat me with their fists, others pelted me with stones, and others tore my clothes. But I kept tight hold of my money, resolved to die rather than surrender any of my winnings to them. For a time I resisted bravely, enduring the blows they dealt me, and the wrenching of my fingers; I was like a Spartan who is being flogged at the altar of Diana. But it was not at Lacedaemon

ἀλλ' Ἀθῆναι, καὶ τῶν Ἀθήνησι κυβευτῶν οἱ ἐξωλέστατοι. Τέλος οὖν λειποθυμήσας ἀφῆκα τοῖς ἐναγέσι λαμβάνειν· οἱ δὲ καὶ τὸ προκόλπιον διηρεύνησαν, καὶ τὰ ἐν τούτῳ ἐγκείμενα φέροντες ᾤχοντο, τοῦτ' ἐμοῦ λώιον ἡγησαμένου τὸ ζῆν ἄνευ χρημάτων ἢ μετὰ χρημάτων τεθνᾶναι.

that I endured this treatment, but at Athens, and at the hands of the most rascally gamblers in the city. At last, I gave up the struggle and left myself at the mercy of the vile wretches, who turned out my pockets and went off with what they found in them. I thought it better to live without money than to die with it in my possession.

LV.

Αὐτόκλητος Ἑτοιμαρίστῳ.

Ὀλίγα ἢ οὐδὲν διαφέρουσι τῶν ἰδιωτῶν οἱ σεμνοὶ καὶ τὸ καλὸν καὶ τὴν ἀρετὴν ἐξυμνοῦντες· τούτους λέγω τοὺς ἐργολαβοῦντας τὰ μειράκια. Οἷον γὰρ, οἷον ἔλαθέ σε συμπόσιον, Σκαμωνίδου γενέσια θυγατρὸς ἑορτάζοντος. Καλέσας γὰρ ἔναγχος οὐκ ὀλίγους τῶν προὔχειν δοκούντων Ἀθήνησι πλούτῳ καὶ γένει, ᾠήθη δεῖν καὶ τοῖς φιλοσοφοῦσι κοσμῆσαι τὴν εὐωχίαν. Παρῆν οὖν ἐν τούτοις Εὐθυκλῆς ὁ στωικὸς, οὗτος ὁ πρεσβύτης, ὁ κουρειῶν τὸ γένειον, ὁ ῥυπαρὸς, ὁ τὴν κεφαλὴν αὐχμηρὸς, ὁ γεγηρακὼς, ὁ ῥυσότερον τῶν βαλαντίων ἔχων τὸ μέτωπον. Παρῆν δὲ καὶ Θεμισταγόρας ὁ ἐκ τοῦ περιπάτου, ἀνὴρ οὐκ ἄχαρις ὀφθῆναι, οὔλῃ τῇ γενειάδι λαμπρυνόμενος. Ἦν δὲ καὶ ὁ Ἐπικούρειος Ζηνοκράτης, οὐκ ἀτημέλητος τοὺς κικίννους, καὶ αὐτὸς ὑπὸ βαθεῖ τῷ πώγωνι σεμνυνόμενος. Ὅτε ἀοίδιμος (τοῦτο γὰρ

LV.

AUTOCLETUS TO HETOEMARISTUS.

THOSE solemn personages, who are always singing the praises of the good and of virtue, differ little or nothing from ordinary individuals; I mean those fellows who go after our young men for money. What a banquet you missed, when Scamonides gave a feast in honour of his daughter's birthday. Having recently invited a number of the wealthiest and noblest in Athens, he thought it his duty also to grace the festivities with the presence of philosophers. Amongst these was Euthycles the Stoic, an old man with a long beard, dirty, filthy-headed, decrepit, with more wrinkles in his forehead than a leather pouch. There were also present Themistagoras the Peripatetic, not an unpleasant person to look at, with a fine curly beard; Zenocrates the Epicurean, with carefully trimmed locks, and a long and venerable beard;

πρὸς ἁπάντων ἐκαλεῖτο), Ἀρχίβιος ὁ Πυθαγορικός, ὦχρον ἐπὶ τοῦ προσώπου πολὺν ἐπιβεβλημένος, πλοκάμους ἀπὸ τῆς κεφαλῆς μέχρι στέρνων αὐτῶν αἰωρῶν, ὀξὺ καὶ μακρὸν καθεικὼς τὸ γένειον, τὴν ῥῖνα ἐπικαμπής, τὸ στόμα ἐπιχειλής, αὐτῷ τῷ πεπιέσθαι καὶ λίαν μεμυκέναι τὴν ἐχεμυθίαν ὑποσημαίνων. Ἐξαίφνης δὲ καὶ ὁ Παγκράτης ὁ Κύων, ῥύμῃ τοὺς πολλοὺς παρωσάμενος εἰσήρρησε, στελεῷ πρινίνῳ ἐπερειδόμενος· ἦν γὰρ ἀντὶ τοῦ πυκνώματος τῶν ὄζων χαλκοῖς τισιν ἥλοις ἐμπεπαρμένην φέρων βακτηρίαν, καὶ τὴν πήραν διάκενον, καὶ πρὸς τὰ λείψανα εὐζώνως ἠρτημένην. Οἱ μὲν οὖν ἄλλοι ἀπ' ἀρχῆς εἰς τέλος παραπλησίαν τινὰ καὶ τὴν αὐτὴν εἶχον τῆς ἑστιάσεως τὴν ἀκολουθίαν· οἱ φιλόσοφοι δέ, προϊόντος τοῦ συμποσίου, καὶ τῆς φιλοτησίας συνεχῶς περισοβουμένης, ἄλλος ἄλλην τερατείαν ἐπεδείξατο. Εὐθυκλῆς γὰρ ὁ ετωικὸς ὑπὸ γήρως καὶ πλησμονῆς ἐκτάδην κείμενος ἔρεγχεν. Ὁ Πυθαγόρειος δὲ τὴν σιωπὴν λύσας, τῶν χρυσῶν ἐπῶν κατά τινα μουσικὴν ἁρμονίαν ἐτερέτιζεν. Ὁ βέλτιστος δὲ Θεμισταγόρας, ἅτε τὴν εὐδαιμο-

the "famous" Archibius the Pythagorean, as he is called, with a very pale face, waving hair that reached down to his chest, a long and pointed chin, a turned-up nose, lips drawn in and tightly compressed, an indication of his reserve. Suddenly Pancrates the Cynic, violently thrusting the others aside, forced his way in, leaning on a staff of holm-oak, which, in place of thick knots, was studded with brass nails, and carrying an empty wallet, conveniently slung for carrying away the remains of the feast. All the other guests, from beginning to end, maintained a uniform and orderly behaviour; but the philosophers, as the entertainment went on, and the wine-cup went round, began to behave in a most extraordinary fashion. Euthycles the Stoic, overcome by his years and having eaten and drunk too much, lay stretched out at full length, snoring loudly. The Pythagorean, breaking through his silence, began to trill the "Golden Verses" to a kind of musical air. The excellent Themistagoras, who, according to the doctrine of the Peripa-

νίαν κατὰ τὸν τοῦ περιπάτου λόγον, οὐ ψυχῇ καὶ σώματι μόνον, ἀλλὰ καὶ τοῖς ἐκτὸς ὁριζόμενος, ἀπῄτει πλείονα πέμματα, καὶ ποικιλίαν τῶν ὄψων δαψιλῆ. Ζηνοκράτης δὲ ὁ Ἐπικούρειος τὴν ψάλτριαν ὡς αὑτὸν ἐνηγκαλίζετο, τακερὸν καὶ ὑγρὸν προσβλέπων ὑπομεμυκόσι τοῖς ὄμμασι, λέγων τοῦτο εἶναι τὸ τῆς σαρκὸς ἀόχλητον, καὶ τὴν καταπύκνωσιν τοῦ ἡδομένου. Ὁ Κύων δὲ πρῶτα οὔρει κατὰ τὴν κυνικὴν ἀδιαφορίαν εἰς σύρμα χαλάσας, καὶ καθεὶς τὸ τριβώνιον, ἔπειτα καὶ Δωρίδα τὴν μουσουργόν, οἷος ἦν ἐν ὀφθαλμοῖς ἀπάντων ὁρώντων ἐνεργεῖν, φάσκων ἀρχὴν γενέσεως εἶναι τὴν φύσιν. Ὥστε ἡμῶν τῶν παρασίτων οὐδείς ἐστι λόγος· τὸ γὰρ θέαμα καὶ τὴν θυμηδίαν παρεῖχεν οὐδεὶς τῶν εἰς τοῦτο κεκληρωμένων, καίτοι γε Φοιβιάδης ὁ κιθαρῳδός, καὶ μῖμοι γελοίων οἱ περὶ Σαννυρίωνα καὶ Φιλιστιάδην οὐκ ἀπελείποντο. Ἀλλὰ πάντα φροῦδα καὶ οὐκ ἀξιόθεα· εὐδοκιμεῖ δὲ μόνος ὁ τῶν σοφιστῶν λῆρος.

tetics, places happiness not in bodily or mental advantages alone, but also in external enjoyment, asked for more pastry, and plenty of different dainties; Zenocrates the Epicurean took the girl who played the harp in his arms, looking at her wantonly and lasciviously with half-shut eyes, declaring that this quieted the desires of the flesh, and was the perfection of enjoyment. The Cynic, with the indifference of his sect, let down his cloak and publicly made water, and then proceeded to copulate with Doris the singing-girl, so that everyone could see him, declaring that nature was the principle of generation. No one took any notice of us parasites; none of those who were invited had a chance of showing what they could do to amuse the company, although Phoebiades, the lute-player, was there, and the comic mimes Sannyrion and Philistiades were not absent. But it was all in vain; these were not thought worth looking at; the nonsense of the sophists was the only thing that met with approval.

LVI.

Θυμβροφάγος Κυπελλίστῃ.

Ἐπαίρεις σεαυτὸν, οὐδὲν δέον, καὶ βαδίζεις ἴσα δὴ, καὶ τύφου πλήρης εἶ, τοῦτο δὴ τὸ τοῦ λόγου, Πυθοκλεῖ, καὶ ἀποφέρῃ μερίδας τῶν ἀρίστων. Οὐκοῦν τὰς σπυρίδας καθημέραν ἐξογκῶν σὺ μεγέθει λειψάνων (καθάπερ πρώην Ἁρπάδης ὁ γραμματικὸς ἐποίει, Ὁμήρου ὡς ἔφασκεν ἐπιλέγων στιχίδιον, εὐμηχάνως αὐτῷ πρὸς τὰς ἁρπαγὰς τῶν βρωμάτων ἡρμοσμένον. Καὶ φαγέμεν, πιέμεν τε, ἔπειτα δὲ καί τι φέρεσθαι) πέπαυσο· κατάβαλε τὴν ἀλαζονείαν, τρισάθλιε, ἢ ἀνάγκη σε γυμνὸν τῆς οἰκίας θύραζε ἐν ἀκαρεῖ χρόνου ἐκβληθέντα ἐκπεσεῖν.

LVI.

THYMBROPHAGUS TO CYPELLISTES.

You are puffed up with pride for no reason at all, and swagger about full of insolence, like Pythocles in the proverb, and yet you carry off your share of breakfast. Give up filling your basket every day with fragments, like Harpades the Grammarian, who quoted a verse from Homer, which was singularly applicable to his own fondness for carrying off food: "To eat and drink, and then carry something away." Wretch, have done with your insolence, or, in a twinkling, we shall be obliged to kick you naked out of doors.

LVII.

Οἰνόλαλος Ποτηριοφλυάρῳ.

Οὐκ εἰς δέον οἰνωμένος ἐσκωψάμην τὸν τροφέα τὸν νεανίσκον Ζώπυρον. Ἐξ ἐκείνου γὰρ ἴσως διαβολῇ τυπεὶς τὰ ὦτα, περὶ τὰς δόσεις κατέστη μικροπρεπέστερος, καὶ φειδωλῷ τῷ μέτρῳ κέχρηται. Εἰωθὼς γὰρ ἐν ταῖς ἑορταστικαῖς τῶν ἡμερῶν, ἢ χιτώνιον ἢ τριβώνιον ἢ ἐφεστρίδα πέμπειν, ἔναγχος Κρονίων ἐνστάντων Ἰφικρατίδας μοι νεουργεῖς ἔπεμψε, τῷ Δρόμωνι δοὺς κομίζειν. Ὁ δὲ ἐπὶ ταύταις ἐβρενθύετο, καὶ μισθοὺς τῆς διακονίας ἀπῄτει· ἐγὼ δὲ δάκνομαι, καὶ τὴν προπετῆ γλῶτταν διαμασσῶμαι, καὶ ὀψὲ τῆς ἁμαρτίας αἰσθάνομαι. Ὅταν γὰρ τὸ ῥεῦμα τῶν λόγων μὴ καθηγουμένης τῆς διανοίας φέρηται, τότε σφάλλεσθαι τὴν γλῶτταν ἀνάγκη. Ἔρρωσο.

LVII.

OENOLALUS TO POTERIOPHLYARUS.

HAVING taken too much wine, I ridiculed Zopyrus, the young master's tutor. From that time, perhaps from listening to accusations against us, he has been less liberal, and treats us rather stingily. On feast days he used to send me a coat, or a cloak, or an upper garment; but lately, just before the Saturnalia, he sent me a pair of new shoes by Dromio. The latter gave himself airs about it, and asked me to pay him for his trouble; but I feel terribly vexed, and bite my hasty tongue, and see that I was wrong, now that it is too late; for, when words flow without reason to guide them, the tongue is bound to make mistakes. Farewell.

LVIII.

Ἀλοκύμινος Φιλογαρελαίῳ.

Οὐδὲν προτιμῶ σου, κἂν ἀπειλῇς ψιθυριεῖν κατ' ἐμοῦ, καὶ καττύῃς διαβολὰς ἀγεννεῖς. Ἁπλοϊκὸς γὰρ καὶ γενναῖος ὁ Μαλιεὺς στρατιώτης ὁ βόσκων ἡμᾶς. Τὰ νῦν δὲ ταῦτα καὶ τοσοῦτον ἀπέχει τοῦ ζηλοτυπεῖν τὰς ἑταίρας, ὡς πρώην λόγου ῥυέντος αὐτῷ ἐπὶ τοῦ συμποσίου, πολλὴν κατέχεε βλασφημίαν τῶν τὰ τοιαῦτα ὑπομενόντων. Ἔλεγεν γὰρ γαμεταῖς ἐπικλήροις οἰκουρίας πρέπειν καὶ τὸν σεμνὸν βίον· τὰς ἑταίρας δὲ δεῖν εἶναι πάντων ἀναφανδὸν, καὶ πᾶσιν ἐκκεῖσθαι τοῖς βουλομένοις. Ὅνπερ οὖν τρόπον τοῖς λουτροῖς καὶ τοῖς σκεύεσι κοινοῖς κεχρήμεθα, κἂν ἑνὸς εἶναι δοκεῖ, οὕτω καὶ ταῖς εἰς τοῦτον

LVIII.

ALOCYMINUS TO PHILOGARELAEUS.

I DON'T mind you in the least, although you threaten to whisper about me, and patch up disgraceful accusations against me. For the Malian soldier, who keeps me in food, is a simple and honourable man. Far from being jealous in the matter of women, only lately, when his tongue began to wag freely at table, he heaped abuse upon those who allow themselves to be jealous. He said that the duty of married women was to look after their household affairs and to lead a chaste life; but that courtesans ought to be looked upon as common property for all who wanted them. Just as we use the baths and their appliances in common, even though they are supposed to belong to one person, so is it with women who have registered themselves

ἀπογραψαμέναις τὸν βίον. Εἰδὼς οὖν τηνάλλως τὴν διαβολήν σου χωρήσουσαν, οὐ τρέμω ἐνδακὼν τὸ χεῖλος, ὡς οἱ τὸν σιγηλὸν Ἥρω παριόντες, μὴ κακόν τι προσλάβωμαι· οὐ γάρ ἐστι τῶν Ἀττικῶν τούτων εἷς τῶν χαύνων μειρακίων, ἀλλ' ἀνὴρ ὁπλομάχος καὶ ἀρήϊος, παρ' ᾧ κολακεία καὶ διαβολῆς τρόπος ἔρρει. Ἀνάγκη δὲ τὸν μὴ διαβολὰς προσιέμενον τοῖς διαβάλλουσιν ἀπεχθάνεσθαι.

courtesans. Therefore, since I know that your accusations will be fruitless, I do not tremble and bite my lip, like those who pass by the silent hero, for fear that some harm may come to me; for this man is not one of those puffed-up Athenian youths, but a gallant soldier, on whom flattery and slander are lost— and he who does not open his ears to slander is bound to be hated by the slanderers.

LIX.

Λιμέντερος Ἀμασήτῳ.

Παρ' ἕνα τῶν τὰ πινάκια παρὰ τὸ Ἰακχεῖον προτιθέντων, καὶ τοὺς ὀνείρους ὑποκρίνεσθαι ὑπισχνουμένων βούλομαι ἐλθών, τὰς δύο ταύτας δραχμὰς, ἅς οἶσθά με ἐν χεροῖν ἔχοντα, καταβαλών, τὴν φανεῖσαν ὄψιν μοι κατὰ τοὺς ὕπνους διηγήσασθαι. Οὐ χεῖρον δὲ καὶ πρὸς σὲ ὡς φίλον ἀναθέσθαι τὸ καινὸν τοῦτο καὶ πέρα πάσης πίστεως φάσμα. Ἐδόκουν γὰρ κατ' ὄναρ εὐπρεπὴς εἶναι νεανίσκος, καὶ οὐχ ὁ τυχών, ἀλλ' ἐκεῖνος (εἶναι) ὁ Ἰλιεὺς ὁ περίψυκτος καὶ περικάλλιστος, ὁ τοῦ Τρωὸς παῖς Γανυμήδης· καὶ καλαύροπα ἔχειν καὶ σύριγγα, καὶ τιάρᾳ Φρυγίῳ στέφειν τὴν κεφαλὴν, ποιμαίνειν τε, καὶ εἶναι κατὰ τὴν Ἴδην· ἐξαίφνης δὲ ἐπιπτάντα μοι γαμψώνυχα καὶ μέγαν ἀετὸν, γοργὸν τὸ βλέμμα, καὶ ἀγκυλοχείλην

LIX.

LIMENTERUS TO AMASETUS.

I INTEND to go to one of those people who hang out placards at the temple of Bacchus, and profess to interpret dreams. I will pay him the two drachmas which you know I have in hand, and give him an account of the vision which appeared to me in my sleep, to see if he can explain it. But it will not be out of place to communicate to you also, as a friend, my strange and incredible vision. I thought I was a handsome young man, no ordinary person, but Ganymede, the son of Tros, the beloved and beautiful boy of Ilium. I had a shepherd's crook and a pipe; my head was encircled with a Phrygian tiara, and I was tending a flock of sheep on Mount Ida. Suddenly, a large eagle, with crooked talons and bent beak, and a savage look, flew

τὸ στόμα, κουφίσαντά με τοῖς ὄνυξιν, ἀφ' οὗπερ ἐκαθήμην πέτρου μετεωρίζειν εἰς τὸν ἀέρα, καὶ πελάζειν τοῖς οὐρανίοις τόποις ἐπειγόμενον· εἶτα μέλλοντα τότε ψαύειν τῶν πυλῶν, αἷς αἱ Ὧραι ἐφεστᾶσι, κεραυνῷ βληθέντα πεσεῖν· καὶ τὸν ὄρνιν οὐκέτι τὸν διοπετῆ τὸν μέγαν εἶναι ἀετὸν, γῦπα δὲ, πικρὸν ὀδωδότα, ἐμὲ δὲ τοῦτον, ὃς εἰμὶ, Λιμέντερον, γυμνὸν πάσης ἐσθῆτος, οἷα πρὸς λουτρὸν ἢ παλαίστραν ηὐτρεπισμένον. Ἐκταραχθεὶς οὖν, ὡς εἰκὸς, ἐπὶ τοσούτῳ πτώματι, ἐξηγειρόμην, καὶ πρὸς τὸ παράδοξον τῆς ὄψεως ἀγωνιῶ, καὶ δέομαι, οἷον φέρει τὸ ὄναρ, μαθεῖν παρὰ τῶν τοιαῦτα ἀκριβούντων, εἰ μέλλοι τις ἀπλανῶς εἰδέναι, καὶ εἰδὼς ἀληθίζεσθαι.

towards me, lifted me up in his claws from the rock on which I was sitting, and flew away with me into the air up to heaven: when I was close to the gates, guarded by the Hours, I fell, smitten by a thunderbolt; and methought the bird was no longer the mighty eagle, swooping down from the clouds, but a vulture, stinking foully, and I was the same Limenterus as I am now, without any clothes on, as if I had been getting ready for the bath or the wrestling-ground. Greatly shaken, as was natural, by such a fall, I awoke. I am still troubled by the strange vision, and I want to find out from those who are experienced in such things what is the meaning of my dream, if anyone really knows for certain, and is willing to tell me the truth.

LX.

Χασκοβούκης Ὑπνοτραπέζῳ.

Οὐκ ἔτι εἰσῆλθον εἰς τὴν Κόρινθον· ἔγνων γὰρ ἐν βραχεῖ τὴν βδελυρίαν τῶν ἐκεῖσε πλουσίων καὶ τὴν τῶν πενήτων ἀθλιότητα. Ὡς γὰρ ἐλούσαντο οἱ πολλοί, καὶ μεσοῦσα ἡμέρα ἦν, στωμύλους ἐθεασάμην καὶ εὐφυεῖς νεανίσκους, οὐ περὶ τὰς οἰκίας, ἀλλὰ περὶ τὸ Κράνειον εἰλουμένους, καὶ οὗ μάλιστα ταῖς ἀρτοπώλισι καὶ ὀπωροκαπήλοις ἔθος ἀναστρέφειν. Ἐνταυθοῖ γὰρ εἰς τοὔδαφος ἐπικύπτοντες, ὁ μὲν φλοιοὺς θέρμων ἀνῃρεῖτο, ὁ δὲ ἔλυτρα τῶν καρύων ἐπολυπραγμόνει, μή που τι τῶν ἐδωδίμων ἀπομείναν διέλαθεν, ὁ δὲ τῶν ῥοιῶν τὰ περικάρπια, ἃ σίδια ἡμῖν τοῖς Ἀττικοῖς προσαγορεύειν ἔθος, ἀπέγλυφε τοῖς ὄνυξιν, εἴ που τι τῶν κόκκων ἐπιδράξασθαι δυνηθείη· οἱ δὲ καὶ τὰ ἐκ τῶν ἄρτων ἀπο-

LX.

CHASCOBUCES TO HYPNOTRAPEZUS.

I HAVE not been to Corinth again; for I soon discovered the disgusting manners of its rich men, and the misery of its poor. After most of them had been to the bath, when it was midday, I saw some talkative and comely young men, who were sauntering, not round the houses, but in the neighbourhood of the Craneium, where the bakers' and fruiterers' shops are. With their eyes bent upon the ground, one picked up beanpods, another carefully examined nutshells, to see if any of the kernel had been left in them accidentally, while another peeled off with his nails pomegranate-skins (which we Athenians call Sidia), to see if he could lay hands on any of the seeds; while others picked up pieces of bread, which had fallen on

πίπτοντα προς πολλών ήδη πεπατημένα αναλέγοντες, έκαπτον. Τοιαύτα τὰ τῆς Πελοποννήσου προπύλαια· καὶ ἡ δυοῖν θαλάσσαιν ἐν μέσῳ κειμένη πόλις χαρίεσσα μὲν ἰδεῖν, καὶ ἀμφιλαφῶς ἔχουσα τρυφημάτων, τοὺς δὲ οἰκήτορας ἀχαρίστους καὶ ἀνεπαφροδίτους κεκτημένη· καίτοι γε φασὶ τὴν Ἀφροδίτην ἐκ Κυθήρων ἀνασχοῦσαν τὴν ἀκροκόρινθον ἀσπάσασθαι· εἰ μὴ ἄρα τοῖς μὲν γυναίοις Ἀφροδίτη πολιοῦχος, τοῖς δὲ ἀνδράσιν ὁ Λιμὸς καθίδρυται.

the ground and been trodden underfoot, and greedily gulped them down. Such is the entrance to Peloponnesus. The city lying between the two seas is certainly agreeable to look at and abundantly furnished with luxuries, but its inhabitants are disagreeable and unamiable; and yet they say that Venus, when she rose from the sea near Cythera, saluted the citadel of Corinth. Perhaps Venus is the protecting goddess of the women only, and Famine is the tutelary god of the men.

LXI.

Ὑδροσφράντης Μεριδᾷ.

Ἡράκλεις, ὅσα ὑπέστην πράγματα, ῥύμματι καὶ νίτρῳ Χαλαστραίῳ χθιξινοῦ ζωμοῦ τοῦ μοὶ περιχυθέντος τὴν γλισχρότητα ἀποκαθαίρων. Καὶ οὐχ οὕτω με ἔδακεν ἡ ὕβρις, ὅσον τὸ παρ' ἀξίαν ὑπομένειν. Ἐγὼ μὲν γὰρ Ἀνθεμίωνος υἱὸς τοῦ πλουσιωτάτου τῶν Ἀθήνῃσι, καὶ Ἀξιοθέας τῆς κατὰ γένος ἐκ Μεγακλέους ὁρμωμένης· ὁ δὲ ταῦθ' ἡμᾶς ἐργαζόμενος, πατρὸς μὲν ἀσήμου, μητρὸς δὲ βαρβάρου, Σκυθίδος οἶμαι ἢ Κολχίδος ἐν νεομηνίᾳ ἐωνημένης, οὕτω γάρ μοι τῶν γνωρίμων τινὲς διηγήσαντο. Ἀλλ' ἐγὼ μὲν ἐν ταπεινῷ τῷ σχήματι τὴν πατρῴαν ἀποβαλὼν οὐσίαν, ἀγαπῶ τῇ γαστρὶ τὴν ἀναγκαίαν πλησμονὴν ἐκπορίζων. Δοσιάδης δέ, ὦ θεοί,

LXI.

HYDROSPHRANTES TO MERIDAS.

O HERCULES, what a job I have had to wash off the sticky soup, which was thrown over me yesterday, with soap and Chalastraean nitre! It was not so much the insult itself that annoyed me as that it was undignified. I am the son of Anthemion, one of the richest men in Athens; my mother Axiothea is descended from Megacles; while the father of the man who treated me like this is some low fellow, and his mother a barbarian, a Scythian or Colchian slave, bought at the monthly fair: at least, some of my acquaintances have told me so. And now I, having lost all the fortune that my father left me, in humble guise am content if I can procure enough to satisfy the cravings of my belly. In the meantime, O ye gods! Dosiades harangues the

τὴν Πνύκα καταλαμβάνει δημηγορῶν, καὶ τοῖς ἐν Ἡλιαίᾳ καταριθμεῖται δικάζουσι, καὶ τὰς ἡνίας ἔχει τοῦ δήμου, παρ' ᾧ Μιλτιάδης ἐδέδετο, ὁ τὸ ἐν Μαραθῶνι τρόπαιον ἐγείρας, καὶ ὁ Ἀριστείδης ὁ δίκαιος ἐξωστρακίζετο. Λυπεῖ δέ με οὐχ ἥκιστα πρὸς τοῖς ἄλλοις καὶ ἡ τῆς προσηγορίας ἀποβολή· οἱ μὲν γὰρ πατέρες Πολύβιόν με ἔθεντο καλεῖσθαι· ἡ τύχη δὲ ἀμείψασα τοὔνομα Ὑδροσφράντην πρὸς τῶν ὁμοτέχνων ἠνάγκασε προσαγορεύεσθαι.

people from the Pnyx, is one of the judges of the Heliaea, and guides that people, who imprisoned Miltiades, in whose honour the trophy at Marathon was set up, and ostracised Aristides the Just. But what most grieves me is the loss of my name: my parents called me Polybius; but Fortune has changed it, and forced me to take the name of Hydrosphrantes[1] amongst those of my profession.

[1] Water-smeller.

LXII.

Χιδρολέπισος Καπυροσφράντῃ.

Ἠπίστασο τὴν αἰτίαν, ἐφ' ᾗ με διεσίλλαινον αἱ γυναῖκες· τελευταῖον δὲ ἡ γραῦς ἡ δούλη ἐλοιδορήσατό μοι, εἰποῦσα, ἀλλ' ἐκκορηθείης, ὅτι ἄκαιρος εἶ καὶ λάλος. Μυστήριον ἐν αὐταῖς στρέφεται ταῖν θεαῖν ταῖν Ἐλευσινίαιν ἀσφαλέστερον, καὶ βούλονται ἡμᾶς ἀγνοεῖν τοὺς εἰδότας, ἢ καὶ οἴονται ἀκηκοότας οὔπω πεπεῖσθαι. Ἐγὼ δὲ οἶδα τὸ δρᾶμα, καὶ ὅσον οὐκ εἰς μακρὰν κατερῶ τῷ δεσπότῃ· οὐ γὰρ βούλομαι χείρων φανῆναι τῶν κυνῶν οἳ τῶν τρεφόντων προϋλακτοῦσι καὶ κήδονται. Μοιχὸς πολιορκεῖ τὴν οἰκίαν ὁ Ἠλεῖος νεανίσκος, ὁ εἷς τῶν Ὀλυμπιάσι βασκάνων· καὶ παρὰ τούτου γραμματίδια ὁσημέραι φοιτᾷ δίθυρα πρὸς τὴν γαμετὴν τοῦ τρέφοντος ἡμᾶς, καὶ στέφανοι ἡμιμάραντοι καὶ μῆλα

LXII.

CHIDROLEPISUS TO CAPYROSPHRANTES.

You know the reason why the women jeered at me. An old slave lately abused me, telling me to go to the devil for a troublesome chatterbox. There is a secret amongst them which they keep more carefully than the Eleusinian mysteries, and they try to conceal it from us, who know all about it, or else think that, although we have heard of it, we do not believe it. But I know what is going on, and I intend presently to tell my master; for I do not want to show myself less grateful than the dogs, which bark in defence of those who feed and take care of them. An adulterer is laying siege to the household—a young man from Elis, one of the Olympian fascinators; he sends neatly-folded notes every day to our master's wife, together with faded bouquets and

ὑποδεδηγμένα. Αἱ δὲ ἀλάστορες αὗται θεραπαινίδες συνίσασι, καὶ ἡ ἐπικήδειος γραῦς, ἣν Ἔμπουσαν ἅπαντες οἱ κατὰ τὴν οἰκίαν καλεῖν εἰώθασιν, ἐκ τοῦ πάντα ποιεῖν καὶ βιάζεσθαι. Ἐγὼ δὲ οὐκ ἔσθ᾽ ὅπως σιγήσομαι, βούλομαι γὰρ ἐμαυτὸν οὐ παράσιτον, ἀλλὰ φίλον ἐπιδεῖξαι· καὶ ἄλλως διψῶ τῆς κατ᾽ αὐτῶν τιμωρίας. Οἶδα γὰρ, οἶδα, εἰ ταῦτα εἰς φανερὸν ἀχθείη, αἱ μὲν θεραπαινίδες δεδήσονται, ὁ μοιχὸς δὲ ἀπολεῖται ῥαφάνοις τὴν ἕδραν βεβυσμένος, ἡ μιαρὰ δὲ γυνὴ τίσει τὴν ἀξίαν τῆς ἀκολασίας δίκην, εἰ μὴ Πολυάγρου τοῦ κυρτοῦ κακώτερός ἐστι τὰ τοιαῦτα Λυσικλῆς· ἐκεῖνος γὰρ λύτρα παρὰ τῶν μοιχῶν ἐπὶ τῇ γαμετῇ πραττόμενος ἀθώους τῆς τιμωρίας ἠφίει.

half-eaten apples. These accursed servants are in the plot, as well as the old woman, with one foot in the grave, whom the rest call Empusa, because she is ready to do and suffer anything. I can hold my tongue no longer; I want to show myself a friend, not a parasite; besides, I thirst to have my revenge upon them. For I am certain, if this affair be brought to light, the servants will be put in the stocks, and the adulterer will be put to death, with a radish stuffed up his backside. And the abandoned wife shall pay the just penalty of her wantonness, unless Lysicles is more stupid in such matters than the hunchback Polyagrus, who, after exacting compensation in money from his wife's lovers, let them go without further punishment.

LXIII.

Φιλομάγειρος Πινακοσπόγγῳ.

Οἷα βουλεύονται καὶ διανοοῦνται αἱ θεοῖς ἐχθραὶ λαικάστριαι. Αὗται τῇ κεκτημένῃ συμπράττουσι· καὶ οἶδε¹ τούτων οὐδὲν ὁ Φαιδρίας. Μηνὶ πέμπτῳ μετὰ τοὺς γάμους τέτοκεν αὐτῷ τὸ γύναιον παιδίον ἄρρεν· τοῦτο μετὰ τῶν σπαργάνων, δέραια τινὰ καὶ γνωρίσματα περιδεῖσαι, ἔδωκαν Ἀσφαλίωνι τῷ συργάστορι κομίζειν ἐπὶ τὰς ἀκρωρείας τῆς Πάρνηθος. Ἡμᾶς δὲ τέως μὲν ἀνάγκη κρύπτειν τὸ κακόν, καὶ πρὸς τὸ παρὸν σιγώην· σιγὴ δέ ἐστι τοῦ θυμοῦ τροφή. Ἐπειδὰν δέ τι κἂν βραχὺ λυπήσωσι, κόλακα καὶ παράσιτον ὀνειδίζουσαι, καὶ τὰς ἄλλας, ἃς εἰώθασιν, ὕβρεις ἐπιφέρουσαι, εἴσεται τὸ γεγονὸς ὁ Φαιδρίας.

LXIII.

PHILOMAGEIRUS TO PINACOSPONGUS.

WHAT tricks these accursed harlots are always devising! They are in league with my mistress, and Phaedrias knows nothing of what is going on. Five months after marriage, the woman had a child— a boy; they wrapped him in his swaddling-clothes, fastened a necklace and some tokens, by which he might be afterwards recognised, round his neck, and gave him to Asphalion, one of the labourers, to carry to the summit of Mount Parnes, and leave him there. In the meanwhile, we were obliged to keep the cruel deed a secret, and I would keep silence now, but silence is the food of anger. If they annoy me ever so little, reproaching me for a flatterer and parasite, and heaping the usual insults upon me, Phaedrias shall be informed of what has taken place.

LXIV.

Τουρδοσύναγος Ἐφαλλοκύθρᾳ.

Ὁ μὲν Κρίτων ὑπ' ἀνοίας καὶ ἀρχαιότητος τρόπου τὸν υἱὸν εἰς φιλοσόφου φοιτᾶν ἐπέτρεψε· τὸν αὐστηρὸν πρεσβύτην καὶ ἀμειδῆ τὸν ἐκ τῆς Ποικίλης ἐξ ἁπάντων τῶν φιλοσόφων καθηγεῖσθαι τοῦ παιδὸς ἀξιώτερον ἡγησάμενος, ὡς ἂν παρ' αὐτῷ λόγων τινὰς σκινδαλμοὺς ἐκμαθὼν, ἐριστικὸς καὶ ἀγκύλος τὴν γλῶσσαν γένηται. Ὁ δὲ παῖς ἐς τὸ ἀκριβέστατον ἐξεμάξατο τὸν διδάσκαλον· οὐ πρότερον γὰρ λόγων γίνεσθαι μαθητὴς, ἀλλὰ καὶ τοῦ βίου καὶ τῆς ἀγωγῆς ἐσπούδασε. Θεασάμενος γὰρ τὸν διδάσκαλον τῇ ἡμέρᾳ σεμνὸν καὶ σκυθρωπὸν καὶ τοῖς νέοις ἐπιτιμῶντα, νύκτωρ δὲ περικαλύπτοντα τὴν κεφαλὴν τριβωνίῳ καὶ περὶ χαμαιτυπίας εἰλούμενον, ἐζήλωσεν ἐν καλῷ· καὶ πέμπτην ταύτην ἡμέραν εἰς ἔρωτα Ἀκαλανθίδος τῆς

LXIV.

TURDOSYNAGUS TO EPHALLOCYTHRAS.

CRITO has been so foolish and such a dotard as to allow his son to go to a philosopher's school; he has sent him to that austere and gloomy old Stoic, whom he thinks the fittest instructor for the youth, that he may learn from him the art of splitting straws, and turn out disputatious and double-tongued. The lad has copied his instructor most faithfully; he has paid more attention to imitating his life and manners than to learning his doctrines. Seeing that his master, during the day, was solemn and severe and always lecturing the young men, while at night he covered his head with his cloak and haunted the brothels, he has admirably copied his model; and for the last four days he has been madly in love with Acalanthis of the Ceramicus. She is a

ἐκ Κεραμεικοῦ κατολισθήσας φλέγεται. Αὐτὴ δὲ ἐπιεικῶς ἔχει πρὸς ἐμὲ, καὶ ἐρᾶν ὁμολογεῖ· τῷ μειρακίῳ δὲ ἐπανατείνεται ἠσθημένη πόθῳ τυφόμενον, καὶ οὐ πρότερον, φησὶν, ἐπιδώσει ἑαυτὴν, πρὶν ἂν ἐγὼ τοῦτο ἐπιτρέψω· ἐμὲ γὰρ κύριον τοῦ τὰ τοιαῦτα προστάττειν ἐποιήσατο. Πολλὰ καὶ ἀγαθὰ δοίης, Ἀφροδίτη πάνδημε, τῇ φιλτάτῃ γυναικί· ἑταίρου γὰρ, οὐχ ἑταίρας ἔργον διεπράξατο. Ἐξ ἐκείνου γὰρ θεραπεύομαι λιπαρῶς ἄλλοτε ἄλλαις δωροφορίαις· καὶ ἤν μοι ῥεύσειεν τοῦ χρόνου προϊόντος δαψιλέστερον, οὐδὲν κωλύσει με, τούτου γαμοῦντος ἐπίκληρον γυναῖκα, ἐν γαμετῆς σχήματι τὴν Ἀκαλανθίδα λυσάμενον ἀναλαβεῖν. Ἡ γὰρ τοῦ ζῆν αἰτία κοινωνὸς τοῦ ζῆν δικαίως ἂν κατασταίη.

friend of mine, and professes to love me; she knows that the youth is mad with desire, but refuses to yield to him, and declares that he shall not enjoy her favours until I give my consent to it, for she has left the decision to me. O Venus, goddess of sensual love, bestow every blessing upon this excellent woman; she has behaved more like a friend than a prostitute! Since that time I have been loaded with handsome presents; if they pour in upon me even more abundantly, as time goes on, nothing shall prevent me from ransoming her from her master and making her my lawful wife. For she to whom I owe my support has every right to share my comforts.

LXV.

Μισόγνιφος Ῥιγομάχῳ.

Μέγα τοῦτο ἀγαθὸν ἡ ἐξ Ἰστρίας ναῦς, ἡ ἐπὶ τοῦ χώματος ὁρμῶσα, εἰς Ἀθήνας ἧκε, φέρουσα τὸν θαυμαστὸν τοῦτον ἔμπορον, ὃς τοὺς πλουσίους τοὺς Ἀθήνῃσι καὶ μεγαλοδώρους, κίμβικας καὶ μικροπρεπεῖς ἀπέφηνεν, οὕτω κεχυμένως πρὸς τὰς δόσεις κέχρηται τῷ βαλαντίῳ. Οὐ γὰρ ἕνα παράσιτον ἐξ ἄστεος, ἀλλὰ πάντας ἡμᾶς μεταπέμψας, καὶ οὐχ ἡμᾶς μόνον, ἀλλὰ καὶ τῶν ἑταιρῶν τὰς πολυτελεστέρας, καὶ μουσουργῶν τὰς καλλιστευούσας, καὶ τοὺς ἐπὶ σκηνῆς ἁπαξαπλῶς εἰπεῖν ἅπαντας, οὐ τὴν πατρῴαν οὐσίαν, τὰ δὲ ἐκ δικαίων αὐτῷ ποριζόμενα σπαθᾷ, καὶ ψαλλόμενος καὶ καταυλούμενος ἥδεται, καὶ τὴν διατριβὴν ποιεῖται χαρίτων καὶ Ἀφροδίτης γέμουσαν, καὶ ὑβρίζει οὐδέν. Ἔστι δὲ καὶ ὀφθῆναι κεχαρισμενώτατος, καὶ τὸ πρόσωπον αὐτοῦ τὰς ὥρας αὐτὰς ἐνορχουμένας ἔχει,

LXV.

MISOGNIPHUS TO RHIGOMACHUS.

THE vessel from Istria, which is anchored off the pier, has brought great good luck. One of its passengers is the wonderful merchant, whose lavish openhandedness makes the wealthiest and most generous of our citizens seem mean and niggardly by comparison. He has invited not one parasite only from the city, but all of us, as well as the most expensive courtesans, the most beautiful singing-girls, in fact, all who perform in public. He is not squandering his patrimony, but all the money he spends has been honestly earned by himself. He is fond of music, makes his stay in the city very agreeable to all, and is never rude to anybody. He is very pleasant to look at; you would say that his face was the dancing-ground of the Hours, and that

ΑΛΚΙΦΡΟΝΟΣ ΡΗΤΟΡΟΣ

καὶ τὴν πειθὼ τῷ στόματι ἐπικαθῆσθαι εἴποις ἄν. Προσπαῖσαί τε γλαφυρὸς καὶ λαλῆσαι στωμύλος. Οὕνεκά οἱ γλυκὺ Μοῦσα κατὰ στόματος χέε νέκταρ· εἰπεῖν γὰρ οὐ χεῖρον κατὰ τοὺς παιδείᾳ σχολάζοντας ἐξ 'Αθηνῶν ὁρμώμενον, ἐν αἷς οὐδὲ εἷς τούτων ἄγευστος

Persuasion was seated on his lips. His wit is refined, his conversation agreeable. "The Muse has poured sweet nectar over his lips," in the words of the poet; for it does not seem inappropriate for a native of Athens to use the language of those who have received a liberal education—which is the case with all of us.

LXVI.

Γαμοχαίρων Φαγοδαίτῃ.

Ἐθεάσω οἷά με εἰργάσατο ὁ κατάρατος οὗτος κουρεύς, ὁ πρὸς τῇ ὁδῷ, λέγω δὲ τὸν ἀδόλεσχον καὶ λάλον, τὸν Βρεντησίου προτιθέμενον ἔσοπτρα, τὸν τοὺς χειροήθεις κόρακας τιθασσεύοντα, τὸν ταῖς μαχαιρίσι κυμβαλισμὸν εὔρυθμον ἀνακρούοντα. Ὡς γὰρ ἀφικόμην ξυριεῖσθαι τὴν γενειάδα βουλόμενος, ἀσμένως τε ἐδέξατο, καὶ ἐφ' ὑψηλοῦ θρόνου καθίσας, σινδόνα καινὴν περιθεὶς, πρᾴως εὖ μάλα κατέφερέ μοι τῶν γνάθων τὸ ξυρὸν, ἀποψιλῶν τὸ πύκνωμα τῶν τριχῶν. Ἀλλ' ἐν αὐτῷ τούτῳ πανοῦργος ἦν καὶ σκαιός· ἔλαθε γὰρ τοῦτο παρὰ μέρος ποιῶν, καὶ οὐ κατὰ πάσης τῆς γνάθου, ὥστε ὑπολειφθῆναί μοι πολλαχοῦ μὲν δασεῖαν, πολλαχοῦ δὲ λείαν τὴν σιαγόνα. Κἀγὼ μὲν οὐκ εἰδὼς τὴν πανουργίαν, ᾠχόμην κατὰ τὸ εἰωθὸς ἄκλητος εἰς Πασίωνος, οἱ συμπόται δὲ, ὡς

LXVI.

GAMOCHAERON TO PHAGODAETES.

You saw how that accursed barber who lives by the roadside treated me; I mean that chattering gossip, who offers his mirrors for sale at Brentesium, who tames jackdaws, and plays a kind of tune with his razors. When I went to him to get shaved, he received me most politely, made me sit down in a high chair, and put a clean cloth round my neck; then he gently drew the razor over my cheeks, and took off my thick hairs. But, in doing this, he was cunning and mischievous, for he only half shaved me, and left one part of 'my face rough, while the other was smooth. I, knowing nothing of the trick he had played me, went as usual to Pasion's house, without waiting to be invited. When the guests saw me, they nearly killed them-

εἶδον, ἐξέθανον τῷ γέλωτι, ἕως ἀγνοοῦντα με ἐφ' ὅτῳ γελῶσιν, εἷς τις εἰς μέσους παρελθὼν, τῶν ἀπολειφθεισῶν τριχῶν ἐπιλαβόμενος εἵλκυσεν. Ἐκείνας μὲν οὖν περιπαθῶς κοπίδα λαβὼν ἀπερρίζωσα, ἕτοιμος δέ εἰμι ξύλον εὐμέγεθες ἀνελόμενος κατὰ τοῦ βρέγματος πατάξαι τὸν ἀλιτήριον. Ἃ γὰρ οἱ τρέφοντες παίζουσι, ταῦτα μὴ τρέφων ἐτόλμησε.

selves with laughing. I could not make
out what had excited their mirth, until
one of them came forward into the
middle of the room and caught hold of
and pulled at the hairs which had been
left. I took a knife, and, feeling greatly
annoyed, uprooted them somehow; and
now I intend to look for a big stick and
go and break the rascal's skull. What
those who keep us do, in order to amuse
themselves, this fellow had the audacity
to do, although he has never contributed
anything to my support.

LXVII.

Διψοφαπαυσίλυπος Πλακουντομύωνι.

Νευρίδα ἰδὼν κανηφοροῦσαν, παρθένον καλλίπηχυν, καὶ εὐδάκτυλον, ταῖς βολαῖς τῶν ὀφθαλμῶν ἀστράπτουσαν, εὐμήκη καὶ εὔχρουν, ἧς αἱ παρειαὶ μαρμαίρουσιν, οὕτως ἐξεκαύθην εἰς ἔρωτα, ὥστε με ἐπιλαθόμενον οἷός εἰμι, προσδραμόντα ἐθέλειν κύσαι τὸ στόμα· ἔπειτα ἐπὶ συννοίας γενόμενον, προςφύντα βούλεσθαι τὰ τοῖν ποδοῖν ἴχνη καταφιλεῖν. Αἲ αἲ τῆς ἀγερωχίας, νῦν ἐμὲ μὴ ἐπιθυμεῖν θέρμων, ἢ κυάμων ἢ ἀθάρας, ἀλλ' οὕτως ὑπερμαζᾶν, καὶ τῶν ἀνεφίκτων ἐρᾶν. Καταλεύσατέ με πάντες εἰς ταὐτὸν συνελθόντες, πρὶν ἢ βριθῆναι τοῖς πόθοις, καὶ γενέσθω μοι τύμβος ἐρωτικὸς ὁ τῶν λιθιδίων κολωνός.

LXVII.

DIPSOPHAPAUSILYPUS TO PLACYNTOMION.

WHEN I first saw Neuris, the maiden who carried the basket, with her beautiful arms and fingers, her eyes flashing glances like lightning, her charming figure and complexion, and her glistening cheeks, I was so inflamed with passion that, forgetting who I was, I ran up and attempted to kiss her; then, when I came to my senses, I was ready to follow her and kiss the marks of her footsteps. Alas, alas, for my insolent folly! to think that I could not be content with lupins, beans, and pulse, but, grown wanton with high feeding, must needs long for what was beyond my reach. Assemble, all of you, and stone me to death, before I am consumed by my desires, and let me have, as a lover's tomb, a mound of pebbles.

LXVIII.

Ἡδύδειπνος Ἀριστοκόρακι.

Θεοὶ μάκαρες, ἱλήκοιτε καὶ εὐμενεῖς εἴητε. Οἷον ἀπέφυγον κίνδυνον, τῶν τρισκαταράτων ἐρανιστῶν λέβητά μοι ζέοντα ὕδατος ἐπιχέαι βουληθέντων. Ἰδὼν γὰρ πόρρωθεν εὐτρεπεῖς ἀπεπήδησα· οἱ δὲ ἀπροβουλεύτως ἐξέχεον, καὶ τὸ θερμὸν ἐπιρρυὲν Βαθύλῳ τῷ οἰνοχοοῦντι παιδὶ ψιλὸν εἰργάσατο· τῆς κεφαλῆς γὰρ ἀπεσύρε τὸ δέρμα, καὶ φλυκταίνας ἐπινωτίους ἐξήνθησε. Τίς ἄρα μοι διαμόνων ἐπίκουρος ἐγένετο; μή ποτε οἱ σωτῆρες ἄνακτες, ὡς Σιμωνίδην τὸν Λεωπρεποῦς τοῦ Κρανωνίου, καὶ μὲ τῶν τοῦ πυρὸς κρουνῶν ἐξήρπασαν;

LXVIII.

HEDYDEIPNUS TO ARISTOCORAX.

O BLESSED gods, be kind and propitious! What a danger did I escape, when those thrice-accursed clubmen tried to throw a kettle of boiling water over me! I saw what they were ready to do when I was a long way off, and jumped out of the way. They poured at random, and the boiling contents, falling over Bathylus, the lad who was handing the wine, completely flayed him; the skin has peeled off his head, and his back is covered with blisters. Who then of the gods was it that protected me? Was it the Saviour princes, who preserved me from the streams of fire, as in time past Simonides the son of Leoprepes at the banquet at Cranon?

LXIX.

Τριχινοσάραξ Γλωσσοτραπέζῳ.

Ἐξηγόρευσα Μνησιλόχῳ τῷ Παιανιεῖ τὴν τῆς γαμετῆς ἀσέλγειαν· καὶ ὃς, δέον βασανίσαι διερευνᾶν τε τὸ πρᾶγμα ποικίλως, ὅρκῳ τὸ πᾶν, ὁ χρυσοῦς, ἐπέτρεψεν. Ἀγαγοῦσα οὖν αὐτὸν ἡ γυνὴ εἰς τὸ Καλλίχορον τὸ ἐν Ἐλευσῖνι φρέαρ, ἀπωμόσατο, καὶ ἀπελύσατο τὴν αἰτίαν. Καὶ ὁ μὲν ἀμηγέπη πέπεισται, καὶ τὴν ὑποψίαν ἀπέβαλεν· ἐγὼ δὲ τὴν φλυαρὸν γλῶτταν ἀποτέμνειν ὀστράκῳ Τενεδίῳ τοῖς βουλομένοις ἕτοιμός εἰμι παρέχειν.

LXIX.

TRICHINOSARAX TO GLOSSOTRAPEZUS.

I HAVE informed Mnesilochus of Paeania of his wife's wantonness; and he, when he ought to have thoroughly sifted and investigated the matter in various ways, like the precious fool that he is, left it to his wife's oath. The woman led him to the well of Callichorum at Eleusis, swore she was innocent, and cleared herself. He was somehow or other convinced, and has abandoned all suspicion; and I am ready to let anyone who pleases cut out my chattering tongue with a potsherd from Tenedos.

1

LXX.

Λιμούστης Θρασοκυδοίμῳ.

Κορύδωνι τῷ γεωργῷ συνήθης ἐπιεικῶς ἦν, καὶ τὰ πολλὰ ἐξεχεῖτο ἐπ' ἐμοὶ τῷ γέλωτι, ἀστικῆς στωμυλίας καὶ ξένης ἢ κατὰ τοὺς χωρίτας ἐπαΐων. Τοῦτον ἰδὼν ἕρμαιον ᾠήθην, εἰ τῶν κατ' ἄστυ πραγμάτων ἀπαλλαγεὶς, εἰς τὸν ἀγρὸν βαδιοίμην, καὶ. συνεσοίμην ἀνδρὶ φίλῳ, γεωργῷ ἀπράγμονι καὶ ἐργάτῃ, οὐκ ἐκ δικαστηρίων, οὐδὲ ἐκ τοῦ σείειν κατ' ἀγορὰν ἀδίκους ἐπινοοῦντι πόρους, ἀλλὰ γῆθεν ἀναμένοντι τὴν ἐπικαρπίαν ἔχειν. Καὶ δῆτα διανοηθεὶς ταῦθ' οὕτω δρᾶν, ᾠκειωσάμην τὸν Κορύδωνα, καὶ στείλας ἐμαυτὸν ἀγροικικῶς, νάκος ἐναψάμενος, καὶ σμινύην λαβὼν, αὐτοσκαπανεὺς ἐδόκουν. Ἕως μὲν οὖν ἐν παιδιᾶς μέρει ἔπραττον ταῦτα, ἀνεκτὸν ἦν,

LXX.

LIMUSTES TO THRASOCYDOEMUS.

I WAS fairly intimate with Corydon the farmer, who often used to laugh heartily at me, since he understood city wit better than country people usually do. When I first saw him, I thought it would be a regular piece of luck for me, if I could give up a city life and retire to the country, and live with a friend who passed his life quietly working on his farm; then I need no longer think about making money by questionable practices in the courts, but could wait patiently to enjoy the fruits of the earth. Having determined to do this, I made friends with Corydon, dressed myself like a countryman, clad myself in a sheepskin, took up a mattock, and got myself up as a regular ditcher. As long as I did this for amusement, it was endurable, and I thought I had made a very good

καὶ μεγάλα ἀποκερδαίνειν ᾠόμην, ὑβρέων καὶ ῥαπισμάτων καὶ τῆς περὶ τὰ ἐδώδιμα τῶν πλουσίων ἀνισότητος ἀπηλλαγμένος· ἐπεὶ δὲ ἐκ τῆς καθημέραν συνηθείας, ἐξ ἐπιταγῆς ἐπράττετο τοὖργον, καὶ ἔδει πάντως ἢ ἀροῦν, ἢ φελλέα ἐκκαθαίρειν, ἢ γύρους περισκάπτειν, καὶ τοῖς βόθροις ἐμφυτεύειν, οὐκ ἔτ' ἀνασχετὸς ἡ διατριβὴ, ἀλλά μοι μετέμελε τῆς ἀλόγου πράξεως, καὶ τὴν πόλιν ἐπόθουν. Ἐλθὼν οὖν ἐπὶ μήκιστον χρόνον, οὐκ ἔθ' ὁμοίως δεκτὸς, οὐδὲ χαρίεις ἐδόκουν, ἀλλά τις ὄρειος καὶ τραχὺς καὶ ἀπηχής, ὥστε αἱ μὲν οἰκίαι τῶν πλουσίων πᾶσαί μοι λοιπὸν ἀπεκέκλειντο, ὁ δὲ λιμὸς τὴν γαστέρα ἐθυροκόπει. Ἐγὼ δὲ αὖος ὢν ὑπὸ τῆς τῶν ἀναγκαίων ἐνδείας, λῃσταῖς τισι Μεγαρικοῖς, οἳ περὶ τὰς Σκειρωνίδας τοῖς ὁδοιπόροις ἐνεδρεύουσιν, ἐκοινώνησα· ἔνθεν ὁ βίος μοι ἀργὸς ἐξ ἀδικίας πορίζεται. Εἰ δὲ λήσω ταῦτα ποιῶν ἢ μὴ, ἄδηλον· δέδια δὲ τὴν μεταλλαγὴν τοῦ βίου· εἰώθασι γὰρ αἱ τοιαῦται μεταβολαὶ οὐκ εἰς τὸ ζῆν, ἀλλ' εἰς ἀπώλειαν καταστρέφειν.

bargain, since I was free from blows and insults, and the unequal footing on which I stood with my wealthy patrons; but when he made a daily practice of ordering me to work, and I had either to plough, clear the stony ground, dig holes, or plant in the ditches, then this kind of life became unbearable; I repented of my foolish act, and longed for the city again. When I returned after my long absence, I did not meet with the same reception as before; instead of being looked upon as a wit, I was considered rough and uncultivated, in fact, a regular boor. All the houses of the wealthy were from that time forth shut against me, and hunger knocked at the doors of my belly. Hard pressed for the bare necessaries of life, I joined a band of Megarian brigands, who lie in wait for travellers near the Scironian rocks; and since then I have gained a dishonest livelihood without working. I do not know whether I shall escape detection; but I am alarmed about my new profession, for such a change of life generally ends in destruction rather than safety.

LXXI.

Φιλόπωρος Ψιχομάχῳ.

Λεξιφάνης ὁ τῆς κωμῳδίας ποιητὴς θεασάμενός με πρὸς ταῖς ἐν συμποσίοις παροινίαις, λαβὼν καθ' ἑαυτὸν, πρῶτα μὲν ἐνουθέτει μὴ τοιαῦτα ἐπιτηδεύειν, ἐξ ὧν ὕβρις τὸ τέλος· ἔπειτα τοῦ φρονήματος ὡς ἔχοιμι διὰ βραχέων ἀποπειραθεὶς, τῷ χορῷ τῶν κωμικῶν συλλαμβάνει· ἐκ τοῦδε τραφησόμενον ἔφασκε καὶ ἐμέ. Ἐκέλευεν οὖν ἐκμαθόντα Διονυσίοις τοῖς ἐπιοῦσι τὸ τοῦ οἰκέτου σχῆμα ἀναλαβόντα, τὸ μέρος ἐκεῖνο τοῦ δράματος ὑποκρίνασθαι. Ἐγὼ δὲ ὀψὲ τοῦ καιροῦ καὶ φύσιν καὶ ἐπιτήδευσιν μεταβαλὼν, δύσκολός τις καὶ δυσμαθὴς ἐφαινόμην· ἐπεὶ δὲ οὐκ ἦν ἑτέρως πράττειν, τὸ δρᾶμα ἐξέμαθον, καὶ μελέτην ἀσκήσει ῥώσας, ἕτοιμός εἰμι τῷ

LXXI.

PHILOPORUS TO PSICHOMACHUS.

LEXIPHANES, the comic poet, seeing me treated with drunken insults, took me aside. He first advised me not to continue my present manner of life, which only ended in insult; and then, having tested my abilities, got me into the comedians' company, which he said would enable me to earn my living. He ordered me to get up the part of a slave for the next Dionysia, at which I was to make my first appearance. As it was rather late in life for me to change my nature and habits, I seemed peevish and hard to teach ; but, as I had no alternative, I learned my part, and, now that I have studied and practised it, I am ready to perform with the rest of the company. You and your friends must be ready to

χορῷ συντελείς. Σὺ δὲ ἡμῖν μετὰ τῶν συνήθων ἐπίσειε τοὺς κρότους, ἵνα, κἄν τι λάθωμεν ἀποσφαλέντες, μὴ λάβῃ χώραν τὰ ἀστικὰ μειράκια κλώζειν ἢ συρίττειν, ἀλλ' ὁ τῶν ἐπαίνων κρότος τὸν θροῦν τῶν σκωμμάτων παραλύσῃ.

start the applause, so that, if I should happen to make any mistakes, the city young men may have no opportunity of hooting or hissing me. Let the clapping of hands in applause drown the noise of the scoffers.

LXXII.

Οἰνοχαίρων Ῥαφανοχορτάσῳ.

Οὐχ οὕτως οἱ τοὺς Ἑρμᾶς περικόψαντες, ἢ τὰ τῆς θεοῦ ἐν Ἐλευσῖνι μυστήρια ἐξορχησάμενοι, τὸν περὶ ψυχῆς ἀγῶνα ὑπέμειναν, ὡς ἐγώ, εἰς χεῖρας ἐμπεσών, ὦ θεοί, τῆς μιαρωτάτης Φανομάχης. Ἐπεὶ γὰρ ἔγνω τὸν ἑαυτῆς προσκείμενον τῇ Ἰωνικῇ παιδίσκῃ, τῇ τὰς σφαίρας ἀναῤῥιπτούσῃ καὶ τὰς λαμπάδας περιδινούσῃ, ὑπετόπησεν ἐμὲ πρόξενον εἶναι τῆς κοινωνίας, καὶ διὰ τῶν οἰκετῶν ἀναρπάσασα, παραχρῆμα μὲν ἐν κυσοδόχῃ δήσασα κατέσχεν, εἰς τὴν ὑστεραίαν δὲ παρὰ τὸν ἑαυτῆς ἦγε πατέρα, τὸν σκυθρωπὸν Κλεαίνετον, ὃς τανῦν δὴ ταῦτα πρωτεύει τοῦ συνεδρίου, καὶ εἰς αὐτὸν ὁ Ἄρειος πάγος ἀποβλέπουσιν. Ἀλλ' ὅταν τινὰ θέλωσιν οἱ θεοὶ σώζεσθαι, καὶ ἐξ αὐτῶν ἀνασπῶσι βαρά-

LXXII.

OENOCHAERON TO RAPHANOCHORTASUS.

THOSE who have mutilated the Hermae, or betrayed the secrets of the Eleusinian goddess, have never endured such agony as I did, when I fell into the clutches of that accursed woman Phanomache. When she found out that her husband was devoted to that Ionian wench, who is clever at tossing up balls and swinging lamps round, she immediately suspected that I was the go-between in the connexion, ordered her servants to seize me, and clapped me into the stocks. The next day, she took me before her father, the sulky Cleaenetus, who is now President of the Council, and held in great respect by the members of the Areopagus. But when it is the will of the gods that anyone should escape, they can draw him up even from the

θρων, ὡς κἀμὲ τοῦ τρικαρήνου κυνὸς, ὅν φασιν ἐφεστάναι ταῖς Ταρταρέαις πύλαις, ἐξήρπασαν. Οὐκ ἔφθη γὰρ τὰ κατ' ἐμὲ ὁ δεινὸς ἐκεῖνος πρεσβύτης τῇ βουλῇ κοινούμενος, καὶ ἠπιάλῳ συσχεθεὶς, εἰς τὴν ἕω ἀπέψυξε. Καὶ ὁ μὲν ἐκτάδην κεῖται, πρὸς τὴν ἐκφορὰν τῶν οἴκοι παρασκευαζομένων· ἐγὼ δὲ [ψύττα κατατείνας], ᾗ ποδῶν εἶχον, ᾠχόμην· καὶ σώζομαι οὐχ ὑπὸ τοῦ τῆς Ἀτλαντίδος Μαίας παιδὸς ψυχαγωγηθεὶς, ἀλλ' ὑπὸ τῶν ποδῶν καὶ τοῦ τολμήματος, τὴν ἐλευθέραν πορίσας ἀτραπόν.

bottom of the pit, just as they saved me from the clutches of the three-headed dog, who, they say, keeps guard before the entrance to the nether world. For, before the terrible old man could bring my case before the Council, he was attacked by the hot ague, and died in the morning. He now lies stretched out in death, and his household are making preparations for the funeral; meanwhile, I ran off as fast as my feet could carry me. I owe my safety and freedom, not so much to the escort of the son of Maia, the daughter of Atlas, as to the swiftness of my feet and my own boldness.

NOTES

These Notes are merely intended to give brief explanations of names or allusions, and do not deal with matters of textual criticism.

BOOK I

The first figure refers to the page, the second to the line of the page.

PAGE LINE

2 20 *Phalerum :* One of the three harbours of Athens, the other two being Piraeus and Munychia.

3 7 *The cask of the Danaides:* These were the fifty daughters of Danaus; they were married to the fifty sons of Aegyptus, and all of them, except one, put their husbands to death on the wedding night. As a punishment, they were sentenced, in the lower world, to keep incessantly pouring water into casks which were full of holes. Hence the expression is used to signify " useless labour."

3 8 *Sea nettles :* Fishes called by this name.

3 18 *In the pool of Eurynome:* There is great doubt about the reading here. Eurynome is supposed to be either the name of a sea-nymph or a place.

PAGE	LINE	
5	4	*Aneisidora :* Corn is said to have been first produced in Attica; hence its inhabitants gave the earth the name of Aneisidora, "producer of gifts."
5	11	*Who hang about the Painted Porch: i.e.,* the Stoic philosophers. The στοὰ ποικίλη was one of the most remarkable of the Στοαί, or porticoes of Athens; it was so called from the variety of curious pictures it contained. Here it was that Zeno, the founder of the Stoic school of philosophy, taught, and for that reason his followers were called Stoics.
5	16	*Aratus :* He wrote two poems on astronomical subjects; he is supposed to have lived about B.C. 270; Cicero translated part of his poems into Latin Verse.
7	15	*The Oschophoria and Lenaea :* Two festivals in honour of Dionysus (Bacchus). The former was properly the name given to a day of the Athenian festival Σκίρα or Σκιροφόρια, on which chosen boys, sons of citizens, in women's dress, carrying vine-branches (ὄσχοι) loaded with grapes, went in procession from the temple of Bacchus to that of ʼΑθηνᾶ Σκιράς. The *Lenaea* was so called from ληνὸς, a wine-press. Dramatic contests, especially between the comic poets, took place on this occasion.
8	1	*Aegina :* A well-known island in the Saronic Gulf, which played an important part in the history of ancient Greece.

NOTES

PAGE	LINE	
9	6	*Darics*: A Persian gold coin, about equal in value to a guinea. Said to have been first coined by King Darius, but the name is probably derived from the Persian darā, "a king"—cf. our "sovereign."
9	7	*Salamis*: B.C. 480, when Xerxes was defeated in a naval engagement by the Athenians under Themistocles.
10	4	*Stiria*: One of the demes or townships into which Attica was divided.
10	14	*Hermione*: In Argolis, in Peloponnesus.
11	8	*Hair-nets*: A woman's head-dress made of net, used to confine the hair with, especially indoors, such as are still used in Italy and Spain.
13	16	*Corycian bark*: So called from a mountain in Lydia, in Asia Minor, which was famous as being the haunt of pirates.
15	3	*After the fashion of Mandrobulus*: That is, from bad to worse. The following is the explanation given of this proverbial expression: Mandrobulus, having had the good luck to discover a vast treasure, in gratitude to the gods, offered a golden ram to them; he afterwards offered one of silver; then one of brass; and, finally, none at all.
15	12	*Sphettus . . . Cholargus*: Two Attic demes.
15	17	*Dionysia*: Festival of Bacchus.
		Apaturia: A festival first instituted at Athens, so called from ἀπάτη, "deceit," because it celebrated the memory of a stratagem by which

Page	Line	
		Melanthius, king of Athens, overcame Xanthus, king of Boeotia.
16	1	*Market-inspectors:* Clerks of the market, who regulated the buying and selling, like the Roman aediles.
17	18	*Malea:* The southernmost point of Greece. It was considered a very dangerous part for navigation. There was a proverb, "When you double Malea, forget those at home."
18	2	*Caphareus:* A promontory of Euboea.
19	4	*Paralus . . . Salaminia:* The two Athenian galleys, reserved for state-services, religious missions, embassies, the conveyance of public moneys and persons, and also frequently as admirals' galleys in sea-fights.
19	16	*Sunium:* In Attica.
19	17	*Geraestus:* A harbour and promontory in Euboea.
22	16	*A Telchinian:* The Telchinians were the first inhabitants of Crete, Cyprus, and Rhodes, and the first workers in metal. They had a bad reputation as spiteful genii; hence, a "Telchinian" was used generally for "a spiteful, mischievous person."
23	4	*The Areopagus:* The highest judicial court of Athens, so called from the Ἄρειος πάγος, or hill of Ares, over against the Acropolis, where it was held.
27	1	*Watcher:* A man whose duty it was to help the fishermen by keeping a lookout and giving them notice of the approach of a shoal of fish.

NOTES

PAGE	LINE	
29	5	*Gulf of Calydon:* Part of the Gulf of Corinth.
29	7	*Crataiis:* A reference to Homer's Odyssey. When Ulysses learns from Circe that he must lose six of his companions at the rock of Scylla, he asks how he can avenge their death; but Circe advises him to flee without delay and invoke Crataiis, the mother of Scylla, to protect him against further loss.
31	6	*Wine from Chalybon:* Wine from a town in Syria, which was a favourite drink of the kings of Persia.
35	13	*A plan worthy of Ulysses:* A proverbial expression, signifying a very clever plan, Ulysses being considered a model of cunning.
36	5	*A couple of obols:* An obol was worth about three halfpence.
38	19	*Propontis:* The Sea of Marmora.
39	7	*Colonus:* One of the boroughs of Attica, famous for the tomb of Oedipus, and immortalised by Sophocles, who was a native of it, in his tragedy of *Oedipus at Colonus*.
39	17	*How many talents?* A talent was worth about £250.
40	7	*For a month:* The interest on borrowed money was paid monthly, and the day of collecting it was the last day of every moon.
40	12	*A wolf:* Wolves were such a pest to the country that a reward was publicly offered for their destruction.
41	8	*Completely ruined me:* Literally, "turned me upside down." The allusion is

PAGE	LINE	
		to casks of wine which, having been drained of their contents, are turned upside down and used for sitting on.
42	6	*Decrepit*: Literally, "as old as three crows."
42	17	*Cecrops*: The oldest legendary king of Athens: hence used for "an old dotard."
43	3	*The Isthmian Games*: So called from the Isthmus of Corinth, where they were celebrated. They were supposed to have been instituted by Theseus, king of Attica, in honour of Neptune.
44	5	*Olympian*: Read "Isthmian."
44	13	*Chremes or Diphilus*: Two characters in Menander's plays.
50	17	*The Festival of Ceres*: The Haloa (Ἁλῶα) was a festival in honour of Demeter (Ceres) as the inventress of agriculture.
52	7	*The Academy*: A gymnasium in the suburbs of Athens, where Plato the philosopher taught: hence his pupils were called Academics.
54	6	*Aspasia*: The mistress of the famous Athenian statesman, Pericles; she is said to have studied under Gorgias of Leontini, a famous sophist and rhetorician.
54	17	*The Lyceum*: A public wrestling-ground in the eastern suburbs of Athens.
56	5	*A poor consolation*: The commentators differ greatly as to the interpretation of this passage. According to some, the reference is not to a "flower," but

NOTES

PAGE	LINE	
		to a lock of hair from Petale's head; others explain it by the Greek proverb, ἐκ τρίχος κρέμαται, implying that a man is in great danger, "hanging by a single hair" or thread. But "the flowers" seems to suit the epithet μαραινόμενον.
57	8	*Myrrhinus*: An Attic deme.
57	9	*The silver mines*: The mines of Laurium, in the neighbourhood of Attica, were famous.
58	10	*Well, my friend*: We find similar suggestions in *Lucian's Dialogues of Courtesans* (xii.).
59	3	*The festival of Adonis*: Celebrated in most of the cities of Greece in honour of Venus, and in memory of her beloved Adonis. See the account in the *Adoniazusae*, the 15th Idyll of Theointus.
65	15	*A staff of figtree wood*: The allusion is obscure; nothing is known of Philo. The proverb itself is said to be used of those who have attained to happiness and fortune beyond their deserts; the idea implied by "figtree wood" is that of weakness and untrustworthiness; but it is not easy to see the application here.
66	14	*A serious dispute*: For a similar contest compare *Athenaeus*, Book xii., and the *Amores of Lucian*.
67	12	*Then she showed*: Lit., but it (πυγή) did not tremble, &c.
68	4	*The Golden Alley*: This topography occurs again in Book iii. letter 8.
68	12	*Colyttus*: An Attic deme.

NOTES

PAGE LINE
68   16   *A dice-box :* Others propose κήριον, "a waxen image."
68   17   *Coral image :* Some take Corallium (κοράλλιον) as a proper name; others interpret it as "counters."

BOOK II

70   6   *Demetrius :* Surnamed Poliorcetes, son of Antigonus, one of the generals of Alexander the Great. He was sent by his father against Ptolemy at the age of 22. He defeated this prince, delivered Athens from the yoke of Cassander, and drove out the garrison established by Demetrius of Phalerum. He seized Cyprus, forced Cassander to raise the siege of Athens, defeated him at Thermopylae, and restored their liberty to the Rhodians and Phocidians. He was appointed commander-in-chief of the Greeks, took part of Thessaly from Cassander, and was defeated at Ipsus (302) by Lysimachus and Seleucus. The Athenians refused to admit him to Athens, but he afterwards forced his way there, took possession of the city, defeated the Lacedaemonians, and ascended the Macedonian throne. He died in B.C. 209.

71   5   *Gnathaena :* A contemporary and rival courtesan.

71   6   *But this does not grieve me :* The meaning of this passage is much disputed; others render ἠλογημένη, "I am greatly perplexed."

NOTES 215

PAGE	LINE	
73	16	*Who behaved like foxes at Ephesus:* There was a Greek proverb, οἴκοι μὲν λέοντες, ἐν μάχῃ δ' ἀλώπεκες. We are told that this was applied to the Lacedaemonians by Lamia, in consequence of their having been corrupted in Ionia by the influence of Lysander.
73	19	*Taygetus:* A mountain in Laconia.
74	3	*Epicurus:* The founder of the Epicurean sect of philosophers, whose motto, roughly speaking, was that pleasure was the chief good, the *summum bonum*. His antithesis was Zeno, the founder of the Stoic school. Consult Zeller's *Stoics, Epicureans, and Sceptics*.
74	13	*His doctrines about nature:* His κυρίαι δοξαι, or special tenets.
75	3	*In his irony:* A reference to the Socratic εἰρώνεια, an ignorance purposely affected to confound an opponent.
75	3	*Pythocles:* The favourite of Epicurus, as Alcibiades was of Socrates.
76	5	*Some Cappadocian:* A reference to the inelegance of Epicurus's style, which is mentioned by Athenaeus.
76	21	*The Lyceum:* A building dedicated to Apollo, on the banks of the Ilissus, one of the three Gymnasia, the other two being the Academy and the Cynosarges.
76	26	*This Atreus:* The following is the comparison drawn. If Epicurus is Atreus, king of Mycenae, Timarchus will represent Thyestes, the younger brother of Atreus, and Leontium Aerope the wife of Atreus, who com-

PAGE	LINE	
		mitted adultery with Thyestes, who on that account was driven out of the kingdom.
77	26	*Sophists :* The so-called "professors of wisdom," who undertook to teach everything for a consideration. There is a celebrated chapter on these people in *Grote's History of Greece.*
79	1	*The Eleusinian goddesses and their mysteries :* These mysteries were celebrated every fifth year at Eleusis, a borough town in Attica, in honour of Ceres and her daughter Proserpine. It was the most solemn and mysterious of all the Greek festivals.
80	7	*The Haloa :* See note on 50, 17.
80	9	*Ptolemy, King of Egypt :* Ptolemy Soter or Lagus (360-283). He had been one of Alexander's most trustworthy generals, and, at the partition of the Empire, was made governor of Egypt. He remained as a nominal tributary to the Macedonian power until 306, when he became the actual king and assumed the title of the Pharaohs. He laid the foundation of the greatness of Alexandria by inaugurating its library and school.
80	13	*Philemon :* A comic poet, contemporary of Menander.
80	18	*Menander* (B.C. 342-290): He was drowned while bathing in the harbour of Piraeus. He wrote more than 100 comedies; but was only crowned eight times, through the intrigues of his rival Philemon. Only a few fragments of his works remain, found in Athenaeus, Suidas, and

NOTES

PAGE	LINE	
		Stobalus; he was the creator of what was called the *New* Comedy.
80	21	*My Heliaea:* The Heliaea was the chief law-court of Athens.
81	18	*Thericlean drinking-cups:* Broad drinking-cups, of black clay or wood, called after Thericles, a Corinthian potter.
81	21	*Our yearly Choes:* The Feast of Pitchers, the second day of the Anthesteria, or Feast of Flowers, the three days' festival in honour of Dionysus (Bacchus) in the month Anthesterion (the eighth month of the Attic year, answering to the end of February and the beginning of March).
82	6	*The legislators:* The θεσμοθέται, or six junior archons at Athens, who after their year of office expired, became members of the Areopagus.
82	8	*The roped inclosure:* In the Athenian law-courts, the judges were separated from the people by a rope. There may also be an allusion to the vermilion-painted rope, with which loiterers were driven out of the Agora into the Pnyx. See Aristophanes, *Acharnians*, 22; and *Ecclesiazusae*, 379.
82	9	*The Feast of Pots:* The third day of the Anthesteria.
		The Ceramicus: Literally, the Potters' Quarter; there were two places of this name, the inner and outer.
82	12	*The Stenia:* A nightly festival in which the return of Demeter (Ceres) from the lower world was celebrated by

PAGE	LINE	
		women. Others propose Στείρια, the name of a deme or borough in the tribe of Pandionis.
82	13	*Psyttalia:* A small island near Salamis.
85	2	*The glorious Mother:* Ceres.
86	14	*Even if an ox were to speak:* That is, if something unnatural were to happen.
87	19	*The promontory of Proteus:* The promontories of the island of Pharos, which was afterwards famous for its lighthouse.
88	11	*Its echoing statues:* Especially the statue of Memnon.
		Its famous labyrinth: For a description, see Herodotus, ii. 148.
88	16	*Bushels:* A μέδιμνος was properly a measure containing *six* bushels.
89	5	*Like another Ariadne:* Ariadne, having fallen in love with Theseus, delivered him from the Minotaur, by giving him a ball of thread, which conducted him out of the labyrinth, after he had destroyed the monster. In return for this, Theseus carried Ariadne with him as far as Naxos, and there abandoned her. She afterwards became the priestess of Bacchus.
90	19	*Those Athenian wasps:* In the well-known play (*The Wasps*) of Aristophanes, the chorus is composed of these creatures, the chief reason given for this being the " irritable and passionate character of the Athenians."
91	1	*Theophrastus:* The tutor of Menander.
91	16	*The stretching of the branches of the broom:* Others read ἄστρων διαθέσει, "the arrangement of the stars."

NOTES

PAGE	LINE	
91	23	*Styrax:* The shrub which produces the sweet-smelling gum or resin used for incense.
94	6	*Your damsel inspired with divine frenzy:* The title of one of Menander's comedies (Θεοφορουμένη). It may simply allude to Glycera herself.

BOOK III

96	1	*Orchomenus:* A city in Arcadia where there was a temple of the Graces.
96	2	*Gargaphia:* A fountain in Boeotia.
96	7	*The Lesbian Sappho:* Who threw herself into the sea for love of Phaon.
97	3	*A dose of hellebore:* Supposed to be a specific for madness. Anticyra was a town in Phocis, on the Corinthian Gulf.
99	7	*Phloea:* One of the Attic demes.
100	11	*Palamedes:* The great inventor amongst the Greeks. Astrology and the measuring of time were two of his notable discoveries.
102	12	*The Leocorium:* The temple of the daughters of Leos, who, in time of famine, sacrificed his daughters in order to put a stop to it.
102	14	*Mendos:* In Egypt. Others understand it of wine from Mende in Thrace.
105	2	*What god unexpectedly interfered?* Lit., acted the part of the *Deus ex machina* (θεὸς ἀπὸ μηχανῆς), a proverbial expression signifying a happier issue of a disagreeable situation than might have been expected.

PAGE	LINE	
107	6	*From the Scyrian quarter:* The common haunt of courtesans.
111	3	*Fall of the leaves:* Plutarch (*Symposiaca*, viii. 10) says: "Dreams are unreliable and false, especially in the months when the trees shed their leaves."
112	5	*Dryads, Epimelides, and Naiads:* The Wood Nymphs, Nymphs of the flocks and herds (or fruits), and the Water Nymphs.
112	10	*Coliades . . . Genetyllides:* Both names of Venus.
114	17	*The son of Calliope:* Orpheus.
		The Edonians: A Thracian people.
119	12	*A Melian or Acarnanian mercenary:* Supposed to be a reference to characters in Menander's plays. Compare the *Miles Gloriosus* of Plautus.
121	13	*The Cordax:* The Athenian representative of the cancan.
124	10	*Oechalia:* There were five towns of this name. This Eurybates was a well-known thief and sharper.
125	9	*The stony field:* The name of a rocky district of Attica.
126	13	*The Eleven:* Composed of one representative from each of the ten tribes of Athens, together with a clerk. They had charge of the prisons, police, and the punishment of criminals.
128	14	*Brilessus:* A mountain in Attica, almost as famous for its honey as Mount Hymettus.
131	5	*That rascal Strombichus:* Lit., Corycian evil spirit. There was a Greek pro-

NOTES

PAGE	LINE	
		verb, " A Corycian has heard him." It had its origin from the brigands who infested Mount Corycus. (See note on 13, 16.)
134	7	*The Meticheum :* The name of an Athenian law-court.
134	12	*A greater chatterer than a turtle-dove :* A proverbial expression. According to Aelian, the turtle-dove kept up a perpetual cooing, not only in front, but also behind.
139	1	*Timon :* Compare Timon the Misanthrope as described by Lucian, and Shakspere's Timon of Athens.
141	1	*The soldier :* A stock character with Greek comic writers; compare Leontichus in Lucian's *Dialogues of Courtesans*.
142	2	*Hermaphroditus :* The special god who presided over the destinies of married people.
142	4	*Alopece :* One of the Attic demes.
144	6	*Numenius :* It was customary at Athens to buy and sell slaves at the commencement of the new moon.
144	13	*Epimenides the Cretan :* This person, being tired with walking, is said to have gone into a cave, where he slept for 47 years.
144	14	*Hercules :* His birth was said to have taken three nights to accomplish.
145	7	*The Thesmophoria :* An ancient festival held by the Athenian women in honour of Demeter (Ceres) Thesmophorus, the law-giver, so called as having introduced tillage and given the first impulse to civil society.

NOTES

PAGE LINE
147　8　*Dogs:* i.e. the Cynics.
148　10　*Draco:* The oldest Athenian legislator. His laws, which were very severe, were afterwards considerably modified by Solon.
149　2　*Decelea:* About 14 miles north of Athens, on a ridge of Mt. Parnes.
150　4　*The goddess of labour:* Especially women's labour. Minerva is meant.
151　18　*The Cynosarges:* A gymnasium outside the city, sacred to Hercules, for the use of those who were not of pure Athenian blood.
153　3　*Serangium:* In Piraeus.
155　2　*Megareans or Aegieans:* Both these people were regarded with contempt, as we learn from Homer, Theocritus, and Erasmus.
155　6　*Crates:* We are told by Diogenes Laertius that he was called θυρεπανοίκτης, that is, the door-opener, because all doors were open to receive him.
155　17　*After he has wiped his hands upon it:* Others take this to mean that "the Graces have wiped their hands upon him," that is, bestowed a part of their grace and powers of fascination upon him. According to the translation in the text, the passage refers to the custom of placing a piece of fine soft bread before each guest at an entertainment, with which he wiped his fingers, and afterwards threw it to the dogs.
158　5　*The Cureotis:* The third day of the Festival of Apaturia, on which the sons of Athenian citizens were ad-

NOTES

		mitted, at three or four years of age, among the φράτορες or tribesmen, and their names entered in their register, which was afterwards a proof of their citizenship.
159	2	*Hermione:* In Argolis.
160	8	*Of Molossian and Cnosian breed:* From Molossus in Epirus. The Cnosian came from Crete.
161	15	*A dog who, &c.:* A common proverbial expression. Cf. *Horace:* Ut canis a corio nunquam absterrebitur uncto.
162	5	*The Propompi:* Possibly the "Seven against Thebes" may be meant; or it is one of the lost tragedies of Aeschylus.
163	1	*Phenea:* A town in Arcadia.
163	14	*His fellow-actors:* Literally, flatterers of Dionysus.
164	8	*Enneacrunus:* Another name for the fountain of Callirhoe, so called from its having "nine springs."
164	16	*Haliartus:* In Boeotia.
164	17	*Dipylum:* The "double gate," the largest in Athens.
165	4	*Pyanepsion:* October-November.
165	8	*The second day:* Which was spent by the bridegroom at his father-in-law's house.
166	6	*His houses:* Properly, houses in which several families live, "flats," or "lodging-houses," answering to the Roman *insulae.* Such houses were a common investment amongst the wealthier Athenians.

NOTES

PAGE LINE

168   2 *Eurotas*: Anciently called the "king of rivers," and worshipped by the Spartans as a powerful god. It rose in Arcadia and flowed through Laconia.

168   3 *Pirene*: A spring near Corinth.

168   6 *Callirhoe*: See on 164, 8.

168 17 *Run the risk of growing thin*: Others render "of being torn to pieces."

170   7 *The oracle of Dodona*: The prophetic oak of Dodona, the most ancient oracle of Greece.

172 11 *The Painted Porch*: See on 5, 11.

174 17 *Like a Spartan*: It was part of the severe discipline which prevailed among the Spartans to flog their young men to make them hardy and able to bear pain.

176   1 *These solemn personages*: This letter bears a very close resemblance to Lucian's *Symposium, or Banquet of the Philosophers*.

176 17 *The Peripatetic*: The Peripatetics were the school of Aristotle and his followers, so called because he taught walking in a περίπατος or walk of the Lyceum at Athens.

177   6 *His reserve*: The Pythagoreans were famous for their silence.

179   3 *Pythocles*: The favourite of Epicurus.

179 10 *To eat and drink*: A quotation from the speech of Eumaeus to Ulysses, *Odyssey*, xv. 377.

180   8 *The Saturnalia*: The festival in honour of Cronus or Saturn, celebrated at

Page	Line	
		Athens on the 12th day of the month Hecatombaeon (July-August).
180	9	*Shoes:* Called Ἰφικρατίδες after the Athenian general Iphicrates.
182	4	*The silent hero:* Probably Harpocrates, the god of silence, who was usually represented with his finger on his lips.
183	12	*Ganymede:* Who was carried up to heaven by an eagle to Jupiter to be his cupbearer.
185	9	*The Craneium:* The market-place of Corinth.
186	9	*Cythera:* The modern Cerigo, where Venus is said to have sprung from the sea.
187	4	*Chalastraean nitre:* From Chalestra, the name of a town and lake in Macedonia. It is highly spoken of by Pliny.
188	1	*The Pnyx:* The place at Athens where the Ἐκκλησίαι or assemblies of the people were held; it was cut out of a hill about a quarter of a mile west of the Acropolis or citadel, and was semi-circular in form like a theatre.
188	5	*Ostracised:* When it was decided to remove a powerful party-leader, after the Senate and Ecclesia had decided that such a step was necessary, each citizen wrote upon a tile or oystershell (ὄστρακὸς) the name of the person whom he desired to banish. The votes were then collected, and if it was found that 6,000 had been recorded against any one person, he was obliged to withdraw from the city within ten days.

NOTES

PAGE LINE
189 17 *One of the Olympian fascinators:* The commentators do not venture upon an explanation. It may simply refer to the athletes who had gained prizes at the Olympic games, and gave themselves airs in consequence.

190 4 *Empusa:* A hobgoblin that assumed various shapes.

190 12 *A radish:* This, as is well known, formed part of the punishment of an adulterer.

191 8 *Some tokens:* The recognition of children in later life through these tokens is a favourite device with Greek and Roman dramatists.

193 7 *Goddess of sensual love:* Venus popularis, or Πάνδημος, the goddess of "common" as opposed to "spiritual" love.

194 1 *Istria:* On the Euxine Sea.

196 1 *That accursed barber:* We are reminded of the barber in the *Arabian Nights*.

198 2 *Who carried the basket:* This basket contained the sacred things that were carried in procession at the feasts of Ceres, Bacchus, and Minerva. The office was highly prized.

199 14 *The Saviour princes:* The Dioscuri, Castor and Pollux. The following is the story of Simonides: He was at a banquet, when someone came to tell him that two young men in the street wanted to speak to him. He went out: and at the same moment, the roof of the house fell in, and destroyed all beneath it. The two young men were supposed

NOTES

PAGE	LINE	
		to have been Castor and Pollux. Simonides of Ceos was the most prolific poet of Greece, and is considered as a first inventor of a mnemonical system.
200	7	*The Well of Callichorum:* Wives suspected of infidelity to their husbands were obliged to declare their innocence at this well.
203	10	*For the next Dionysia:* At which new plays were performed.
205	1	*Hermae:* Figures of Hermes (Mercury) in the public streets, which it was considered a heinous offence to mutilate or remove.
205	2	*Betrayed:* Literally, "danced out," apparently referring to certain dances which burlesqued these solemn rites.
205	7	*That Ionian wench:* Ionian girls were famous for their wanton dances.
207	1	*The three-headed dog:* Cerberus, who guarded the gates of the nether world.
207	12	*The son of Maia:* Hermes (Mercury), who escorted the souls ($\phi\upsilon\chi\alpha\gamma\omega\gamma\epsilon\hat{\iota}\nu$) of the dead to Hades.

BIBLIOGRAPHY

1 The Aldine edition, Venice, 1499: the "editio princeps."
2 Recensuit, emendavit, versione ac notis illustravit S. Bergler, Lipsiae, 1715.
3 Cum Bergleri commentario integro, cui aliorum criticorum et suas notationes, versionem emendatam indiculumque adiecit J. A. Wagner, Lipsiae, 1798.
4 Recensuit cum Bergleri integris, Meinekii, Wagneri, aliorum selectis, suisque annotationibus edidit, indices adiecit E. E. Seiler, Lipsiae, 1853.
5 Translated from the Greek with annotations, by T. Monro and W. Beloe. [Apparently the only English version published.]
6 Lettres grecques; traduites en François [par J. Richard], avec des notes historiques et critiques. Amsterdam, 1785.
7 Lettres grecques traduites en Français, par S. de Rouville, Paris, 1874.
8 A's Briefe, aus dem Griechischen übersetzt von J. F. Herel, Altenburg, 1767.
9 Letteri di Alcifrone: tradotte dal Greco per F. Negri, Milano, 1806.

www.ingramcontent.com/pod-product-compliance
Lightning Source LLC
Chambersburg PA
CBHW022133300426
44115CB00006B/173